Landscape Gardener
Ogawa Jihei and His Times

JAPAN LIBRARY

Landscape Gardener Ogawa Jihei and His Times

A PROFILE OF MODERN JAPAN

Suzuki Hiroyuki

Translated by **Hart Larrabee**

Japan Publishing Industry Foundation for Culture

Note to readers: In this book, long vowels in Japanese words are indicated by the use of macrons, except in commonly known place names and words already adopted into English. Japanese names are written in the conventional Japanese order: family name followed by given name. Factual errors discovered in the process of translation have been corrected.

Landscape Gardener Ogawa Jihei and His Times: A Profile of Modern Japan
Written by Suzuki Hiroyuki. Translated by Hart Larrabee.

Published by Japan Publishing Industry Foundation for Culture (JPIC)
3-12-3 Kanda-Jinbōchō, Chiyoda-ku, Tokyo 101-0051 Japan

© 2013 Suzuki Tokiko

First English edition: March 2018

English translation © 2018 Japan Publishing Industry Foundation for Culture
Foreword to the English edition © 2018 Ebara Sumiko

Originally published in Japanese under the title *Niwashi Ogawa Jihei to sono jidai* by the University of Tokyo Press in 2013.

English publishing rights arranged with the University of Tokyo Press.

The Japan Publishing Industry Foundation for Culture wishes to express its deep appreciation to Associate Professor Ebara Sumiko of Chiba University for her full and generous cooperation and guidance in the production of this book.

Jacket and cover design: Point & Line Co., Ltd.
Jacket and cover photograph: The garden at Murin-an. Photo © Nimura Haruo

As this book is published primarily to be donated to overseas universities, research institutions, public libraries and other organizations, commercial publication rights are available. For all enquiries regarding those rights, please contact the publisher of the original Japanese edition at the following address:
Rights and Permissions, University of Tokyo Press
4-5-29 Komaba, Meguro-ku, Tokyo 153-0041 Japan
info@utp.or.jp

All rights reserved. Printed in Japan.
ISBN 978-4-86658-019-7
http://www.jpic.or.jp/japanlibrary/

Preface

Landscape Gardener Ogawa Jihei and His Times: A Profile of Modern Japan was my husband Suzuki Hiroyuki's final book. He was in his twenties when we got married and seemed on his way to becoming an expert on the architecture of the Victorian period. One day about a decade later, though, I noticed that his shelves held a growing number of books related to modern Japan. Most appeared to have come from used book sellers and covered history, architecture, and biographies of figures both famous and obscure.

When I saw how his book collection had evolved, I remember thinking that things were moving in the right direction. The reason was that I had never thought of Suzuki Hiroyuki as the sort of person to follow the standard pattern for a Japanese scholar of Western culture, that is, to work at a university in Japan and find time amid his duties to further his own understanding by traveling overseas for study or to conduct research. He showed no signs of restlessly reserving tickets for flights as holidays approached, and indeed seemed to show greater interest in the old shrines, temples, and gardens that he visited during trips within Japan and in the inscriptions that he found in cemeteries while out for a walk. It seems to me that this inclination of his was probably tied to a powerful awareness of his own roots, of ancestors who were modest shogunal retainers and of the numerous civil servants, physicians, and legal professionals who subsequently populated the family line.

He did, of course, spend a year during his twenties at The Courtauld

Institute of Art in London on a study abroad program arranged through the British Council, and later had the opportunity to travel abroad a few times a year either to lead architecture-related tours or to attend international conferences, but Suzuki Hiroyuki was, at heart, a person oriented toward Japan.

I think he was fortunate that the prime of his working life fell at the end of the twentieth century, a time when the profile of Japanese architects was rising, many talented people were coming to Japan, and he had the opportunity to look after students from overseas at the University of Tokyo, thereby placing himself firmly in the midst of global trends without ever leaving Japan for very long. Perhaps it was the nature of the times, too, that most of the dozen or so students who he taught for a short period at Harvard University during the early 1990s later came to Japan for one reason or another.

Still, there is no doubt that Suzuki Hiroyuki's research on the Victorian period in his youth established a foundation for his later interest in modern Japan. When he was still a middle-ranked researcher I once asked what he thought his life's work would be. His answer was, "Ogawa Jihei and Josiah Conder." When he was in the hospital for the last time he said, "When I get out of here, my next book will be on Conder." I cannot help but think that had he only been given another year or two of life, he might have achieved both of the ambitions of his youth. At the same, I also feel grateful that he was able to complete *Landscape Gardener Ogawa Jihei and His Times* the year before he passed away.

I regret that he is not here himself to see the publication of this book in English, and I wonder what readers in the English-speaking world will think of the process by which a single landscape gardener shaped, for those who built modern Japan, what the author calls the "totalities of their private realms."

I wish to thank the Japan Library at the Japan Publishing Industry Foundation for Culture (JPIC) for making publication of this English edition possible, the University of Tokyo Press for acting as an intermediary, and Chiba University Associate Professor Ebara Sumiko for providing editorial assistance and a foreword to the English edition.

6

Contents

Foreword to the English Edition

Architectural historian Suzuki Hiroyuki, a keen-eyed critic of contemporary architecture throughout his life and someone who threw himself into numerous architectural preservation movements, published this book just eight months before his untimely death. In it, he talks not about buildings but about gardens.

Having begun as a scholar of Victorian Gothic architecture, Suzuki published *Kenchiku no seikimatsu* (The fin de siècle in architecture) in 1977. At roughly the same time, while translating the first volume of Nikolaus Pevsner's *Studies in Art, Architecture, and Design* into Japanese with his wife Tokiko, he hit upon the concept of genius loci ("spirit of the place"). The approach of deciphering social and historical memory from the land was one that reconnected architecture—which had, during the twentieth century, lost any sense of place through an excessive, machine-inspired insistence on rationality, functionality, and universality—to the cultural substrata. Suzuki was looking for a way to understand modernization in non-Western countries, and reexamining modern Japan by looking at the history of the land brought a new image into focus.

In 1982, Suzuki both wrote the *Yamagata Aritomo kyūtei Odawara Kokian chōsa hōkokusho* (Report on the survey of Koki-an, the former residence of Yamagata Aritomo in Odawara) and published "Meiji kara shōwa ni itaru sukiya: Ueji no sekai" (Sukiya architecture from the Meiji through Showa periods: the world of Ueji). In this, he touched upon the breadth of landscape designer Ogawa Jihei's gardens, which began with Yamagata Aritomo's Murin-an villa in Kyoto.

The garden at Murin-an literally had its source in the Lake Biwa Canal, which brought modernization to the ancient capital of Kyoto. A portion of the water from the canal, which was expected to serve multiple purposes including power, transport, irrigation, rice polishing, firefighting, drinking, and sanitation, was diverted to Murin-an, the Kyoto villa whose owner had contributed so much to the canal's construction. Yamagata is known as the dominant figure at the foundation of Japan's pre-war political regime. A man of refined tastes who got a somewhat late start in the world of *sukisha* connoisseurs, he preferred to apply his resources to the building of gardens rather than to the tea ceremony with its emphasis on exceptional objects. In doing so, together with Ogawa Jihei, Yamagata experimented with gardens composed of flowing water, a variety of tall trees, low-trimmed azaleas, broad lawns, and stones laid flat. Such gardens had a naturalism that contrasted with the symbolism of traditional Japanese gardens and conveyed a modern sensibility.

Suzuki also observed that the period during which the garden at Murin-an was created corresponds to the point at which the Empire of Japan, victorious in the Sino-Japanese War, was shifting from the assimilation of Western culture that had begun with the opening of the country to more proactive efforts. Within this shift there was a drive, a longing, to find a way to express the Japanese spirit in a modern context. Meeting this demand by adjusting the techniques of traditional Japanese gardens, Ogawa Jihei ultimately created what could be called the model for the modern Japanese garden. Taking part in the construction of the Fushimi Momoyama Mausoleum is thought to have shown him that even the imperial household was in the midst of a transition to the modern, while the work itself is believed to have had a major influence on the perfection of his own style. Soon, many politicians and distinguished gentlemen were commissioning him to create gardens for their own private villas.

Roughly fifty years after the completion of the garden at Murin-an, however, the Empire of Japan collapsed in 1945. Just before Konoe Fumimaro, who led three cabinets beginning around the start of hostilities in China in 1937, committed suicide at his Tekigai-sō villa in Ogikubo, he visited Kōden-sō, the primary residence of Nagao Kin'ya in Sakura Shinmachi, which had a garden designed by Ogwa Jihei.

The entire rise and fall of modern Japan can be seen clearly against the background of Ogawa Jihei's gardens. The image this brings into relief is neither clear nor simple, and at times may seem enigmatic or illogical. Nevertheless, Suzuki describes a new vision of modern Japan seen through the private world of gardens, one that includes things that conventional accounts of modern history have left behind.

To describe things in this way may leave the impression that Ogawa Jihei's gardens are somehow inapproachable, but this is not the case at all. His gardens are, above all, open spaces where the sound of flowing water falls pleasantly on the ear. As with the garden at the former primary residence of Iwasaki Koyata in Toriizaka (now the International House of Japan), some live on without any sense of incongruity even after an original Japanese-style building has been replaced by one constructed in the International Style. Suzuki writes, "Gardens, perhaps, have longer lives than buildings." The gardens of Ogawa Jihei, having watched over modern Japan, continue to be imprinted with new memories of the land today.

Ebara Sumiko, Associate Professor
Chiba University Department of Architecture

The Philosopher's Walk

In this book I intend to tell the tale of landscape gardener Ogawa Jihei VII and the times in which he lived. It is a story, however, about more than just Japan's proud culture of landscape gardening. By looking at the people who were captivated by gardens in the midst of Japan's modernization, and at the kind of gardens they created, I hope to consider the very character of the country's modernization.

Ogawa Jihei was born in April 1860 as the second son of Yamamoto Yahei in a village that is now part of the city of Nagaokakyō in Kyoto Prefecture. Since his mother died when he was still very young, he was raised by his father. In 1877 he was made the adoptive heir of the Ogawa family of landscape gardeners in Kyoto and later succeeded to the family business. By creating a group of gardens that drew water from the Lake Biwa Canal, he introduced a new garden culture to modern Kyoto. He also created the gardens at Heian Jingū shrine and a garden for Meiji elder statesman Yamagata Aritomo. Ogawa Jihei's work was also favored by Sumitomo Shunsui, head of the Sumitomo zaibatsu; Saionji Kinmochi, the last of modern Japan's *genrō* "founding fathers"; Iwasaki Koyata, head of the Mitsubishi zaibatsu; and Konoe Fumimaro, who served multiple terms as prime minister during the early Showa period (1926–1989).

Ogawa Jihei passed away in December 1933 at the age of seventy-three. Spanning from the Bakumatsu period (1853–1868) at the end of the Tokugawa shogunate through the early years of the Showa period, his life encompassed the history of Japan's modernization and his gardens embodied the transformations that swept Japan during that time.

I will begin with a discussion of the history of Japan's modernization that provided the context for Ogawa Jihei's gardens. In doing so I will look at the construction of the Lake Biwa Canal, a model example of a national project that contributed to the achievement of Japan's modernization, and one that was symbolic, too, in that it was accomplished through the efforts of Japanese alone without relying on engineers hired from overseas. I would like to start by visiting a cultural landscape that emerged from the Lake Biwa Canal many years later because it serves as something of a twin to the gardens of Ogawa Jihei.

There is a path in Kyoto known as the Philosopher's Walk. It follows the banks of a branch of the Lake Biwa Canal that flows slowly from Nanzen-ji temple to just before Ginkaku-ji temple, and exudes a particularly beautiful charm during the autumn foliage season (Fig. I-1). It is such a wonderful place for a pleasant stroll that there is little need to give much thought

Fig. I-1: The Philosopher's Walk

about the origins of its name. When we walk the path from the Ginkaku-ji side, the waters of the canal murmur softly as they flow to meet us, and as we continue along against the current we eventually emerge just below Nanzen-ji temple. Approaching Okazaki Park, the atmosphere on the streets descends to something more worldly, but then the area opens up onto a district lined with large estates, and heading in that direction returns us to another stretch of beautiful scenery. Passing large homes with expansive, cherished gardens such as the current primary residence of the Sumitomo family and another estate that once served as a second home for Nomura Tokushichi II, the founder of Nomura Securities, brings us practically to the gate of Nanzen-ji temple. Today, the route is one of Kyoto's best-known walking paths.

Kyoto is often described as the "thousand-year capital," but the scenery along the Philosopher's Walk to Nanzen-ji temple is somewhat newer. Rather than conveying some ancient Heian period (794–1185) landscape or views dating back to the Kamakura (1185–1333), Muromachi (1336–1573), or even Edo (1603–1868) periods, it took shape instead between the Meiji (1868–1912) and Showa periods. Rather than showing traces of the thousand-year capital, it reflects a culture born of modern Japan, which is easy enough to imagine given that the Philosopher's Walk follows the branch canal.

The Lake Biwa Canal was Meiji Japan's first monumental public works achievement in Kyoto, built to drive the modernization and revitalization of the city in the wake of the Meiji Restoration of 1868. The name "Philosopher's Walk," however, did not appear until much later, during the postwar years, in an apparent reference to the frequent strolls taken by philosopher and area resident Nishida Kitarō. It was only in 1972 that a stone marker erected to commemorate improvements made to the path along the canal was inscribed with the name of the walk.

The waters of the branch canal disappear into the hills around Nyakuō-ji Shrine, where there is a house that was once occupied by the philosopher Watsuji Tetsurō. It was built during the mid-Meiji period by Furugō Tokimachi, head clerk to the wealthy Yokohama merchant Hara Sankei, who gave his name to Sankei-en Garden. Later named Mitsugo-an, it is now home to the philosopher Umehara Takeshi. That Watsuji, who developed the concept of *fūdo* [milieu], should have lived near the Philosopher's Walk is perhaps evidence of the favorability of the area's scenery. Modern intellectuals discovered a utopia here, and this landscape born of modern Kyoto is now a magnificent *fūdo* of its own.

I know I repeat myself, but the Philosopher's Walk is a typical product of modernity. The Lake Biwa Canal is a classic example of a national land improvement project undertaken in the course of Japan's modernization, an ambitious venture designed to infuse Kyoto with a modern vitality by building a modern canal to provide transportation facilities and water for industrial use—new urban infrastructure that the city previously lacked.

As part of such a project, what role was the branch canal intended to play? Flowing over the Suirokaku, a brick aqueduct on the grounds of Nanzen-ji temple, and on toward Ginkaku-ji, its waters served two main purposes. The first was as irrigation for farmland in Kyoto's eastern suburbs and the second was as a source of power for industrial use. The latter may require some explanation. The period from the end of the nineteenth to the beginning of the twentieth century when the Lake Biwa Canal was being built was the heyday of waterwheel power, of running factories using hydraulic turbines driven by flowing water. The branch canal, then, would supply water for power, and the area from Nanzen-ji to Ginkaku-ji was supposed to become an industrial area lined with factories driven by water turbines.

The arrival of practical hydroelectric power while the canal was being built, however, changed its function from turning waterwheels that would drive factories to generating hydroelectric power. Japan's first hydroelectric power station was built in the Keage area near Nanzen-ji, and the branch canal, having lost its role of providing water to drive factories, came to be used primarily for irrigation.

It was the philosophers of Kyoto who found in this area an environment suitable for contemplation, transforming a path that was supposed to be lined with factories into the Philosopher's Walk. Every visit to the area makes me think of the serendipity that influences where and how such ideal locations are born.

But the modern landscapes generated by the canal are not limited to the Philosopher's Walk, and indeed are spread surprisingly wide. Just as a drop of water poured into a stream is capable of spreading across millions of acres of farmland, the impact of the canal extended broadly not only across modern Japan's industry and transport but also across its cultural history. In this it embodies Japan's history from the Edo and Meiji periods through the end of prewar Japan and represents the lives and talents of so many people who lived during that time.

Less than a century separates the Meiji Restoration from Japan's defeat in the Pacific War, yet the country's transformation over that period was greater and more tumultuous than any other hundred years in history. It was during this period that Japan experienced the process of modernization. Whether this is seen as a miraculous transformation or as one whose merits and demerits largely balance out no doubt depends on where one stands. Nevertheless, was there not, in the expressions of culture demanded by modern Japan over the course of that century, a certain continuity? Is it not within this basso continuo that the essence of Japan's modernization can be found? The canal relates to these points of departure.

In drawing water from the Lake Biwa Canal, landscape gardener Ogawa Jihei VII used something originally intended for industry to create a group of colossal gardens showcasing the stylishness of modern Japanese culture. Desired by members of the Japanese ruling class—from Yamagata Aritomo to Konoe Fumimaro—who continued to pursue modernization, these were expressions that underpinned the totalities of their private realms. To understand this world, however, we must first look at the history of the development of the Lake Biwa Canal itself as well as its world historical context.

Chapter One

Modernization and the Development of the Lake Biwa Canal

The Role of Water in Modernization

How were canals characterized in the course of modernization at the end of the nineteenth century, that is, at the time when Tanabe Sakurō presented his plans for constructing the Lake Biwa Canal?

Globally, the nineteenth century was an age of waterpower. The industrial revolution was made possible by the United Kingdom's abundant waterpower, which touched areas so diverse as to be almost unimaginable to us today.

First, prior to the advent of the steam engine, industry was sustained by waterpower in its most basic form. If you look for harbingers of the industrial revolution in New Lanark near Glasgow in the United Kingdom, you will no doubt be impressed to find that the textile mills that were run by Robert Owen still exist. Most impressive, however, is the overwhelming volume of tea-colored water flowing swiftly along the River Clyde, all but lapping at the mills that stand close along its banks (Fig. 1-1). Seeing this surely brings a sudden sense of reality to an industrial revolution that people today otherwise know only in their heads.

Water, of course, had previously been used in all sorts of ways. Since ancient times, it was used first for drinking but also for transport and as the lifeline of agriculture. Its strength in modern times, however, and particularly the new potential it gained in the nineteenth century, was as a source of power. If civil engineering student Tanabe Sakurō hoped to give full play

Fig. 1-1: The textile mills of New Lanark and the River Clyde

to water's potential, then it is perfectly natural that his conception would spread so much further than the excavation of a waterway.

Just around the time that Tanabe Sakurō appeared there was another person in Kyoto advocating for the potential of waterpower: Kawashima Jinbei II. As owner of the Kawashima Orimono textile company, he occupied an important position in the world of Kyoto textiles and was one of those who sought to build new industry on the foundations of tradition. While traveling abroad in 1886 he visited the industrial city of Holyoke in the United States and was greatly impressed with the use of water there as a source of power for industrial use.

The city of Holyoke is located in Massachusetts, roughly 100 kilometers due west of the state capital of Boston. The appeal of the city and its significance in terms of urban history lies in its river. As is well known, New England's growth was the result of taking advantage of the topographical conditions of fall line cities located on geological terraces. A typical fall line city, Holyoke applied the abundant waters of the rapids flowing through it to develop its textile and papermaking industries. What these industries needed more than anything else was water, and Holyoke's was provided by the Connecticut River, which wraps around the town flowing in from the northwest and out to the southwest. Its course was precipitous, with a waterfall located on the city's northeast that came to be known as Hadley Falls (Fig. 1-2).

Industry in Holyoke was made possible by drawing water from the Connecticut River as a source of power to drive hydraulic turbines, and this is what attracted the notice of Kawashima Jinbei. But what form did industry driven by the waters of the Connecticut take? For those for whom waterwheels conjure only pictures of gristmills, this is something that can be difficult to imagine. The reason that even those who are interested in the Lake Biwa Canal can find its essence difficult to grasp is that today we have trouble visualizing what the water-driven industrial production of the nineteenth century on which it was based looked like.

The industrial canals that run through the city of Holyoke were constructed from 1847 through 1900. A wooden dam was built on the Connecticut River in 1849 to draw water into them and the Hadley Falls Company, later the

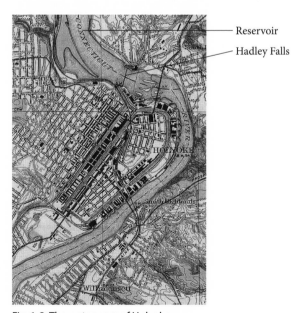

Reservoir

Hadley Falls

Fig. 1-2: The waterways of Holyoke

Holyoke Water Power Company, was established. The company built three canals on which thirty-six waterwheels were installed. These were "power canals," used not as a means of water transport but to generate hydraulic power, and their development spurred the rapid growth of Holyoke as an industrial city. The most important precondition for an industrial city at the time was a location where waterways for power could be secured. Waterways supplied the water that turned the waterwheels that powered the factories and made them more productive. The number of waterwheels was a direct index of the scale of a city's industrial output.

Although once numbering thirty-six, by the mid-1990s only a single waterwheel still remained in operation in Holyoke, used by the Parsons Paper Mill, a company known for manufacturing high-quality papers. The location advantage of a canal town was that the water could be used not only as part of the papermaking process but also as a source of power. Holyoke grew together with its twin industries of textiles and paper. Kyoto textile-maker Kawashima Jinbei took an interest in Holyoke because he paid attention to the leading regions in his own industry.

The power to run the machinery in any given factory came from a single large waterwheel whose torque was conveyed throughout the factory by means of shafts and belts. Tracing the source of power for the Parsons Paper Mill, we can see that it came from a massive bevel gear attached to a shaft that descended into the factory's basement, and beyond that to a waterwheel that was turned by the flowing water (Fig. 1-3). Really too large to be called a waterwheel, the turbine roared as it rotated beneath the floor. With a vertical axis of rotation, the turbine measured perhaps two meters in diameter with a rotating portion on its upper half that took the form of a cylindrical bladed wheel and a lower half that tapered to a shape like a giant pot.

But how did the water that turned such a turbine find its way beneath the floor of the mill? The canals of Holyoke meander broadly through the city (Fig. 1-2). After backtracking to run parallel to the original waterway, the water level is much lower. In other words, the canals are designed such that there are parallel flows at successively lower elevations. Factories were constructed between the two parallel waterways, with water turning their turbines as it flowed from the upper canal to the lower through their basements. When you stop to think about it, the mechanism is really plain and simple, and yet this very plainness and simplicity characterizes the source of power for the early days of the industrial revolution.

At the same time, this must also have been the principle underlying plans to use the waters of the Lake Biwa Canal. The Holyoke I visited, however, was a city that time had left behind with the restructuring of industry. Its bleak streets taught me that the speed of urban growth in America could be matched by the speed of its decline. Water was once an unparalleled source of power, yet when it lost this position and the mantle passed to electricity, this city structured around its canals lost its vitality.

Fortunately, there are few signs of such decline at the Lake Biwa Canal. Although the incline, a device for transporting boats over land on a flat car, is no longer used, the canal as a whole has not been abandoned. The Suirokaku aqueduct found near Nanzen-ji, where the Philosopher's Walk ends, is so atmospheric that it now appears on Kyoto tourism posters and captivates people as an artistic work of civil engineering (Fig. 1-4).

Fig. 1-3: Bevel gear (foreground) and waterwheel (background)

Fig. 1-4: The Suirokaku aqueduct at Nanzen-ji

What is the secret to the Lake Biwa Canal's continued vitality in the neighborhoods of Kyoto? The canal almost appears intended from the start to transcend its origins as a product of civil engineering and give rise to a measure of artistry. The character of the canal seems like something both anticipated at the time of its birth and nurtured over history since its completion. If we trace the path of the whole, we may find that the formation of the Philosopher's Walk is but one byproduct of the expansive canal.

Tanabe Sakurō and the Lake Biwa Canal

At the age of six-and-a-half years, Tanabe Sakurō, who would go on to design the Lake Biwa Canal as an engineer for the Ministry of Domestic Affairs, experienced the fall of Edo Castle in 1868. When looked back on from a Meiji perspective, the life of a samurai during the last days of the shogunate must have seemed like a dream. The son of a shogunal retainer, during the Taisho period (1912–1926) Tanabe recalled his most vivid memory of childhood to have been the moment of his escape from Edo during the confusion of the Restoration when he ran into twenty or thirty thugs armed with bamboo spears, gripped his short sword, and shouted, "Well, there is nowhere safe in this land. Come at me and I'll cut you down." Born in Edo (later renamed Tokyo) in 1861, he was part of a generation that lived through a period of profound swings in values such as has rarely been seen in Japanese history.

Tanabe Sakurō's father Magojirō had studied under Takashima Shūhan and become a master of gunnery. Although said to have been responsible for establishing the shogunate's military school, he passed away in 1862, the year after Sakurō's birth, at the age of 42 having contracted measles during an epidemic. Deprived of his father at an early age, Sakurō was raised by his mother and eventually determined to make his living as an engineer like his father. By that time, however, the shogunate had fallen and the world had radically changed.

Having seen political upheaval firsthand, the path of an engineer was perhaps the only one in which this son of a shogunal retainer could believe, and Sakurō chose to enter the Imperial College of Engineering that had been established by the Ministry of Industry. Learning new science and technology must have seemed the surest way to make his way in the world based on his talents without relying on clan favoritism. In this, it is easy enough to imagine that the life of the father he lost so early must have cast a long shadow. Magojirō had adopted the art name Butsudō, said to be a reference to the saying, "Those ignorant of guns must not speak of soldiers. Those who speak of soldiers must not forget guns." In this one senses both his pride in being a gunner and a certain engineer's sensibility in warning against becoming a grandiloquent jingoist.

Tanabe Sakurō would graduate from the School of Civil Engineering at the Imperial College of Engineering on 15 May 1883, but well before then, from a very young age, he had studied the Chinese classics under Ōkubo Kansai and French under Fukuchi Gen'ichirō. Such opportunities came to young Sakurō through Tanabe Taichi, the head of a branch of the Tanabe clan who was friends with both men.

Immediately following the Meiji Restoration, Sakurō followed Taichi to Numazu where he studied at elementary school through the age of eleven, a move precipitated by Taichi's appointment to teach at the Numazu Military Academy that had been established by the Tokugawa clan. Taichi had already been to France as a member of shogunal missions during the Bakumatsu period and, after the Restoration, would accompany the 1871–1873 Iwakura Mission to the United States and Europe as a first secretary and later serve as a diplomat. (Fukuchi Gen'ichirō was also among the first secretaries who accompanied the delegation.)

The Numazu Military Academy was the most advanced institution of Western learning in the early years of the Meiji period. Nishi Amane was installed as head of the academy, overseeing a teaching staff made up of the best educated among the former shogunal retainers. The elementary school where Tanabe Sakurō studied was affiliated with the military academy, giving him the opportunity to enjoy the finest intellectual heritage of the former shogunate. The school produced many individuals, such as Shimada Saburō, who would be active players in the world of Meiji letters and politics. Sakurō, too, can be counted among the many notable persons who studied at the Numazu Military Academy's elementary school.

For his graduation thesis at the Imperial College of Engineering's School of Civil Engineering, Tanabe Sakurō took on the subject of planning the construction of the Lake Biwa Canal. The precise reasons for his interest in the topic are unclear but, as discussed later, he set about the project at the urging of Ōtori Keisuke. It is evident, though, that he was motivated by more than just a fascination with water-use technology. Indeed, Tanabe aspired to promote industry throughout the entire city of Kyoto and took on the Lake Biwa Canal project as part of a comprehensive national policy to that end. Stretching the imagination, one can even think this may have been due to a certain sympathy he felt, as the son of a former shogunal retainer, for the old capital of Kyoto as a city on the decline.

The actual plan for a national project to construct the Lake Biwa Canal, however, was not an emotional or sentimental effort but one that was conceptually very rigorous. Seen from the perspective of the present, we can conclude that it had the character of a national project that could only have been devised in Meiji Japan.

What, then, was the substance of the Lake Biwa Canal construction project? In simplest terms, it was a plan to draw the waters of Lake Biwa from Shiga Prefecture to Kyoto by way of a canal. And yet, looking at the details of this plan it becomes clear that it was all but overloaded with deeper purpose—so much so that one might say this very thirst for more marked the spirit of the Meiji period.

Indeed, plans to excavate a waterway from Lake Biwa date back to the Edo period; a petition presented to the authorities in 1841 imagined such a waterway used for the passage of boats and the irrigation of farmland. The construction prospectus for Tanabe Sakurō's plan, meanwhile, adopted seven objectives, as summarized below.

1. Manufacturing Machinery
   Hydraulic power—the prospectus reads, "Starting industries requires large, sophisticated machinery, and relying on hydraulic pow-

er is the most convenient and beneficial means of driving such machinery." The plan, in fact, was to use the water to drive waterwheels. The prospectus also notes, "Not only does the Shirakawa River run below the area around Nyakuōji and the village of Shishigatani, but the grade of the land is also very steep, no doubt making it an ideal location for the installation of waterwheels." This was the major objective for developing the Lake Biwa Canal. However, because practical realization of hydroelectric power ultimately made this aspect of the scheme unnecessary, such topographical features instead set the stage for the creation of Ogawa Jihei's gardens.

2. Transportation

This section describes a canal to realize the Edo period dream of allowing the passage of boats. The prospectus is accompanied by a calculation of how far freight charges would be reduced by completion of the canal.

3. Farmland Irrigation

This, too, was a dream held since the Edo period. The prospectus estimates yields would increase by more than 16,000 *koku* of rice.

4. Waterwheels for Polishing Rice

At the time, many waterwheels were used to polish rice. Recognizing latent demand, the prospectus suggests completion of the canal would prompt a flood of interest in installing such waterwheels.

5. Fire Prevention

The plan suggests that distributing water from the canal throughout the city of Kyoto using a number of branch waterways would be helpful in fire prevention.

6. Drinking Water

The canal is promoted as a source of drinking water.

7. Sanitation Matters

The prospectus asserts that sending the abundant waters of the canal through the sewers in the city of Kyoto would help them flow smoothly, preventing sanitation-related problems such as the spread of infectious disease. (Items 6 and 7 can both be seen to position the canal as something that would lead to further improvements to waterworks and sewers.)

The Lake Biwa Canal designed by Tanabe Sakurō teaches us that the plans of Meiji engineers were much more than just products of the application of technology for technology's sake in the pursuit of Westernization.

The reason Tanabe Sakurō selected the Lake Biwa Canal as the topic for his graduation thesis is said to have been because the principal of the Imperial College of Engineering, Ōtori Keisuke, when consulted about the idea by Kyoto governor Kitagaki Kunimichi, recommended Tanabe as a student who was expected to graduate the following year. Known for coming up with the word *bijutsu* as a translation for "fine arts," Ōtori was a former shogunal retainer and a survivor of the final battle of the Boshin War at Goryōkaku fortress in Hakodate. He was probably familiar with Tanabe Taichi, another enlightened shogunal retainer who worked for the Meiji government. If so, given that students in the School of Civil Engineering at his Imperial College of Engineering numbered fewer than ten per class year, he was certainly also aware that Taichi's nephew was a talented student among them. When approached by Governor Kitagaki about a civil engineering project, Ōtori must have felt it to be a most agreeable coincidence that a student connected to Tanabe Taichi should be enrolled in the School of Civil Engineering. Such is the connection linking Tanabe Sakurō and Kyoto.

Beginning in 1881, two years before his graduation, Tanabe Sakurō began measuring the water level of Lake Biwa at Mihogasaki in Ōtsu and the following year began surveying the elevation between Ōtsu and Kyoto. By determining that the surface of Lake Biwa was nearly 43 meters higher than the area near Nanzen-ji in Kyoto, he demonstrated that the waters of Lake Biwa could be used in Kyoto as long as a waterway could be practicably constructed.

Having graduated from the Imperial College of Engineering with the submission of his graduate thesis *Biwako sosui kōji no keikaku* (A plan for construction of the Lake Biwa Canal) on 15 May 1886, Tanabe Sakurō immediately began working to make the canal a reality. On 22 May, just a week after his graduation, he was announced as an employee of the Kyoto prefectural government in the capacity of a junior official with a monthly salary of 40 yen, and arrived in Kyoto on 27 July.

The Lake Biwa Canal was intended to serve many purposes: to provide water for irrigation, to allow the passage of boats, and to supply drinking water. Its most important function, however, was to provide water to power industry. The multipurpose plans for the canal sought to satisfy all of these many objectives. Moreover, a canal prioritizing the passage of boats would need to be much larger in scale than a waterway intended only to supply water.

All previous modern waterways in Japan had been designed for irrigation. A prime example is the Asaka Canal, which drew water from Lake Inawashiro for use in irrigating farmland. The first modern waterway constructed in Meiji Japan, its construction was led by Dutch civil engineer Cornelis van Doorn.

With its aim of drawing water for multiple purposes, the Lake Biwa Canal was significantly larger than the Asaka Canal and its plans entailed the excavation of long tunnels. Van Doorn was critical of the Lake Biwa Canal project as being extremely difficult both technically and in terms of construction costs. Indeed, the project was expected to be a challenge. After all, the plan involved drawing water from Lake Biwa into a waterway at Ōtsu and sending it through three tunnels—including the roughly 2.4-kilometer long Nagarayama Tunnel (Tunnel No. 1)—to the Nanzen-ji area on the eastern edge of Kyoto. Given that the Nagarayama Tunnel would be the longest in Japan at the time, that a Japanese engineer had drawn up the plans, and that no consideration had been given to enlisting the aid of foreigners, it is perhaps perfectly reasonable that van Doorn would express apprehension.

Not only was the Nagarayama Tunnel to be excavated from both the Ōtsu and Kyoto ends, its construction also involved digging shafts midway so that excavation could proceed in both directions from the center as well. This was, of course, intended to reduce the length of the construction period. Because the necessary materials and contractors were unavailable, almost all of the construction work ultimately had to be managed directly. A purpose-built factory, for example, had to be constructed to manufacture the bricks used to finish and reinforce the inside of the tunnels, and the situation was similar with other materials and technologies. Overcoming such challenges, construction moved forward in earnest, driven by a mission to build facilities that would check Kyoto's decline in the wake of the shift of the nation's capital to Tokyo while also contributing to making Japan a wealthy nation.

Kitagaki Kunimichi's Support for the Canal Project

While civil engineer Tanabe Sakurō devoted himself to executing the project, others who recognized the importance of constructing the Lake Biwa Canal applied themselves to getting the project approved by the national government, budgeted, and up and running. Kyoto governor Kitagaki Kunimichi was the driving force behind Kyoto's post-Restoration revival and it may be said that the project came to fruition only due to his promotion of the plan as governor.

Having spent the turbulent Bakumatsu period before the fall of the shogunate supporting pro-imperial nationalists on the ground, Kitagaki Kunimichi pushed ahead with a career as a public servant once the Restoration government was established. In 1870 he was sent to Hokkaido charged with serving as a senior inspector with the Danjōdai police agency, also traveling at that time to Sakhalin. Later he became a seventh-grade official with the Hokkaido Colonization Office and lived the life of a bureaucrat in Hokkaido and Sakhalin until November 1874.

While posted to Hokkaido during the early Meiji period, Kitagaki is said to have made the acquaintance of Enomoto Takeaki, Ōtori Keisuke, and other former shogunal retainers who had made a last stand at Goryōkaku fortress in Hakodate during the Bakumatsu period because they had also become officials with the Hokkaido Colonization Office. Indeed, here lies the reason that Ōtori, as principal of the Imperial College of Engineering, would ultimately connect Tanabe Sakurō with Kyoto. The relationship between Enomoto and Kitagaki, meanwhile, would develop to the point that Enomoto took on the role of go-between when Kitagaki's daughter and Tanabe later married.

It could be said that Kitagaki's ability to get the Lake Biwa Canal project up and running was due to his ties to the Hokkaido of the Bakumatsu and Restoration periods. The reason these ties should bring such a result is that the Goryōkaku fortress was where the technocrats of the shogunate had assembled. Indeed, it was their confidence in their own knowledge and technical skills that led them to carry on the resistance as far as Hokkaido. Ultimately, those who survived would make what they knew available to the Meiji government.

Among those making their stand at Goryōkaku, these were men of a completely different mindset than Hijikata Toshizō of the Shinsengumi, who went there in search of a place to die. Hijikata knew that the arrival of the Restoration would render him and people like him "useless to both heaven and earth," bereft of any philosophical meaning. Or perhaps it would be better to say that he understood from the time he left Kyoto that he was already dead to history. A similar state of mind could be found in the elite shogunal Shōgitai troops who had come to Hokkaido from Edo after being defeated at the Battle of Ueno.

Even among the shogunal retainers, there was an enormous gulf between fighters like the Shōgitai troops or Hijikata and those who had technical skills such as Enomoto Takeaki, Ōtori Keisuke, or Tanabe Sakurō's father Magojirō and uncle Taichi. It is not, of course, as if the educated class among the shogunal retainers who survived the Restoration were sustained by a sense of elitism alone. Indeed, we can see them as having a kind of convoluted spirit of self-relativization that can truly be called modern. Unlike the simple focus on national wealth and military strength of the pro-imperialist nationalists of the Satsuma-Chōshū alliance, or the fighters martyring themselves to the former shogunate, these men must have held in their hearts a sense of modernity that concealed their bitterness. Perhaps it was this very spirit that managed to invest the civilization and enlightenment of the Meiji period with cultural depth.

To Enomoto Takeaki and the others we can add the names Kurimoto Joun and Narushima Ryūhoku. These men lived through the Meiji period feeling useless, but in some ways their existence gave their era greater cultural complexity. These former shogunal retainers withdrew from the world of politics after the Restoration and lived through the new age in a way completely unlike Joseph Fouché or Charles Maurice de Talleyrand-Périgord after the French Revolution. That Japan had such people can surely be counted among the distinctive characteristics of Japanese modernity.

Be that as it may, we must trace the path that Kitagaki Kunimichi followed later. After Hokkaido, he continued his career as a regional bureaucrat in Kumamoto and Kōchi before becoming the third governor of Kyoto Prefecture in January 1881. Inheriting a policy of modernization initiated by his predecessor Governor Makimura Masanao, Kitagaki began making various efforts to bring about the construction of a canal. During his second month as governor, Kitagaki ordered prefectural cartographers to begin a preliminary survey for a canal, having them measure the difference in elevation between Kyoto and Lake Biwa and evaluate possible routes. This was when Tanabe Sakurō, prior to graduation, began measuring the water level of Lake Biwa at Mihogasaki in Ōtsu. The results, as we have already seen, showed that its elevation made the water perfectly suitable for use provided that a waterway could be practicably constructed. At this stage, the purpose of the canal was still weighted toward agricultural irrigation. Although it is unclear exactly when Kitagaki and Tanabe first met, Tanabe's name appears in Kitagaki's diary entry of 20 April 1882 with a note identifying him as a student at the Imperial College of Engineers. In discussing the Lake Biwa Canal, Tanabe introduced Kitagaki to tunnels in the Alps linking Italy and France (Kitagaki's account makes mention of "the Alks [sic] range between Italy and France"). Tanabe enthusiastically described their ventilation systems, presumably because he anticipated people being sent through the tunnels in connection with boat transport.

If the canal were to be used primarily for agricultural irrigation, it would fall under the jurisdiction of the Ministry of Agriculture and Commerce. If the canal were to be used primarily for water transport, it would fall under the jurisdiction of the Bureau of Civil Engineering at the Ministry of Domestic Affairs. Kitagaki Kunimichi had originally envisioned a canal devoted primarily to irrigation, but he eventually leaned toward positioning it as an industrial development project that prioritized water transport. Doing so, however, naturally meant a huge increase in the required width of the waterway relative to a canal devoted to irrigation alone, and a corresponding increase in construction costs. The projected budget for the draft plan considered by the Ministry of Agriculture and Commerce was 600,000 yen, but that would not be nearly enough. Things progressed, taking on the aspect of a power struggle between the Ministry of Agriculture and Commerce and the Ministry of Domestic Affairs. Finally, on 20 January 1885, four years after Kitagaki assumed office as governor, the Ministry of Domestic Affairs, which had become the authority in charge, granted permission to begin construction of the Lake Biwa Canal. Examination by the Ministry of Domestic Affairs prompted a change in the canal route to incorporate multiple tunnels. The new projected budget was roughly 1,250,000 yen, more than double the amount of the Ministry of Agriculture and Commerce plan. The minister of domestic affairs at the time was Yamagata Aritomo of the Chōshū faction. It is said that in those days the Chōshū faction dominated the Ministry of Domestic Affairs while the rival Satsuma faction dominated the Ministry of Agriculture and Commerce, hence the inter-ministry power struggle. The relationship between Yamagata and the canal would take a new direction after the canal's completion through the work of landscape gardener Ogawa Jihei, but this is where it began.

Establishing the Canal Route

Construction of the canal entailed building a waterway made up of facilities including, from the Lake Biwa end at Ōtsu, the Ōtsu Canal (Fig. 1-5), Tunnel No. 1 (Nagarayama Tunnel), Tunnel No. 2, Tunnel No. 3 (Hinooka Tunnel), the Fujio Canal, the Yamashina Canal, the incline, and the Ōtō Canal. Numerous books have been written that describe the project's chal-

Fig. 1-5: The Ōtsu Canal

lenges and Tanabe's accomplishments in overcoming them. Oddly, though, few works have touched on the significance of the route itself. Nevertheless, it was this choice of route that set the stage for the activities of landscape gardener Ogawa Jihei.

As seen today, the canal divides at Keage; the main canal then falls through water pipes to drive the Keage Power Station before continuing on toward the Kyoto City Zoo in Okazaki, while the branch canal wraps around behind Nanzen-ji temple to flow behind Eikan-dō temple on its way toward Nyakuōji. The Suirokaku aqueduct was built to serve the branch canal. The area from Nanzen-ji to Nyakuōji that the branch canal courses through is a historic one with many old shrines and temples. Efforts were made, therefore, to preserve Kyoto's scenic beauty by running the canal through unobtrusive tunnels and by designing structures like the Suirokaku aqueduct with great care. In fact, the design of such structures was a collaborative effort involving not only civil engineers but also Ohara Masutomo, a graduate of the School of Architecture at the Imperial College of Engineering.

Why was such care taken in the construction of the branch canal? The answer lies in its function as a power canal. Although it is impossible to trace the entire route of the branch canal on foot, we can follow it on a map (Fig. 1–6). After wrapping around behind Nanzen-ji temple, the branch canal enters a tunnel, threads along the mountain's edge past Eikan-dō and Nyakuōji, and then resurfaces to continue aboveground toward Ginkaku-ji along what is now the Philosopher's Walk. Without losing any of its potential energy, the branch canal maintains its elevation by weaving along the foothills, continuing toward the village of Tanaka and the Seifū-sō villa, which was originally built as a second home for Saionji Kinmochi and is now the property of Kyoto University.

The branch canal is a narrow waterway, too small for the passage of boats. You can confirm this for yourself by climbing above the Suirokaku aqueduct beside Nanzen-ji and observing the channel that flows over it.

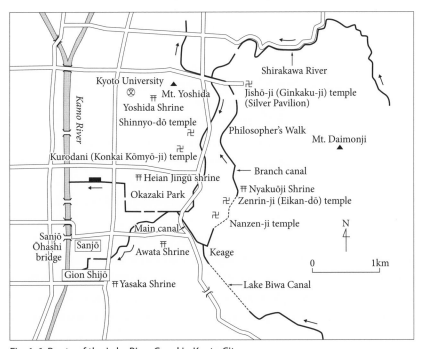

Fig. 1-6: Route of the Lake Biwa Canal in Kyoto City

Fig. 1-7: The branch canal above
the Suirokaku aqueduct

The water is abundant and fast moving but incapable of supporting even a small craft (Fig. 1-7). The branch canal clearly was not designed for transportation but rather for power and irrigation. Indeed, it does provide water for agriculture to northeast Kyoto. Here, too, we can see an effort to make the most of the water by using it in multiple ways.

Although planned under the jurisdiction of the Ministry of Domestic Affairs as an industrial waterway, the Lake Biwa Canal's branch canal retains the character of an irrigation channel that should have fallen under the jurisdiction of the Ministry of Agriculture and Commerce. This is illustrated by an episode relayed in *Tanabe Sakurō hakase rokujūnenshi* (A sixty-year history of Dr. Tanabe Sakurō).

In November 1907 the mayor of the village of Shirakawa, Nishimura Tomesaburō, sent Tanabe a thank-you letter that said, "Since the completion of the Lake Biwa Canal we now have abundant water for our village's fields and waterwheels and remain ever grateful for the magnitude of your accomplishments." The body of the letter continues, "As a small token of our true feelings we sought to present you with a stone lantern made using stone from our village. Since you have declined to accept it, please under-

stand that we have instead inscribed the lantern with words commemorating your accomplishments and donated it to Shinnyo-dō temple in
Higashiyama." In relaying this episode, *Tanabe Sakurō hakase rokujūnenshi*
further notes that "the lantern mentioned is the one currently [1924] found
adjacent to the Benten-dō hall at the north end of the precincts of Shinnyo-dō temple in eastern Kyoto."

A visitor to Shinnyo-dō today finds no Benten-dō on the temple
grounds, which are lined with numerous stone monuments. Nevertheless,
it is possible to discern the following inscription on a stone lantern found
in front of the Gansan Daishi-dō hall that stands to the left of the temple's
main hall:

Presented to Shinnyo-dō
Commemorating the merits and virtues of Tanabe Sakurō, Doctor of
Engineering
November 1907
Nishimura ■rō, Village of Shirakawa

Although the inscription immediately following "Nishimura" is now il-
legible, it seems certain that it completes the name of the mayor of Shirakawa village, Nishimura Tomesaburō.

The phrase *shōtoku kinen* ["commemorating the merits and virtues
of"] suggests both the depth of the gratitude that the people of the day felt
toward Tanabe Sakurō and the breadth of the uses to which the waters of
the Lake Biwa Canal were applied.

And yet we must ask again whether the branch canal was really a waterway primarily for irrigation. When the mayor of Shirakawa writes of
"abundant water for . . . fields and waterwheels" he probably means waterwheels used to pump water or those used for milling flour, which would
make the branch canal a typical agricultural waterway.

I suppose it would be best to take another look at the Lake Biwa Canal
and its branch canal as originally envisioned by Tanabe Sakurō, that is, at
the power canal described at the beginning of the prospectus. Water from

the branch canal was supposed to drop into the Shirakawa River, providing a source of power for waterwheels that would drive factories. The feasibility of hydroelectric power made this unnecessary and the branch canal ended up being used more for irrigation. Accordingly, the gratitude of the mayor of Shirakawa may have made Tanabe somewhat uncomfortable. Perhaps such feelings were behind his refusal to accept the stone lantern.

Construction on the canal is known to have begun on 2 June 1885 while its completion was marked with a sluice opening ceremony on 9 April 1890. During the fourth year of construction, from 20 October 1888 to 23 January 1889, Tanabe Sakurō traveled to North America to inspect canals with Takagi Bunpei, a member of the canal survey committee in Kyoto. Sakamoto Norimi, director of the canal office, had ordered them to go to America to research the latest in methods for arranging waterpower. Through this trip we ought to be able to get a clearer picture of Tanabe's view of canals.

The Canal Cities of North America

The itinerary for Tanabe Sakurō's trip to North America was meticulously planned to make the most of each and every day. Leaving Yokohama on the 2,800-ton *Abyssinia*, he went out on deck every night to survey the ship's position and distance traveled by observing the moon and the stars. Notably, he did this twice on 28 October, the day the ship crossed the international date line, recording its positions as 179° 40' east longitude and 172° 12' west longitude. This suggests both the tenacity of a born engineer and a real love of surveying. Tanabe seems to have taken great pleasure even in such tedious measurements and calculations.

Arriving in Vancouver at three o'clock in the morning on 4 November 1888, by one o'clock that afternoon he was on the Canadian Pacific Railway bound by way of Montreal for New York, where he arrived on 11 November. Unbelievably long by current standards, the journey had taken more than twenty days.

On the 14th he arrived in Washington, D.C. where he visited the Patent

Office and inspected the Patowmack Canal. On the 21st he inspected the Morris Canal before returning to New York on the 23rd. Both the Patowmack and Morris canals were transportation canals designed for the passage of boats. The Patowmack Canal is famous today for the blossoming cherry trees, sent from Japan, that line its banks.

Tanabe Sakurō's inspection of the Morris Canal, meanwhile, was intended to provide a model for the incline he intended to use in the Lake Biwa Canal. As is well known, such inclined planes are designed to facilitate the passage of boats between canals with height differentials by loading them onto cradle cars that were pulled up or down slopes. The Lake Biwa Canal incline was a Kyoto attraction for a long time and has been retained to the present day although it is no longer in use.

A typical North American transportation canal, the Morris Canal went from Port Delaware in Phillipsburg on the banks of the Delaware River to the Hudson River by way of New York's neighbor cities of Newark and Jersey City. The canal had a total length of just over 102 miles, which can be thought of as twice the length of the Panama Canal or about as long as the Suez Canal.

One of the characteristics of the Morris Canal was its change of elevation, which reached as high as 914 feet, the largest of any canal in the world. The Suez Canal is nearly level and although differences in elevation are said to have complicated the construction of the Panama Canal, the difference there is no more than 85 feet. The Panama Canal, then, could clear its change in elevation by raising boats using locks. The more dramatic change in elevation at the Morris Canal could not be overcome in this way, so inclined planes—both single and double types—were installed at 23 locations in addition to the canal's twenty locks.

Planning for the Morris Canal began in the early nineteenth century. Surveying was initiated in 1822 by Columbia University professor James Renwick and a company was established in 1824 to handle construction and financing. Construction began in 1825 and was completed in 1831. Total construction costs were initially estimated to be $817,000 but by the time the canal was completed had grown to $2,104,413. The Morris Canal was designed for the passage of 10-ton boats but enlarged in 1860 at a cost of $1,700,000 to enable the passage of boats as large as 70 tons. It was the canal of this period that Tanabe Sakurō would have seen. Based on looking through a book of historical photographs of the Morris Canal, it appears that the cradle cars used for the inclined planes incorporated wooden trusses and that navigation along the canal involved the boats being pulled by horses or donkeys. Compared to the steel cradle cars and the use of electric power for traction at the incline on the Lake Biwa Canal, the facilities were already outdated.

The Morris Canal was used for a long time, recording its heaviest usage in 1867, the year before the Meiji Restoration. After this, however, the canal's position was gradually eroded by the development of the railroad and it was shut down in the 1920s. Today only a very small portion has been preserved. Seeing it in its heyday, Tanabe Sakurō no doubt made his inspection of the canal with enthusiasm. In Newark, however, where the Morris Canal literally ceded the road to automobile traffic and subway tracks, all that remains to convey what it looked like are some tile murals on the subway station walls.

After concluding his two-day inspection of the Morris Canal, Tanabe Sakurō returned to New York on 23 November 1888. Four days later, on 27 November, he appeared in Boston where he began an inspection of canals and industries in the state of Massachusetts. In Boston he inspected electric and water utilities before going to Lynn to inspect an electric railway on 3 December, something intended to serve as reference for Kyoto's municipal streetcar plans.

After visiting Lynn, Tanabe Sakurō headed to Lowell on the following day, the 4th, and then on to Holyoke, described at the beginning of this chapter, on the 5th. There he inspected canals designed not for water transport but for power generation. *Tanabe Sakurō hakase rokujūnenshi* (A sixty-year history of Dr. Tanabe Sakurō) records Tanabe's behavior during this period as "seeing waterpower in these cities," a concise illustration of the fact that he was interested not in the canals per se but in their use in supply-

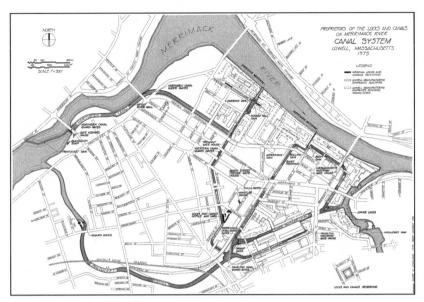

Fig. 1-8: The canals of Lowell

ing water for power. According to this book, Tanabe met someone named Francis in Lowell and someone named Herschel in Holyoke. Clemens Herschel was the president of Holyoke Water Power Company, which essentially ran everything in the city. The Francis in Lowell, on the other hand, was British-born engineer James B. Francis, who completed the city's network of canals. After serving as Chief Engineer of the Proprietors of Locks and Canals, the company that constructed and managed the canals, in 1855 he authored the book *Lowell Hydraulic Experiments*. At the age of just 28, Tanabe was able to gain insights about water-use techniques directly from this giant in the field. At the time, Lowell was a civil and mechanical engineering mecca that offered engineers an unparalleled place to learn.

The canals of Holyoke were the most heavily engineered, diverting the waters of the Connecticut River, with its large drop at Hadley Falls, through entirely artificial channels to create a tidily organized industrial site. The canal system at Lowell, by contrast, was somewhat more empirical, diverting the waters of the Merrimack River into a number of successive branches—including the Pawtucket Canal, Merrimack Canal, feeder canals, and

Northern Canal—each constructed in turn and applied to the generation of power. In this way, distributary channels were created with different water levels, and water falling from upper canals to lower canals was used to turn the waterwheels generating power for industrial use (Fig. 1-8).

The town of Holyoke was first created in 1847 as a planned city founded on well-organized waterways. Historically older (even if dating only to 1813), Lowell differs in offering a picturesque network of canals that were built one after the other. Nevertheless, its canals form much the same sort of system, one that relies on water falling from a higher-level flow to one at a lower level.

Looking at the Lake Biwa Canal in this light, and particularly the plans for its branch canal, we can see that the design marvelously incorporates a nuanced reading of the topography. That is, the branch canal maintains a high position in the foothills as it moves from Nanzen-ji to Nyakuōji by way of Eikan-dō. After ducking through tunnels behind both Nanzen-ji and Eikan-dō, the water reveals itself again in front of the shrine at Nyakuō-ji. Here a reservoir has been provided to regulate water volume, just prior to which there is a discharge channel connected directly to the Shirakawa River. The branch canal then flows on below Reikan-ji temple, the tomb of Emperor Reizei, and Hōnen-in temple before arriving in front of Ginkaku-ji temple. There, the natural Shirakawa River flows in the opposite direction, heading from Ginkaku-ji toward Nanzen-ji (Fig. 1-6).

Something odd, though, occurs on the streets in front of Ginkaku-ji where the branch canal and the Shirakawa River intersect. The waters of the former pass below while those of the latter cross above, even as both continue to flow in opposite directions. In other words, the flow of the Shirakawa is positioned below the waters of the branch canal after passing Ginkaku-ji. Along this section, then, it would be possible to turn waterwheels using water dropped from the branch canal into the Shirakawa. The branch canal is constructed in such a way that it can serve as an upper canal to a lower canal formed by the natural Shirakawa River.

Tanabe Sakurō's concept of creating a power canal system not by dividing a single flow or causing it to backtrack to create different elevations but instead by connecting a branch of the Lake Biwa Canal with the natural Shirakawa River was truly genius. It was a plan grounded in inspired design based on topographical characteristics, and one not seen in the canal systems of Holyoke or Lowell. Surely in this we find evidence of Tanabe Sakurō's talents as an engineer. The scope of this plan for the power canal system extended from Nanzen-ji into Shishigatani. This stretch, in other words, was intended to be lined with factories—a far cry from a "philosopher's walk." This was what the text of the first objective in the prospectus—Manufacturing Machinery—meant when stating, "Not only does the Shirakawa River run below the area around Nyakuōji and the village of Shishigatani, but the grade of the land is also very steep, no doubt making it an ideal location for the installation of waterwheels."

Holyoke and Lowell were model cases for the establishment of industrial sites using such canal systems, but Tanabe Sakurō's inspection visits to Holyoke and Lowell took place in 1888, fully three years after construction on the Lake Biwa Canal had begun. This is much too late for him to have been researching canal systems. By then, his ingenious plan for the canal was complete and construction was already winding down. The year before his trip, the Nagarayama Tunnel—the canal's most difficult section—had been completed and the design for the Suirokaku aqueduct at Nanzen-ji temple was also complete. Although Tanabe's trip to North America has been explained as being for the purpose of investigating methods of arranging waterpower in the United States (Holyoke), perhaps his true reason for taking the trip lay elsewhere, in something other than waterway research—something related to the new hydroelectric systems about which information was arriving during construction of the Lake Biwa Canal.

Tanabe Sakurō wrapped up his inspections of Holyoke and Lowell in just one day each, departing Boston on 6 December and returning to New York, where he examined electric companies. On the 17th, he headed back to the Morris Canal to see its inclined planes. On the 23rd he left New York, arriving five days later on the 28th in Aspen, Colorado, where he saw the construction of a hydroelectric power installation under the guidance of a man named Devereux. It was news of this application of hydroelectric power that had drawn him to the spot, but in recording his impressions he described it as "very small-scale." Already, Tanabe had a clear concept in mind for the hydroelectric station at Keage.

Aspen is a classic example of a town created overnight during America's history of pioneering. A mining town formed in 1878, the population exploded beginning in 1887 with a boom in silver mining. A major conflagration in 1884 brought home the need for water to fight fires. Waterway planning began the following year, with plans for hydroelectric power also being undertaken at about the same time. The first visible fruit of hydroelectric power was a demonstration of electric lamps on 19 May 1885. Ultimately, the plan called for a 150-horsepower hydraulic turbine that would make use of a 49-foot vertical drop to turn two generators, and this was constructed in the fall of 1888 just two or three months before Tanabe's visit. The Devereux that Tanabe met was James H. Devereux, the younger brother and business associate of Walter B. Devereux, a metallurgical engineer who worked as the right-hand man to Jerome B. Wheeler, owner of the Aspen Mining and Smelting Company, Aspen's largest mining company. An 1873 graduate of Princeton University, Walter was Aspen's first true engineer and served as Wheeler's financial and technical advisor.

Interestingly, a shareholders meeting for the Aspen Mining and Smelting Company was held on 11 December 1888 at the company's headquarters at 54 Wall Street in New York City. Tanabe Sakurō was in New York on that day, "seeing electric companies there." Given that he later left directly for Aspen suggests that he may have heard about the shareholders meeting and even met one of the Devereux brothers in New York. The timing is surprising, as is Tanabe's information-gathering ability.

After his inspection in Aspen, Tanabe Sakurō saw and sketched an eclipse in Nevada on the 31st while he was on his way to the west coast. Giving free rein to his engineering spirit, he surely made various other observations, too. He was a restless man, indeed.

Early in the new year, on 2 January 1889, Tanabe Sakurō arrived in San Francisco. The following day he headed to the Pelton Water Wheel Company to discuss waterwheel plans—specifically, those for water turbines to be used for generating electric power. Unlike turbines designed for water-driven power whose shafts were positioned vertically, this type had a horizontally oriented shaft and received water from the side. Tanabe placed an order for waterwheels that would turn the generators at the Keage Power Station. The Pelton Water Wheel Company had manufactured the waterwheels used to generate hydroelectric power in Aspen and was the principal developer of the technology they used. For inventing a water wheel whose shaft was oriented horizontally, the company's Lester A. Pelton would later receive the Elliott Cresson Medal from the Franklin Institute. It was this type of waterwheel that Tanabe ordered, although those he ordered were far larger than the ones used at Aspen. The power station at Aspen generated just 150 horsepower, but plans for Keage called for eventually generating 2,000 horsepower. At the Keage Power Station, two Pelton turbines were initially used to turn two generators, each producing 80 kilowatts of power.

Having completed his work, Tanabe Sakurō began his journey home to Japan aboard the 3,000-ton *Belgique* at three o'clock in the afternoon on 5 January, arriving in Yokohama on the 23rd and returning to Kyoto on the 31st. Although his return was ten days earlier than originally planned, the roughly three-month trip had been a full one. Taking little time for rest, on 10 February he began work on *Suiryoku haichihō chōsa hōkokusho* (Investigative report on methods of waterpower arrangement), thereby beginning the formal incorporation of plans for hydroelectric power.

After this whirlwind crossing of the American continent, Tanabe had returned home with satisfactory results. Nevertheless, his inspection visits to Holyoke and Lowell in the midst of a busy itinerary can perhaps be seen as driven by the force of circumstance. Both were industrial cities powered by waterwheels. You could say that from the moment plans for the Lake Biwa Canal switched from the use of waterwheel-driven power to hydroelectric power, visiting these cities became meaningless. In fact, although Tanabe visited the Morris Canal twice to study its inclines, he allocated but a single day each for Holyoke and Lowell. That Tanabe's busy itinerary included as many days as possible for inspections of inclines and electric companies, including his trip to Aspen during the year-end rush, reinforces the sense that his brief visits to Holyoke and Lowell were tacked on only for appearances sake. They were probably no more than insurance visits after having already made the decision to abandon the notion of a power canal system. In fact, in Tanabe's telegram of 25 November, immediately following his inspection of the Morris Canal, and again in writing on 9 December upon returning to New York after visiting Holyoke and Lowell, he asked the canal office to suspend work on the incline until his return to Japan. Once the plan for electricity generation was within sight, he needed to stop and reassess the incline, too.

Although Holyoke would bear cultural fruit in the form of Mount Holyoke College, the city today has declined as an industrial area whose day has passed. Industry changes with the times, but my impression is that the college, having transformed the wealth generated by industrial strength into culture, stands alone in sustaining the city today. In the same way, Lowell has also completely lost its strength as an industrial city, and is a classic example of an industrial city in decline. Lowell, though, having developed without the overly orderly block planning found in Holyoke, has more varied scenery and a canal network with a picturesque charm. Today, Lowell promotes itself as a former factory town and a tourist spot for industrial archaeology. Enormous gears once used in the city's factories have been placed on the streets like public sculpture and routes have been developed for touring old mills that give visitors a glimpse of nineteenth-century industrial systems.

Lowell also seeks to market itself as the town where Beat novelist and poet Jack Kerouac (1922–1969) was raised, and there is a small park that bears his name. Born the son of French-Canadian immigrants, Kerouac lived in Lowell through high school. He is said to have spoken only French until entering elementary school. He died before reaching the age of fifty, leaving behind the seminal *On the Road*, an expression of the feelings of impending ruin experienced by young people in post-Second World War America as the country headed toward war in Vietnam. The city of Lowell represented an archetypal landscape for such young people, a devastated factory town bereft of any hint of culture.

The more functional a system of waterways was, the less capable it was of keeping pace when things changed. With the end of the age of water-power, a network of waterways perfectly aligned to a particular purpose became a system empty of utility value. Such is the nature of the functionalist lifespan. Lowell's network of waterways was still under development when it fell from use and remained incomplete, which is why it was possible to transform its scenery into a site for tourism. In Holyoke, however, where the waterway network had been perfected, there was no land left for factory expansion and the functional, mechanical waterways have not generated much appeal as a tourist destination.

That Tanabe Sakurō sought to use the power of water not to turn water-wheels but to generate electricity shows his perceptive insight on changing times. Given the time period, it would not have been at all surprising had the Lake Biwa Canal been Japan's first and last example of a power canal. Had it been completed as a power canal, the area from Nanzen-ji to Nyakuōji would have become an industrial area similar to Lowell, though on a smaller scale, and one that would surely stand in decline today. Tanabe's gamble on hydroelectric power—which he happened to see in Aspen just after that installation's completion and before it had spread elsewhere around the world—determined everything. Ultimately, it made possible the supply of electricity and brought Japan's first streetcar to Kyoto. The late 1880s when Tanabe visited the United States was both the heyday of power canals and the turning point when they began their decline. It is probably impossible to give Tanabe too much credit for his foresightedness. Shortly after Tanabe's visit, Aspen lost momentum with the collapse of silver prices in the 1890s. It was not until the 1930s that Aspen finally recovered when it reinvented itself as a city of culture and recreation. Tanabe seems to have had the good fortune to visit just the right places at just the right times.

But what of the ingenious plans for the branch canal that Tanabe Sakurō had already formed before heading to the United States—the idea that, stretching from Nanzen-ji to Nyakuōji, it would serve as an upper canal casting water into the lower canal of the Shirakawa River? The design of the Suirokaku aqueduct had been finalized prior to his departure and construction was proceeding apace on the branch waterway itself. Ultimately, however, the completed branch canal would serve not as an upper canal but as a simple irrigation channel.

Canal Function and Design

The volume of water that would flow through the Lake Biwa Canal was calculated in terms of cubic *shaku* (that is, the volume of a roughly 30 cm-square cube) per second. Roughly 300 cubic *shaku* of water would be drawn per second at Ōtsu, traveling at a speed of between three and four *shaku* per second. Roughly one-sixth of this water—that is, roughly 50 cubic *shaku* per second—would be directed to the branch canal. This represented an abrupt reduction to the amount that was originally expected to drive turbine-style waterwheels as it fell into the Shirakawa River around Shishigatani. Indeed, the branch canal had initially been planned as a trunk canal conveying a high volume of water—104 cubic *shaku* per second—to drive waterwheels powering a variety of factories constructed along three or four stepped levels provided between the canal and the Shirakawa.

A plan drafted in March 1890 and approved by Governor Kitagaki Kunimichi—*Sosui oyobi hennyū chiiki o chūshin to suru shigai kakuteian* (A city planning proposal centered on the canal and the newly incorporated areas)—can be found in *Biwako sosui oyobi suiryoku shiyō jigyō* (The lake Biwa Canal and hydropower project), compiled by the Kyoto Municipal Electric Bureau. Expectations that completion of the canal would bring new development to the surrounding area demanded a plan to cope with such future growth, and this document describes a vision of the future city centered primarily on land for roadways ranging from 18-meter wide first-class roads to fourth-class roads measuring 5.4 to 7.2 meters wide.

According to this plan, the optimal approach was for both commercial and industrial interests to utilize the canal along the roads on both sides of the main canal between the incline and the Kamogawa River and from

Nyakuōji to the point where the branch canal meets the north-side road. This roughly corresponds to what today is the Philosopher's Walk, a neighborhood originally destined to be dominated by factories and the canal. In addition, three other neighborhoods were also mentioned as suitable for commerce and industry: "from the south corner of Kamogawa Ranch to the gate of Kurodani Temple in Shōgoin-chō," "from the gate of Shōren-in temple in Awata on Sanjō-dōri street through Yoshida-chō to the Higher Middle School," and "from Bukkō-ji temple on the east side of the Fujii Spinning Company on Nijō-dōri street across Shōgoin to the west-side road at Hyakumanben intersection."

The interesting thing is that while the area leading from the gate of Nanzen-ji temple to the gate of Ginkaku-ji temple by way of Eikan-dō and Nyakuōji is described as slightly less desirable for commercial and industrial use than the other areas, the report also notes that favoring the area was only natural given its status as home to some of Kyoto's finest scenery and as a draw for those seeking to enjoy views of the beloved eastern mountains in the Higashiyama district. This shows that the authorities at the time understood that the Higashiyama foothills, though slated to become an industrial area, should also develop as a place of scenic beauty. The promotion of Kyoto was moving forward with a comprehensive view.

The plan was to provide first-class roads in all of these areas, although in fact this changed with changing circumstances. When plans to use the canal for industrial purposes switched from using waterwheels to using hydroelectric power, the branch canal, originally planned as a power canal, was repositioned as something for only irrigation and agricultural waterwheels. Although the villagers of Shirakawa had sent Tanabe Sakurō a stone lantern inscribed with an expression of their gratitude for such benefits as the canal brought them, Tanabe's feelings upon receiving it were surely mixed. After all, contrary to his initial plans the branch canal did no more than supply water for agriculture. His decision not to accept this lantern, ultimately presented instead to Shinnyo-dō temple, no doubt speaks to his state of mind.

As mentioned above, when planning the canal its basic water volume was measured in cubic *shaku* per second. For the Lake Biwa Canal, each cubic *shaku* per second was called "one unit." The canal as a whole, then, was described as carrying 300 units, of which 50 were carried by the branch canal.

Notions of water volume can also be found at the power canals of North America, where it was expressed in terms of "mill-power," that is, as a unit of potential energy needed to turn a waterwheel. Mill-power, then was an amount of energy determined by multiplying water volume by the length of the drop. The concept of mill-power was first developed in Lowell, where one mill-power was defined as 25 cubic feet of water per second flowing over a 30-foot drop, or 45.5 cubic feet per second flowing over a 17-foot drop, or 60.5 cubic feet per second flowing over a 13-foot drop. Mill-power, then, was not so much a measure of water volume as an empirical unit of energy. This concept born in Lowell spread to other towns, and mill-power rights were registered and traded just like ownership rights to real estate.

By comparison, the "unit" used at the Lake Biwa Canal was not a representation of motive energy but strictly a measure of static water volume. For a branch canal whose role as a power canal had been abandoned, this was probably sufficient. The old units based on the *shakkan* system of weights and measures are no longer used today, and water volume contracts are measured in liters per second. For example, the Rakusui Garden, whose contract I was able to review, draws four liters of water per second. One cubic *shaku* works out to roughly nine liters, so perhaps the units used in water volume contracts today encourage water conservation more so than in the past.

Seen as a whole, the Lake Biwa Canal covered just about every possible function such a canal system could perform. First, as symbolized by the incline, it functioned as a transportation canal. As a power canal, it went a step beyond waterwheels to put together a hydroelectric power system. It also supplied water for drinking and irrigation, and would later provide water for firefighting at the Imperial Palace and Higashi Hongan-ji temple. In this multifunctional waterway we find a virtual catalog of canal functionality. We could say that it represents both the genius of Tanabe Sakurō and the essence of the Meiji period's industrial spirit. Although thoroughly functional, the Lake Biwa Canal's pursuit of a complex of functions rather than focusing on just one ensured its longevity. And at the end of its long life, it gave birth to both the Philosopher's Walk and the gardens of landscape designer Ogawa Jihei.

Of particular interest is the design of the structures built at various points along the canal. The entrances and exits of each tunnel are provided with solidly formed arched portals. Constructed after the completion of the canal itself, the pump house built to divert water from Keage to the Imperial Palace adopts a classical style with a Tuscan order. The Suirokaku aqueduct, Japan's only continuous arch bridge from the period, is a popular site for tourists in part because its stylistic details are so true to the Roman aqueducts that inspired it.

These canal facilities were some of the first structures built in the true classical style in Japan. It is fascinating, too, that the Keage pump house's most elaborately detailed elevation is found not at the building's entrance but rather facing the canal's waterway (Fig. 1-9). This illustrates how everything was centered on, and designed to face, the waterway.

It may seem odd that these works of civil engineering should incorpo-

Fig. 1-9: The pump house at Keage (at the old Kujōyama Water Purification Plant)

rate an authentic style more often associated with palaces and government buildings. Indeed, this was a period when countless Western-style structures appeared throughout Japan that were done by halves and went no further than the realm of pseudo-European conceit.

This puzzle can be solved by recognizing that authentic styles were used for these structures not *despite* but rather *precisely because* they were works of civil engineering. Arches, vaults, and tunnel portals exhibiting authentic style and composition were adopted because such style and composition was considered part and parcel of the civil engineering systems brought by the West.

Works of architecture were often subjected to creative compromise out of consideration for Japan's culture and history, and such stylistic alterations or simplifications can be seen to represent a certain kind of originality. Meanwhile, for civil engineering structures—manifestations of technological fields—the formal language of the West was adopted perfectly. In this we see a difference in the way forms were assimilated across artistic and technological fields in the course of Japan's modernization.

For example, when Kamiya Denbei, owner of the Kamiya Bar in Asakusa so famous for his iconic Denki Bran cocktail, set out to fulfill his long-held dream of undertaking the entire winemaking process from grape cultivation to bottling by building Chateau Kamiya (now Ushiku Chateau) in Ushiku, Ibaraki in 1903, the winery buildings included a storehouse, a fermentation building, bottle storage, and an underground nursery, and were designed as authentic Western architecture in the French style. To think that an authentic Western architectural style was adopted *despite* the buildings being a winery would be odd; rather, it is better to consider that an authentic Western architectural style was adopted *precisely because* it was understood to be an element of French winemaking technology. The buildings were constructed not as an expression of architecture as art but as a faithful rendering of parts of a technological system.

Another similar example can be found in drawings held in the collection of the Shōko Shūseikan Museum, originally built by the Satsuma domain in the latter days of the shogunate as a model factory designed to introduce Western technology. The museum today exhibits drawings, done on Japanese washi paper by Japanese draftsmen, of a steam engine frame, one that while no doubt made of cast iron is composed in the Gothic style. One characteristic of the Gothic style is pointed arches that combine two arc segments, and such pointed arches frequently appear in windows and ceilings. The drawings on washi at the Shōko Shūseikan Museum include vivid depictions of pointed arches. The Bakumatsu period when the Shōko Shūseikan was working so hard to introduce modern Western technologies corresponded to the high point of the Gothic Revival in Europe. At the time, nearly everything was dressed up in the Gothic style, which influenced even the design of machinery. The samurai of Satsuma who worked to introduce Western technology no doubt diligently copied the steam engine frame with its pointed arches from some master drawing without giving the Gothic style any thought, and were no doubt unaware that pointed arches were one of the style's distinguishing features.

Construction of the Lake Biwa Canal began roughly thirty years after the Shōko Shūseikan, so Tanabe Sakurō and his colleagues understood the significance of the classical styles used to embellish their works of civil engineering. Many had been quick to realize that the canal would tie together some of Kyoto's most scenic locations, and the American Ernest Fenollosa had spoken before the people of Kyoto in 1886, subsequent to the start of construction on the canal, to argue the importance of the arts. Kitagaki

Fig. 1-10: Lake Biwa Canal tunnel entrance

Kunimichi, too, is said to have come to believe that it was necessary to work to preserve and improve Kyoto's scenic spots. Tanabe is said to have suggested "doing art on the tunnel entrances" and, as mentioned above, entrusted their design to Ohara Masutomo, a graduate of the School of Architecture at the Imperial College of Engineering, upon learning that he was working for Shiga Prefecture. In this, the civil engineers opted to employ such styles accurately, with neither simplification nor modification (Fig. 1-10).

The Fine Arts and Technology

Here, though the transition may seem abrupt, I would like to talk about the concept of *geijutsu* from the latter days of the shogunate through the Restoration. The reason is that, much like our concept of philosophy (*tetsugaku*), our current concept of the fine arts (*geijutsu*) is a product of modernity; the word *geijutsu* existed, but meant something different, during the Edo period.

Sakuma Shōzan, an enlightened scholar of the Edo period, argued for *tōyō dōtoku seiyō geijutsu* [Eastern morals, Western *geijutsu*], where the word *geijutsu* represents a concept similar to "science and technology." The artistic forms found at the Lake Biwa Canal, then, are perhaps best seen as structures built using *geijutsu* as it was understood by Sakuma Shōzan with the new addition of an artistic sensibility grounded in the concept of *geijutsu* as it came to be understood in the Meiji period.

In general, however, the sense with which the word *geijutsu* was used during the Edo period differed slightly from the way Sakuma Shōzan used it. The 1855 books *Geijutsu hiden zue* (Illustrated secrets of the arts), written by Ōmori Masatomi, and *Geijutsu nogake kyō* (Lessons from excursions in the arts), translated by Ōsho Sanjin, were treatises on gunnery. At the time, the word *geijutsu* referred to the military or martial arts, including gunnery. For example, Hirahayashi Masasuke wrote a treatise on swordsmanship called *Geijutsu manbyōen* (A cure-all for the arts) in 1773 and Kokenken Ryokusui's *Geijutsu yōran* (A survey of the arts) was included as part of *Honchō kyūba yōran* (A survey of Japanese archery and horsemanship) in 1787. Other works on swordsmanship include Niwa Chozan's *Tengu geijutsu ron* (On the arts of the mountain goblins) from 1729 and the Masaki School text *Geijutsu bukō ron* (On the arts and martial accomplishment) by Kashibuchi Arinori. As a gunner, Tanabe Sakurō's father Magojirō would have been known as a *geijutsuka* (artist) in his day.

Even into the Meiji period, books such as *Kyōikugaku* (Pedagogy) by Isawa Shūji, published in 1882, contained statements like, "Many of them have developed robust physiques through training in these various martial arts. Such *geijutsu* vary with different systems of physical education." Here, too, the word *geijutsu* is used to mean the martial arts.

Given this Edo period equivalence between *geijutsu* and the martial arts, how was the concept of "fine arts" as expressed in English understood? The word devised—and attributed to Ōtori Keisuke—as a Japanese translation for "fine arts" was *bijutsu*. A pamphlet soliciting works to be exhibited at the Vienna International Exposition of 1873 defines *bijutsu* as "including works of music, painting, sculpture, and poetry." Of note is that the concept of *bijutsu* is described as covering not only visual arts such as painting and sculpture but also music and poetry. Here the term *bijutsu* describes something closer to the concept that *geijutsu* represents today.

Ōtori Keisuke's writings also include *Nihon bijutsu* (The arts of Japan), published in 1877, in which he writes, "*Bijutsu* means crafts such as drawing and painting, sculpture, modeling, and interior decoration." Here the concept of *bijutsu* conforms well to today's notion of the visual arts. In this we can see that the concept of *bijutsu* changed slightly as it took root in the early years of the Meiji period. Ōtori had been a typical shogunate technocrat. As technological systems were constructed and concepts adopted during the Meiji period, the former shogunate had gained the potential to become a driving force for civilization and enlightenment. Had he lived to see the Restoration, Tanabe Sakurō's father might also have played an active role as a man of talent like Ōtori. I cannot help imagining that Tanabe, as he set off on his own path as an engineer, must have secretly harbored thoughts of the man his father might have become.

The science and technology of the Meiji period is often criticized as something imported directly from the West, as intent on adopting easily obtained applied methods but divorced from the ways of thinking that led to their establishment. Such a lack of originality, so it goes, led to the present day's denigration of basic research and a posture of merely imitating results and putting them to practical use.

And yet, was that really the case? It is well known that many Japanese translations of conceptual terms took hold during the early years of the Meiji period in the form of Chinese character compounds. Nishi Amane's coinage of the word *tetsugaku* for "philosophy" is a well-known example, while Tanaka Fujimaro established the word *kōkogaku* for "archaeology" and Itō Chūta, during the middle of the Meiji period, established the word *kenchikugaku* for "architecture," replacing the word *zōkagaku* ("house-building") that had been used until then. Indeed, many of the conceptual terms we use today became fixed through the efforts of people during the Meiji period. It is unimaginable to think that this process was free of either conflict or distress. They carefully considered the meaning of each concept, wandered widely across the landscape of existing Japanese and Chinese terms, and translated the concepts conceptually. The phrase *wakon yōsai* [Japanese spirit and Western learning], a play on the *wakon kansai* [Japanese spirit and Chinese learning] of a previous age, is often said to express the spirit of the Meiji period. The application of Japanese spirit—and knowledge of the Chinese classics—to Western learning, however, must surely have required considerable thought. It is difficult to imagine such a thing occurring completely divorced from underlying ways of thinking, grounded only in a simple belief in the supremacy of technology.

Is it even possible, as argued by the modernists of a certain period, to adopt technology only after first comprehending the depths of its underlying ideas? If so, what would this look like? Had Western science and technology been adopted only after understanding Western thought, would there have been any room for we non-Westerners to retain our own originality? Is it not the case that mastering the modern science of the West without any sense of the rift suggested by *wakon yōsai* would be merely *yōkon yōsai* [Western spirit and Western learning], gaining us little more than the status of "honorary whites"? For a country like Japan located outside the Western European sphere to achieve modernization without colonization, wasn't the proper application of Japanese spirit and Western learning an inevitable path?

But here an additional problem arises. Does Western technology have an expression? If technology itself is nothing but the realization of objective principles and there is no room for expressive breadth, then how were we Japanese supposed to express our own image as we pursued modernization? Merely bringing in the Western arts just as they were would not express a modern Japan, and continuing to use Japan's traditional artistic expressions unchanged would hardly constitute an expression of modernity.

The Lake Biwa Canal provides a fascinating historical answer to the question of how *wakon yōsai* came to be expressed. Through his gardens, landscape gardener Ogawa Jihei gave shape to the cultural aspirations of a modernizing Japan and of the people at the core of this modernization. Such an expression was indispensable to ensure that modernization was more than just a synonym for Westernization.

Tanabe's phrase "doing art" is interesting in how perfectly it conveys the notion of unsentimental engineers adding stylistic decoration to the products of technology. Engineering technology and the language of classicism were taken in together as a part of a single continuity. In the eyes of the engineers, the design of the tunnel portals with their pediments and keystones may have seemed just part of the technology. Dressing up the tunnel portals in the classical style was probably, in the minds of the engineers, an unsentimental means of "doing art."

In fact, the designs used for the tunnel portals were nearly exact copies of examples found in various locations in Europe and the United States. According to *Biwako sosui no hyakunen* (A century of the Lake Biwa Canal), the following correspondences can be found:

Tunnel No. 1 East Portal and Tunnel No. 3 West Portal:
Hauenstein Tunnel, Central Railway, Switzerland (1853–1857)

Tunnel No. 1 West Portal and Tunnel No. 2 East Portal:
Hoosac Tunnel, Troy and Greenfield Railway, United States (1874)

Tunnel No. 2 West Portal:
Ippensen Tunnel South Portal, Kreiensen-Holzminden Railway, Germany (1863–1864)

Tunnel No. 3 East Portal:
Altenbeken Tunnel West Portal, Holzminden-Altenbeken Railway, Germany (1861)

Branch Canal Tunnel
Altenbeken Tunnel East Portal, Holzminden-Altenbeken Railway, Germany (1861)

Each of these designs was taken from illustrations contained in the back of Henry S. Drinker's *Tunneling, Explosive Compounds, and Rock Drills* (2nd edition, 1882), a reference book that had been purchased by the canal office. From the standpoint of creativity and originality, the motifs are beside the point, suggesting a truly nonchalant approach to design. This, then, was the meaning of "doing art." Nevertheless, the result was to bring an orthodox classicism to Japan without any oddly inventive additions.

The engineers, however, also seem to have felt that "doing art" alone was insufficient. To confer cultural significance on their works of civil engineering, they made an addition that took a very Eastern approach: inscribing the tunnel portals with poetic phrases reminiscent of the framed tablets often hung at the entrances of temples and other buildings. The calligraphy for each was done by a politician who had supported this massive national civil engineering project.

Tunnel No. 1 East Portal:
Kishō bansen [How magnificent this ever-changing landscape!] (Itō Hirobumi)

Tunnel No. 1 West Portal:

Kaku to shite sore iruru koto ari [This land that keeps the canal filled is deep and vast.] (Yamagata Aritomo)

Tunnel No. 2 East Portal:

Jin wa yama o motte yorokobi chi wa mizu no tame ni yorokobu [The virtuous find pleasure in mountains. The wise find pleasure in water.] (Inoue Kaoru)

Tunnel No. 2 West Portal:

Yama ni shitagaite suigen ni itaru [Follow the mountain to reach the source.] (Saigō Jūdō)

Tunnel No. 3 East Portal:

Kau shōshoku o miru [The greenery is more vivid after the rain.] (Matsukata Masayoshi)

Tunnel No. 3 West Portal:

Uruwashiki kana sanga [How beautiful these mountains and rivers!] (Sanjō Sanetomi)

In addition, calligraphy by Governor Kitagaki Kunimichi (*Yūkan kisō* [Beautiful views and great ideas] (Fig. 1-11) and *Yōki hassuru tokoro* [Exude a positive spirit]) adorns both ends of the Nejirimanpo pedestrian tunnel at Keage, and later, when the Second Canal was built, Tanabe Sakurō contributed calligraphy alongside that of Prince Kuni Kuniyoshi.

The prominence of those who contributed their calligraphy speaks again to the Lake Biwa Canal project's importance as a national endeavor. All were politicians who exercised influence over the construction of the canal and drove the project forward, and we should note among their names that of Yamagata Aritomo, owner of the Murin-an villa that would mark Ogawa Jihei's starting point as a landscape gardener. That they chose to inscribe such words, too, suggest the approach that Japan took when seeking to adopt Western civil engineering systems in those days.

In a word, even while introducing Western technological systems as a complete set right down to their formal aspects, there was still an effort to add a sense of Japanese cultural identity in some final flourish. It could be said that this was the essence of the oft-noted posture of *wakon yōsai* that formed the ideological grounding for Japan's policy of Westernization.

And yet we must also be careful because what we regard as the domain of "Western learning" leads to enormous differences in which domains and forms are seen as expressive of "Japanese spirit." At the Lake Biwa Canal, the formal elements—including those with classical designs generally understood as belonging to artistic fields—were all adopted together as parts of a Western technological system, that is, as a system of "Western learning." This is precisely why each tunnel portal carried, as both a finishing touch and an expression of the "Japanese spirit," calligraphic inscriptions done in the manner of framed tablets.

Fig. 1-11: Calligraphy by Kitagaki Kunimichi on the Nejirimanpo pedestrian tunnel

Perhaps because it was a national project imbued with such a consciousness, the Lake Biwa Canal also came to exert—on a scale comparable to its place in the history of modern technology—an influence on the cultural expressions of modern Japan. In this, when construction of the canal as a whole is seen as the fruit of "Western learning," it also seems to represent a corresponding manifestation of "Japanese spirit." Although still far off, it also marks the beginnings of the Philosopher's Walk and the gardens of Ogawa Jihei.

New Uses for the Canal

Here we need to return once again to a broad overview of the canal's construction.

In 1881, Kitagaki Kunimichi, who had been appointed governor of Kyoto, went to Tokyo to present plans for the Lake Biwa Canal project to decision-makers such as Itō Hirobumi, then a member of the Council of Advisors, and Matsukata Masayoshi, then minister of domestic affairs. Surveying work began in earnest the following year and all survey plans were completed by 1883. At the end of that year, for the first time, Kitagaki petitioned the minister of domestic affairs, minister of finance, and minister of agriculture and commerce for permission to begin work on the Lake Biwa Canal. After a series of adjustments were made, the minister of domestic affairs issued the official order authorizing construction of the canal on 29 January 1885. The minister of domestic affairs at the time, that is, the minister in charge who gave permission for construction to begin, was Yamagata Aritomo. Groundbreaking ceremonies were held on 2 June 1885 at the Mio Shrine in Ōtsu and again on the following day at Yasaka Shrine in Kyoto.

Construction continued for five years, concluding in 1890. On 15 March of that year, water was passed through the entire waterway with favorable results. On 1 April, ceremonies were held at shrines in Ōtsu and Kyoto to mark the end of construction, and a ceremony was held on the 9th to celebrate the completion of the canal.

The completion ceremony on the 9th in Kyoto was attended by the emperor and empress as well as the prime minister, the minister of the navy, the minister of finance, and the minister of education. At the time, the prime minister was Yamagata Aritomo and the ministers of the navy, finance, and education were Saigō Jūdō, Matsukata Masayoshi, and Enomoto Takeaki. As you can see, many of the names correspond to those whose calligraphy adorned the tunnels of the canal. Requests to contribute calligraphy were a mark of appreciation from those involved in the construction of the canal to the politicians who contributed the most to the project.

Biwako chisui enkakushi (A history of flood control on Lake Biwa) describes the construction as "a project unprecedented in scale for our country. Because it was undertaken with no such previous experience, the opinions of government authorities were divided at the outset when authorization to start construction was sought, and rumor has it that word even reached the ears of the emperor, but here, honored by the emperor's presence, we must acknowledge how far we have come from such beginnings." The power of the politicians, and particularly that of the minister of domestic affairs who decided to approve the construction, must have seemed enormous to those involved in building the canal. The minister of domestic affairs who made that decision, Yamagata Aritomo, would attend the completion ceremony as prime minister and was a presence that loomed particularly large to those involved with the canal.

I have written that the purpose of the Lake Biwa Canal was to facilitate water transportation, to supply waterpower as a source of energy, and to provide water for irrigation, firefighting, and drinking. And yet the shift in plans in 1887 for the use of its waters as a source of energy from waterwheels to hydroelectric power resulted in surplus water volume, particularly for the branch canal. As already noted above, the branch canal only carried 50 units of water, a reduction from the original plans, and yet even this was more than was needed at the time.

Eventually there were moves to use the waters of the branch canal for purposes other than those for which it was previously intended. The pioneer in this was cloisonné artist Namikawa Yasuyuki, who lived at 24 Horiike-chō, Sanjō Shirakawa-suji Higashi-iru 1-chōme in Shimogyō-ku and drew water from the canal into his own garden. Namikawa was, together with Namikawa Sōsuke, one of the most renowned cloisonné artists of his day. Born in Kyoto on 1 September 1845, he married Kaji, the daughter of Namikawa Seizen (who served Prince Kuni Asahiko), joining the Namikawa clan as an adopted son. His original family name was Takaoka. In addition to serving the family of the prince, Namikawa learned cloisonné from Momonoi Eishō and by 1876 had progressed to the point of dealing with foreign traders in Yokohama. Emboldened by exhibiting his work at the Paris International Exposition of 1878, he left the service of Prince Kuni Asahiko and struck out on his own. In 1890 he won first prize at the Third National Industrial Exhibition while the pair of vases in a purely Japanese style that he exhibited at the World's Columbian Exposition in Chicago in 1893 also earned a favorable reception. These vases found a buyer at 2,000 yen, which grew to 2,600 yen by the end of the event as the result of currency exchange fluctuations. His outstanding achievements are said to include the invention of transparent black enamel and the inclusion of motifs from ancient works in his cloisonné designs. Drawing on famous works

Fig. 1-12: The garden at the home of Namikawa Yasuyuki

of antiquity such as those held at the Shōsō-in Imperial Repository, he introduced Japanese designs to the world of cloisonné. In 1896 he was appointed, together with Namikawa Sōsuke, as an Imperial Household Artist. In his later years he was also active in business, serving among other roles as an auditor for the Kyoto Trade Bank.

Namikawa Yasuyuki had drawn water from the canal into his residence on Shirakawa-suji for purposes of polishing cloisonné in 1894, and also came to use a portion of this water for his pond (Fig. 1-12). In 1896, Kyoto journalist Kuroda Tengai, in his *Meika rekihō roku* (A record of visits to distinguished homes), described the garden of Namikawa's home as "the pinnacle of seclusion and tranquility, its waterspout emitting a voluble stream whose considerable vigor astonishes the viewer."

Although the Namikawa residence is said to have used water from the canal, it stands on the banks of the Shirakawa, just off what is now the Jingū-michi road that serves as the approach to the Heian Jingū shrine. Drawing the waters of the Shirakawa to use for both cloisonné polishing and the garden would have been a simple matter of installing a sluice gate along the river. Surely the water originally used for the Namikawa garden came from the Shirakawa. Of course, since the Shirakawa was supposed to play a role as the branch canal's lower canal, and because it diverges from the canal as it continues south into the city, it would certainly be possible to mistake its waters for those of the canal. Today, water for the pond at the Namikawa residence is drawn from the canal proper through steel pipes.

The use of water from the canal exclusively for the purpose of feeding the garden of a private dwelling, though, would be pioneered not by Namikawa Yasuyuki but by Yamagata Aritomo.

CHAPTER TWO

Yamagata Aritomo as the Beginning

The Third Murin-an Villa

Yamagata Aritomo, the minister of domestic affairs who approved construction of the Lake Biwa Canal and then later the prime minister who received the emperor and empress at its completion ceremony, dominated the foundation of Japan's pre-war political system. In the introduction to his short biography, *Yamagata Aritomo*, political historian Oka Yoshitake wrote:

> *Imagine for a moment a kind of historical distribution map depicting the many figures that moved across the political stage during the Meiji and Taisho periods. Yamagata Aritomo would no doubt occupy the position of a central mountain range, both by virtue of the many roles he played during his long life and because of the extensive factional network at whose center he stood. At the base of this towering range we would find the bedrock of the imperial system as constructed since the Meiji Restoration. To tell the tale of Yamagata's life, then, is to relate the history of the Meiji and Taisho periods, and tracing its course is a useful way to illuminate the process and structure of our country's modern history from a unique viewpoint.*

Many people have accepted the idea that the political history of modern Japan can be seen through the life of Yamagata Aritomo as an individual. Oka Yoshitake said that in Yamagata one could see a *Homo politicus*, that is, someone for whom politics went beyond ideas and encompassed their pattern of behavior. There was certainly an aura about Yamagata, in his manner and as an individual. As minister of domestic affairs when ground was broken and prime minister at the time of completion, he had a profound relationship with the Lake Biwa Canal, which is why those involved in its construction would deliver its waters to him.

In 1894, work began on a garden just down from Nanzen-ji temple as part of the construction of Yamagata's Murin-an villa in Kyoto. Having previously visited Namikawa Yasuyuki's garden, Kuroda Tengai wrote of Yamagata that "he spends his free time in tasteful ease, tending to his garden." In other words, Yamagata had found a lifelong pastime in his gardens.

This was not the first time that Yamagata had built a residence named Murin-an. As a young man he had erected a villa by that name in Yoshida in Chōshū (present-day Yamaguchi) and in 1891 built another near Kyoto's Nijō Bridge. It seems that Yamagata initially wanted to expand this second Murin-an to create a somewhat larger-scale garden but for reasons related to city planning the owner, Kyoto Prefecture, refused to sell him the adjoining land. As a consequence, he gave up on the property soon after buying it and pulled out completely in November 1892. He promptly found another site in the city of Kyoto, the location of the Murin-an that remains to this day. In other words, the villa near Nanzen-ji temple was the third to bear this name.

During construction of this third Murin-an, Yamagata was in the field in northeastern China for the Sino-Japanese War. In his absence, he left orders for Kuhara Shōzaburō to oversee construction. Kuhara Shōzaburō might be best recognized today as the father of Kuhara Fusanosuke, but he was also both the older brother of Fujita Denzaburō and a well-connected businessman who laid the foundation for the Kuhara zaibatsu. In this, too, we see a glimmer of the political influence of Yamagata the military man. According to research by Amasaki Hiromasa, Yagasaki Zentarō, and others, it was not until 1896 that Yamagata formally took personal ownership of the Murin-an site. Until that time it had been the property of Kyoto City.

Fig. 2-1: The garden at Murin-an, Yamagata Aritomo's villa in Kyoto

Yamagata, in other words, began building his villa and garden on leased land. It was even later, in 1902, that he finally took possession of the site's eastern section. Given, as we will see later, that the east side of the property includes the part where water drawn into the garden forms its waterfall, the Murin-an garden that we see today did not fully take shape until after 1902 (Fig. 2-1).

Water from the canal was drawn into the Murin-an garden in the name of providing water for firefighting. Regardless of the circumstances, it was probably impossible to state openly that the waters of the canal were being given over for purposes of a garden pond. Perhaps because the nominal purpose was firefighting, assistant engineers from the Kyoto Municipal Office of Water Supply handled the installation of steel pipes and other construction required to draw water from the canal. Meanwhile, Yamagata Aritomo submitted an application to the Kyoto City Council to "donate 200 yen for fiscal 1902 to ensure that Kyoto City water supply projects continue to flourish in the future." Yamagata wanted water for his garden pond and Kyoto City cooperated as much as it could in the name of supplying water for firefighting. Had the city found a new way to use the water from the canal, or was this simply an exception made on behalf of Yamagata as an important benefactor?

In hindsight, it seems clear that Kyoto City had seen new potential for the water for the canal, but in fact it is probably more likely that such prospects played less of a role than the desire to make an exception by providing the influential Yamagata with water for "firefighting." The natural interpretation is that others followed this precedent later as the charms of Yamagata's garden became more widely known.

The *Sukisha* Connoisseurs of the Meiji Period

The time from the middle of the Meiji period into the Taisho period is known as an age when those with new influence in the wake of the Restoration steadily accumulated power and turned their attention to cultural pursuits such as calligraphy, painting, antiques, landscape gardening, and the tea ceremony. The tea ceremony, in particular, gained tremendous popularity among the powerful in business and politics. Inoue Kaoru (art name: Segai) was a central figure in this movement, known both for transporting the Hassō-an tea ceremony room to his home at Uchidayama in Tokyo and for his extensive collection of artwork.

The acquisition by Masuda Takashi (art name: Don'ō), head clerk of the Mitsui zaibatsu that Inoue favored most, of a sixteen-character portion of Kōbō Daishi's calligraphic transcription of the mottos of Cui Ziyu in 1895 led to the establishment of a tea ceremony called the Daishi-kai the following year. Because the annual event gained a reputation for including only those who were both first-rate businesspeople and sophisticates of exceptionally good taste, people competed for invitations.

In addition, Matsura Akira (art name: Shingetsu) launched the Wakei-kai tea ceremony in 1898 with the idea that its members, nicknamed the Sixteen Arhats, would each host tea ceremonies in turn. At one point, the Sixteen Arhats were: Ishiguro Tadanori (art name: Kyōō), Itō Shunkichi (art name: Sōyū), Kanazawa San'emon (art name: Sōten), Yoshida Tanzaemon (art name: Fūken), Takeuchi Sennosuke (art name: Kansui), Uryū Shin (art name: Hyakuri), Yasuda Zenjirō (art name: Shōō), Masuda Takashi (art name: Don'ō), Makoshi Kyōhei (art name: Keshō), Aoji Ikujirō (art name: Tankai), Matsura Atsushi (art name: Ranshū), Mitsui Hachirōji-rō (art name: Shōrai), Mitsui Takayasu (art name: Kasei), Hisamatsu Katsu-shige (art name: Ninsō), Higashikuze Michitomi (art name: Chikutei), and Takahashi Yoshio (art name: Sōan). All were members of the business elite who were known as men of refinement during the Meiji and Taisho periods. Members added later include Hara Tomitarō (art name: Sankei), Nezu Kaichirō (art name: Seizan), Dan Takuma (art name: Rizan), and Nozaki Kōta (art name Gen'an). Many of these men kept company with Yamagata Aritomo. Masuda and Nozaki, in particular, socialized with him frequently as fellow owners of vacation homes in Odawara. Nevertheless, Yamagata himself is said to have never gotten deeply involved with matters of tea. He described the situation to Takahashi Yoshio, who was something of a spokesman for the way of tea as practiced among connoisseurs at the time, as follows:

Once when I was feeling bored at Murin-an it occurred to me to invite guests from Kyoto for a tea ceremony so I had old Matsuoka, who has now passed away, visit and came to understand that expensive-looking tea implements were frowned upon and that it would be enough to put together a complete set even if they happened to be newly made. But when I invited tea lovers from the area like the late Ijūin Kanetsune, their merry conversations in the tea ceremony room concerned the wonderful bowls they had seen at such-and-such a gathering or the paintings or calligraphy that so-and-so had recently purchased. They talked of tea ceremonies elsewhere but paid little mind to the one they were taking part in that day. I felt as though I had loaned out my own tea ceremony room just so they could chat about tea ceremonies hosted by others. I came to the realization that it is impossible to draw the interest of tea lovers without using antique utensils attached to famous names and, deciding that the impoverished were unqualified to serve as hosts, gave it up completely.
[From *Kokian no hannichi* (Half a day at Koki-an)]

The criticism here of tea ceremonies that focused on antique utensils is fascinating for its penetrating insight into the trends of the time. Yamagata Aritomo clearly had no patience for tea ceremonies that centered on comparing the objects used. One theory is that Yamagata disparaged the tea ceremony simply because he had gotten a late start on his own collection of tea utensils, but even if that were the case he still breaks here from the idea of emphasizing celebrated tea ceremony items. Perhaps he did feel that such "famous things" were linked too directly to wealth, but even more than this he no doubt preferred landscape gardening as a means for expressing his sensibilities and talents. Yamagata was a powerfully self-reliant man. Gardening required far greater financial resources than the tea ceremony but brought the pleasure of recreating the world. Moving a project forward might require leveraging one's authority, but this could be understood as a means for displaying the clarity of one's taste and sensibility. This is one reason the powerful love gardens.

The Naturalism of Murin-an

Even in his gardens, Yamagata Aritomo did not favor the use of "famous things." In broadest terms his gardens were naturalistic. While traditional gardening methods sought to create symbolic landscapes centered on a number of "key stones" with specific functions, his were clearly the opposite. It was in anticipation of this that Yamagata was given water from the canal.

At the point where the waters of the canal split, dropping into the hydroelectric station at Keage on one hand and forming the branch canal that winds around Nanzen-ji temple on the other, the water is also drawn across the road toward the Murin-an property on the other side. The Murin-an lot is shaped like an irregular triangle that tapers to the east, and is located just across the street from the main entrance to Nanzen-ji temple. There, the waters of the canal bend at the base of the incline as they head toward Okazaki Park and what is now the approach to the Heian Jingū shrine. That the property is bounded by the curve of the canal also explains its irregular shape.

A pond was built on the site through which water drawn from the canal flowed gently from east to west, crossing the garden diagonally before leaving the property. The pond is shallow and the garden of which Yamagata Aritomo was so proud is an open one with expansive views.

In the completed garden, tall trees were planted beginning from the buildings on the west side of the property and growing more numerous toward its depths on the east, effectively incorporating the Higashiyama mountains in the background while leaving the foreground open through the use of water from the canal. Stones were only positioned horizontally rather than on end. The result was an otherworldly tranquility in a space that was modest by the standards of larger gardens.

The tall trees included many firs, the result of a creative choice by Yamagata. Notable as a means of generating contrast, the firs are concentrated on the left as one looks out on the depths of the garden from the Japanese-style main building, while many chinquapin are planted along the boundary on the right. The other boundary areas, meanwhile, incorporate numerous cryptomeria.

Other tree placements that draw the eye include the pines (red pines) on the far shore of the pond and near the waterfall, the two mountain cherries planted at the rear of the garden (Yamagata said that he himself planted three leafy cherry trees there), and the single persimmon, camphor, and bayberry trees planted near the main building. The use in the foreground of such trees, which are rarely found in traditional gardens, suggests that this was also an idea that originated with Yamagata. In fact, trees such as firs, persimmons, and bayberries frequently appear in other gardens built by Yamagata such as those at Chinzan-sō—his primary residence in Mejiro, Tokyo—and Koki-an in Odawara. The main trees in the garden at Murin-an, however, are maples.

Turning to stones, one notices among the stepping stones that stretch from the sitting room to the garden what seems to be a *garan ishi* ("temple stone") placed at the junction of the path, a technique often seen in gardens of the period. Originally used at the base of temple pillars, such stones can be identified by the flat raised section on which the pillar would have rest-ed. Many temples were devastated during the anti-Buddhist movement that swept through Japan in the early Meiji period, and there was little resistance to digging out the foundation stones from the ruins.

One of the great debates in Japanese history concerned whether or not Hōryū-ji temple was a reconstruction. At issue was whether the temple had actually burned down and, if so, when it had been reconstructed. Excavation of the Wakakusa Garan temple at Hōryū-ji provided evidence to resolve the matter, indicating that Hōryū-ji had indeed burned down. By uncovering earlier temple buildings whose footprints overlapped with those standing at the time, the excavation demonstrated that Hōryū-ji was a reconstruction. This excavation was undertaken in 1939, prompted by the return to the temple of the foundation stone from the pagoda's central pillar, which had been located at the villa of Nomura Tokushichi II (art name: Tokuan) in Sumiyoshi, Hyōgo. Although unthinkable today, at the time even foundation stones of such historical importance were traded from one person to another and found their way to the second homes of distinguished gentlemen. This episode alone illustrates how popular such temple stones were at the time.

Temple stones do not, however, play a very important role at Murin-an. Indeed, in the composition of the garden as a whole one finds no "key stones" like triad stones or crane and tortoise islands. Everything is naturalistic and conceived as scenery. There is, however, one massive stone in the garden that stands out prominently, one that even the great Toyotomi Hideyoshi had been unable to quarry from its original location in Daigo. Positioning it deep in the garden was intended to create a kind of natural landscape.

How were the buildings positioned in relation to the garden at Murin-an? Both Western-style and Japanese-style buildings were erected to serve as Yamagata's retreat in Kyoto, but his interests seem to have been focused entirely on the garden. In his aforementioned conversation with journalist Kuroda Tengai, he said, referring to the Western-style building, "It isn't much to look at, but I had it built because I needed a place to store things. My plan is that it will eventually be hidden as the trees grow in."

Sure enough, today the building is completely cut off from the garden by the trees. From the beginning it was not a particularly impressive sight, more of a defensive structure that might indeed be described as a storehouse. Yamagata probably slept in this Western-style building when staying at Murin-an overnight. The way it is built could be said to betray an evident fear of assassination, and speaks to an almost complete distrust of others.

Such structures are occasionally seen elsewhere, as at the villa of Tanaka Mitsuaki, a member of the Yamagata faction who lived to the ripe old age of ninety-five. A profligate builder who constructed many homes, in Tanaka's final years he constructed two villas in Shizuoka Prefecture. One was a vast estate known as Kokei-sō built in Iwabuchi, while the other was a smaller villa named Hōju-sō located just a short distance away in Kanbara. Although the escape route hidden behind the hanging scroll in the drawing room at Hōju-sō is charming, it is the bedroom that is most surprising. Built much like an earthen storehouse, it could be locked firmly from the inside. To enable communication with the outside, there was a mail slot in the wall between the bedroom and the hallway. When Tanaka was in his bedroom, his servants would feed him letters through the slot from the hallway. Compared to the literal storehouse in which Tanaka slept, the Western-style building at Yamagata Aritomo's Murin-an was surely an improvement.

The Japanese-style main building at Murin-an consists of a great tatami space, made up of one 10-mat room and a 7-mat antechamber, connected to a two-story wing by an interior garden. The building is positioned to afford views of the main garden. Looking back at the building from the main garden, one can see that the roof over the second story is inelegant, with one end hipped and the other gabled.

In this way, the garden's composition makes wonderful use of the elongated triangular site but lacks a "looking back" perspective. There is no suitable place to cast a glance back at where you came from while walking through it. The landscaping approach seen here seems to resemble a military strategy, sustained by a policy of expansion through marching ever forward. The garden's openness to the borrowed landscape of the mountains to the east and its sense of stretching out without fading out is characteristically modern, but also the result of its entirely unidirectional perspective. In this sense, then, the garden at Murin-an is not truly modern. Yamagata Aritomo was fond of describing himself as "a mere soldier," and his garden does reflect the tastes of a military man.

Kuroda Tengai, having visited Murin-an in 1900, recorded the following as Yamagata's words:

> *The gardens of Kyoto value a sense of seclusion but have no appreciation for the grand or magnificent. Most are small-scale tea gardens of which much is made about who designed them, about Kobori Enshū or whoever, and are of very little interest, so I decided to make a garden of my own devising.*
>
> *At first, the gardeners said the problem was mine for not having reviewed the copybooks that laid out the rules for placing stones, for how to combine yin stones and yang stones or the five stones and the seven stones. Well, this is what I said. "It's true I know nothing about the rules of yin stones and yang stones, but I can see plainly enough by looking at what's before me that the focal point of the garden will be the soaring green Higashiyama mountains. And because the garden sits at a point where the foothills protrude, the mountains will also supply water for a waterfall. If so, then surely the placement of the stones and the arrangement of the trees must be calculated on this basis. I don't know what you think, but surely you agree?" [...]*
>
> *Other gardeners seemed to find strange the idea of planting ferns among the rocks of the waterfall. I planted about 30 firs here but at the time the gardener had only 1 or 2 firs on hand, none of which seemed worth using, but now they have dozens.*
>
> *Along the stream here I planted flowers that bloom often in the fields—called, uh, quince, yes, that's it, quince—but even after three years they have yet to take root, even though out in the fields they bloom just fine even when trod upon. That's all the more reason I plan to plant some azaleas that will cling low to the rocks along the*

stream, and have asked the gardeners to trim them close.

Gardens in Kyoto value the quiet simplicity of moss and rarely incorporate grass, but it would be a great deal of trouble to cover this whole garden with moss, and relying on moss isn't particularly interesting, so I was determined to plant a lawn. Originally Kuhara (Shōzaburō) planted one on this side of the stream so I had onishiba grass planted on the far side and have it cut now and then. This is fairly expensive but it's better this way. For trees I'm planning to rely mainly on cryptomeria, maple, and leafy cherries. How does that sound? As for water, people in the past preferred ponds but I think streams are more appealing. When you go out into mountain villages you come upon winding streams with clear water murmuring along like the one you see here. Thinking this was more atmospheric, I had a stream put in here. [From *Zoku kōko kaishin roku* (A record of pleasant scenes in and around the capital, Vol. 2) by Kuroda Tengai]

Yamagata Aritomo chose not to build a garden composed around "key stones" but one that was an extension of the natural landscape. It remains unclear whether this was due to a lack of knowledge or was something grounded in a stubborn aesthetic conviction. It was probably a mix of the two. Still, he had clearly defined preferences. The shallow stream, the combination of firs, maples, and mountain cherries, the low-trimmed azaleas, and the planting of a lawn can all be said to reflect his tastes. In these we find a prototype for large Japanese-style gardens built beginning in the Meiji period, one that originates at least in part in Yamagata's preferences. His remark above that he thought streams were "more atmospheric" is particularly interesting. After all, the garden at Murin-an, of which the stream is an essential part, is only made possible by drawing water from the Lake Biwa Canal.

Expressions of "Japanese Spirit"

There are a number of theories about when the garden at Murin-an was completed. One is that both the buildings and the garden were completed in 1896, but Yamagata seems to have already been using the site before then. We know this because he signed a letter to Tanaka Mitsuaki dated 23 October 1895 "Sincerely yours, Tomo, Master of Murin-an, near Nanzen-ji temple." In this same letter Yamagata writes, "The Higashiyama landscape is as it ever was, and although the leaves of the maple have not yet turned color it is most pleasant to walk outside." [From *Seizan yoei: Tanaka Mitsuaki haku shōden* (Traces of Seizan: A short biography of Count Tanaka Mitsuaki) by Kumazawa Ichie]

While building the garden at Murin-an, Yamagata Aritomo was rewarded for his distinguished service during the Sino-Japanese War with the title of marquis, made a member of the Order of the Golden Kite (Second Class), and received the Grand Cordon of the Order of the Rising Sun with Paulownia Blossoms. He also received 50,000 yen from the imperial household on 5 August 1895, and it is thought that this was the source of funding for Murin-an. Having secured victory in the Sino-Japanese War, Yamagata's heart no doubt brimmed with feelings of pride and self-confidence as he walked in the Higashiyama foothills. Directly or indirectly, Murin-an was born with the Sino-Japanese War as its father and the Lake Biwa Canal as its mother.

The period of victory in the Sino-Japanese War was one of particular importance to the Japanese-style culture of the Meiji period and beyond. In 1895, the same year Murin-an was being constructed, the Heian Jingū shrine was also built in Kyoto. As is well known, the Heian Jingū shrine was built to commemorate the 1,100th anniversary of the foundation of the capital in Kyoto. Its main hall is a smaller-scale reconstruction of the Heian period Great Hall of State and was designed by Kyoto-born master craftsman Kiko Kiyoyoshi and Itō Chūta, who had just graduated from the Imperial College of Engineering and would later go on to teach at the Imperial University. This was the first time a university-educated architect had designed a work of traditional architecture.

That same year, the prefectural government office in Nara, the other ancient capital, was also built in the Japanese style. There, too, the design

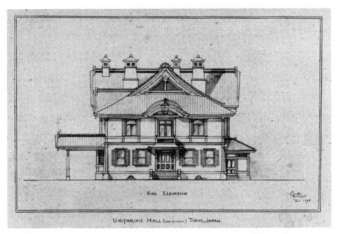

Fig. 2-2: Yuiitsu-kan [Unitarian Hall] (Designed by Josiah Conder)

was undertaken by a graduate of the Imperial College of Engineering, Nagano Uheiji. It may seem perfectly natural that buildings of a strongly public nature would be designed in the Japanese style in the ancient capitals of Kyoto and Nara, but the Imperial College of Engineering was an institution for acquiring Western technology so it is hugely significant that the architects it graduated—that is, architects grounded in "Western learning"—should be called upon to undertake Japanese design.

In addition, architect Josiah Conder, the first foreigner recruited to teach Western architecture to those such as Itō Chūta and Nagano Uheiji, had designed the Yuiitsu-kan (Unitarian Hall) the previous year in 1894. This building blended Japanese and Western styles in a way that was unique in his body of work. The exterior followed the Japanese *shinkabe* style in using plaster walls with exposed pillars and had a Japanese-style roof that even incorporated an undulating gable (Fig. 2-2).

The most famous of Conder's architectural works in Japan was the Rokumei-kan guesthouse, but he also designed buildings such as the Ueno Museum and a sales office and reception rooms for the Hokkaido Colonization Office. Although Conder experimented in accordance with his own sense of style, he had not designed any buildings in the Japanese style before Yuiitsu-kan, where for the first time he shows the utmost consciousness of Japan and a willingness to incorporate its style. What does this mean?

I find it hard to believe it was merely a coincidence that both Josiah Conder, an architect recruited from overseas, and the Japanese architects to whom he had taught Western architecture began to produce Japanese-style buildings in 1894 and 1895. The Japanese ideal at the time was to become one of the world's wealthy nations, a strong country that ranked with the European powers. Wasn't there a need to acquire, as the trimmings of state, architecture that was faithful to the Western tradition? Surely that was the "Western learning" demanded by the Imperial College of Engineering. Yet both Conder, who was the very embodiment of "Western learning," and the Japanese architects who had mastered it began designing Japanese-style buildings. This is extraordinary.

I suspect that this period, one overlapping with the Sino-Japanese War, marked the development of Japanese architecture to a point where its absorption of Western architecture was complete and it was capable of actively pursuing new efforts of its own. Defining exactly where this point was, however, is difficult, and might ultimately be dismissed as a subjective question. First, it is easy to imagine that even while "still learning," Japanese architecture might have begun to seek forms appropriate to architectural expression in Japan. Even if imperfect, there could certainly have been efforts to pursue a national identity. Rather than thinking of Japanese-style architectural expressions as precursors, having achieved a certain level of accomplishment, to matters of practical application, it is probably better to think of them as an irresistible expression of Japanese spirit. Such "Japanese spirit" seemed inevitably to emerge in the tension between it and "Western learning."

For a Japan that was rapidly modernizing in the Meiji period, the ideology of *wakon yōsai* [Japanese spirit and Western learning] was an unstable foothold from which to balance its own cultural identity with the work of modernization—a shaky foundation ever susceptible to collapse from below.

With the success of the Meiji Restoration, the patriotic commoners who had been its driving force found themselves with nowhere to go as bureaucratic institutions took shape. Aoyama Hanzō, the protagonist of Shimazaki Tōson's *Yoake mae* (*Before the Dawn*), dreams of the Restoration in a remote Kiso region post town as a way of reviving the spirit of Hirata Shinto, but when his dreams are cruelly dashed he dies in madness. Saigō Takamori, who perished during the Satsuma Rebellion, chose a death that cast his lot in line with the will of such patriots.

Modernization is the process by which other countries adopt the international values fostered in the West beginning with the industrial revolution. Such, at least, was the process in nations like Japan that acquiesced to modernization under foreign pressure.

Even if "Japanese spirit" could be described as something still held deep in the heart, the world in its outward forms—technologies, systems, and even the arts—was shaped entirely by "Western learning." With the Restoration, the construction of large Japanese-style ships was prohibited, medicine turned in the direction of Western medical science, and both law and litigation moved toward conformance with Western systems. Perhaps the only way to protect "Japanese spirit" amid such a process of modernization was to define the world of outward forms and systems as mere techniques.

For a time there were many who argued that what made Japan's modernization so off-balance was that it never went beyond understanding Western civilization as a kind of technique and failed to truly understand the depth of its ideas, but this is incorrect. For the Japanese people of the Meiji period, confining Western civilization to the domain of technique was a desperate means of preserving their own cultural identity.

Eventually, however, a time came when it was no longer possible to write off the world of outward forms as mere technique. "Japanese spirit" and "Western learning" cannot, at heart, be so readily separated, and "Japanese spirit" soon began seeking its own forms. Such is the nature of cultural identity, and it had an urgency that exceeded any desire to understand the ideology or worldview hidden beneath the surface of Western technology.

Through a foreigner's eyes, Josiah Conder perceived this spirit of the Japanese people, writing that much in their culture belongs "to their past rather than to their present civilization" and that "there is no more patriotic nation under the sun."

We need to reexamine the notion that the shape of Japanese culture beginning in the Meiji period followed some urge to give form to "Japanese spirit," that while Western forms were expressions of the public, of institutions, Japanese culture expressed the private, one's true intentions. Things were never so simple in reality, and there was a surge of efforts to introduce Japanese style into the public domain as an expression of Japan's cultural identity.

If we were to seek the shape of 1894–1895 in the lineage of the Heian Jingū shrine, the Nara Prefectural Office, Yuiitsu-kan, and Yamagata Aritomo's Murin-an, we could probably discern a certain current of the times that might be called an impulse for Japanese style. This was a period corresponding exactly with the Sino-Japanese War. Just as Japan—running headlong through the process of modernization—was demonstrating its acquisition of "Western learning" on the field of battle, this impulse for Japanese style was emerging even in representations of public facilities and spaces.

On 21 March 1896, the Daishi-kai mentioned above was launched in Tokyo. Although the acquisition by Mitsui-affiliated industrialist Masuda Takashi the previous year of a sixteen-character excerpt from the mottos of Cui Ziyu as transcribed by Kōbō Daishi himself had been merely coincidental, it was no accident that this tea gathering named in its honor would go on to exert enormous influence as a salon for the business elite. Inoue Kaoru, who had previously executed a policy of Westernization at the Rokumei-kan in an effort to get the Unequal Treaties revised, also frequently hosted tea gatherings in Tokyo around that same year, in which he turned sixty, and often included many of the same guests as Masuda's Daishi-kai.

In this way, the tendency toward the expression of "Japanese spirit" came to flow gently among the powerful in the world of politics and business. Rather than a rejection of modernization by means of "Western learning," this tendency was premised upon development through "Western learning." The move toward expressing "Japanese spirit" was not limited to the pastime of tea but also revealed itself in a variety of fields, one of which was the gardens born of the Lake Biwa Canal. Yamagata Aritomo may have gotten off to a late start in the world of the tea ceremony, but he reigned supreme when it came to landscape gardens, a realm that was, at least in one sense, larger in scale. Both the tea ceremony and the landscape garden were truly suitable forums for expressing the Japanese spirit.

Even today in the twenty-first century, when speaking of Japanese culture in an international context, the three key words of Shinto, Zen, and the tea ceremony still wield enormous influence. Indeed, these suggest the cultural images that people from overseas hope to see in Japan. When presenting an image of Japan that follows the expectations of others, it is only natural that it should be well received. To go on about Shinto and Zen and the tea ceremony—things most contemporary Japanese are not really all that familiar with—actually represents nothing less than the loss of one's cultural identity, but this is a rut from which we seem to have difficultly breaking free.

Well, then, was the shape of 1894–1895 the same sort of "performance of an expected image of Japan" that we see today? I do not think so. There was a more urgent drive, a longing for identity. The *wakon yōsai* [Japanese spirit and Western learning] slogan, recited together with *fukoku kyōhei* [national prosperity and military power], labored under the heavy burden of modernization. Tea and gardens were there for the powerful to brush aside the uneasiness of their own positions, which grew more insecure the more actively they pushed ahead with modernization. Gardens, in particular, provided a place where the mind could feel most at ease, and since great gardens required enormous wealth to create, they had a magical ability to bestow comfort, pride and encouragement upon those with the wherewithal to own them.

Making a bit of a leap, we could say that while modernity ushered in the thoroughly ungrounded "spaces" of Western architecture, landscape gardens were "places," firm and unmovable. To stand in such gardens was to enjoy a sense of security, pride, and comfort.

The garden at Murin-an was the first indication, by a Japan that had begun to walk the path of modernization, of a new Japanese identity. Neither adopted from the West nor a return to tradition, it was the first expression through which the people of influence who furthered Japan's modernization could project themselves.

The Beginnings of Ogawa Jihei VII

The garden world of Yamagata Aritomo, one that brought new possibilities for utilizing the waters of the Lake Biwa Canal, was not the product of Yamagata's efforts alone. The gardeners he mentions were indispensable, and he spoke of Ogawa Jihei VII.

Ogawa Jihei VII was born the second son of Yamamoto Yahei in a village that is now part of the city of Nagaokakyō in Kyoto Prefecture on 5 April 1860. His name in childhood was Gennosuke. In November 1877, at the age of 17, he married Mitsu, the fourth daughter of the Ogawa family, into which he was registered as an adoptive heir. In 1879 he took over as head of the family and succeeded to the name Ogawa Jihei VII. Mitsu was born in the same year as her husband, although on 26 February so she was slightly older. Her father, the previous Ogawa Jihei, retired upon relinquishing the mantle of family leadership, taking the name Ninkō, but passed away on 9 May 1879. He, too, had been adopted into the Ogawa family. He was born the third son of a farmer, Kamejima Kurōbei, in the village of Yamamoto in the Kawabe district of Settsu Province on 5 May 1816, married Ito (born 3 October 1815), the eldest daughter of the Ogawa family, in March 1832, and with her had one son and four daughters. The youngest daughter, Mitsu, became the wife of Ogawa Jihei VII. The name Jihei has been passed down from generation to generation in the Ogawa family. The Ogawa Jihei in which we are most interested here should properly be referred to as Ogawa Jihei VII, but going forward I will simply refer to him as Ogawa Jihei except where doing so would cause confusion.

Because the Ogawa family business was gardening, Jihei was also called "Jihei the gardener" (*uekiya no Jihei*), which became shortened to Ueji.

Gardening was the Ogawa family business but, while the details are un-clear, it is said not to have been especially thriving. With Kyoto's economy reeling from the upheaval of the Restoration, no doubt there were few who sought to squander their fortunes on gardens.

Landscape gardener Ogawa Jihei's encounter with Yamagata Aritomo had a decisive impact on his life and career, one that he described to Meiji period journalist Kuroda Tengai by saying, "I am who I am today thanks to three men: Mr. Yamagata, Mr. Nakai Hiroshi, and Mr. Ijūin Kanetsune." [From *Zoku zoku kōko kaishin roku* (A record of pleasant scenes in and around the capital, Vol. 3)]

According to this account, "Mr. Yamagata decided to build Murin-an" and then, after its completion, "when it came time to build the gardens at Heian Jingū shrine, the call went out to send for Mr. Yamagata's gardener." After struggling to complete that project, Ogawa Jihei "was asked to do a garden for a museum." The scope of his work broadened and "it was around that time that my name started to get around.

"Next, I designed a series of gardens for Mr. Kuhara (Shōzaburō), Mr. Shimizu (Kichijirō), and Mr. Ichida (Yaichirō), and fixed up the Tanaka (Ichizō) garden, too. Today I have people here in Kyoto, of course, but also in Momoyama, Osaka, Suma, Tarumi, and Mikage, generally with one or two gardens underway at a time. And at the end of March this year I de-signed a garden for the guesthouse at the prefectural offices in Toyama."

Such was the history of Ogawa Jihei's expanding world of landscape de-sign as recounted to Kuroda Tengai during an interview published in 1913, by which time we can see that his business had already broadened beyond Kyoto and throughout the entire Kansai region, and that his starting point was Yamagata Aritomo's Kyoto villa, Murin-an.

Ogawa Jihei's garden at Murin-an embodied the shape of 1894–1895, a time when Japan consciously drove forward its own modernization, in the realm of gardens. It came to express the spirit of the age on a national scale that transcended the history of landscape gardens. Just as Yamagata Ari-tomo was the architect of the Meiji system of state, his garden at Murin-an was an expression of the times in the Japan of a Meiji period that had cho-

Fig. 2-3: The Western-style house at Murin-an

sen modernization.

A Western-style building was constructed in a corner of the garden at Murin-an in 1898, the one about which Yamagata said, "It isn't much to look at, but I had it built because I needed a place to store things. My plan is that it will eventually be hidden as the trees grow in." Defensive in posture, its exterior so thoroughly shut out outsiders that it seemed symbolic of Yamagata's political stance of not trusting anyone (Fig. 2–3). Nevertheless, this unobtrusive Western-style building is famous as the setting for what is known as the "Murin-an Conference."

On 21 April 1903, as the relationship between Japan and Russia grew increasingly unsteady, three important people gathered at the Western-style building at Murin-an, each arriving at a slightly different time: Itō Hirobumi, president of the Seiyūkai political party; Katsura Tarō, the prime minister; and Komura Jutarō, the minister of foreign affairs. Gathering at the home of elder statesman Yamagata Aritomo to confirm the basic line for the government's policy toward Russia, they set the course for the Russo-Japanese War.

The Fifth National Industrial Exhibition was being held at that time in Osaka and both Emperor Meiji and Prime Minister Katsura were scheduled to make an appearance, making it natural to arrange a meeting in Kyoto. According to Katsura, "I spoke with Marquis Itō and Foreign Minister Komura, and we visited Marquis Yamagata at Murin-an in Kyoto on the

21st." Murin-an was a place for politics, and the garden of Ogawa Jihei was a political garden. An Ueji garden would once again be seen as a political garden nearly half a century later in connection with Konoe Fumimaro. In this sense, too, Ogawa Jihei's garden was an expression of a Meiji period Japan that had chosen modernization.

Incidentally, while both Itō Hirobumi and Yamagata Aritomo are described above as marquis at the time of the Murin-an Conference, as the result of victory in the Russo-Japanese War both men, as well as Katsura Tarō, were made princes while Komura Jutarō was made a count.

Yamagata Aritomo loved Murin-an and its garden, visiting frequently in his later years. Many of the *waka* poems that he wrote suggest as much. Even after Yamagata's death, his widowed mistress Yoshida Sadako continued to love the garden. Among her *waka* from 1940 that were included in the collection *Shinshinshū*, one reads:

More than twenty years after first coming
  to Murin-an in Kyoto, the skies darken.
Snow falls furiously in peony flakes and
  the beauty of Higashiyama is indescribable.
It is as though the snow falls for me, and I look
  upon these mountains in the east with longing.
Time has passed, and seeing the black carp in the pond
  often reminds me of their master.
Speaking with Takimoto, who has
  looked after Murin-an for nearly fifty years,
Tending its garden and serving my late husband daily,
  I wish the old man well.

At the risk of repeating myself, it would not have been strange at all for Kyoto to offer great thanks to Yamagata Aritomo, who had been minister of domestic affairs at the time the ministry was responsible for approving construction of the Lake Biwa Canal and then visited the site as prime minister on the occasion of the canal's completion. It would not have been strange at all had there been a move, in gratitude for a civil engineering project so decisive to Kyoto's modernization, to present him with a Japanese-style garden as a byproduct of modernization.

In this way, the Lake Biwa Canal, a crystallization of the technology that propelled modernization, also opened up another new world of possibilities.

The Gardens of Yamagata Aritomo

In *Sankō iretsu* (Distinguished deeds of the late Prince Yamagata), a collection of essays memorializing Yamagata after his death, author Takahashi Yoshio wrote, "Prince Yamagata had a secret talent for making gardens. He was particularly fond of water, whose sound could be heard from anywhere in his residence." Indeed, Yamagata had water drawn into the gardens at all of his homes, not just Murin-an. The same book reports that Yamagata spoke as follows about the Sentōbaku waterfall at the center of the garden at his Koki-an villa in Odawara, where he spent the last years of his life: "One expects the shape of the waterfall to always remain the same, yet it seems different every time I look. I never grow tired of watching, and sometimes stand here gazing at it for a long while."

Here, Yamagata Aritomo is the very picture of a solitary man of influence absorbed in his garden. He was a politician of such power that Oka Yoshitake would write at the beginning of his critical biography that "every move of the Yamagata faction followed his direction, the political world danced to the tune of his 'magic flute,' and the moods of politicians rose and fell with his every smile or frown." Still, to imagine him gazing in untiring fascination at the waterfall suggests the icy essence of people in such positions. For them, a garden is a source of consolation and pride.

To what end, though, are gardens built at all? *Sakuteiki* (Records of garden making), said to be the oldest text on garden making, contains many references to "the art of erecting stones," "how to erect a stone," and "the oral tradition of erecting stones," which suggests that the act of setting stones is at the heart of gardening. Yet it remains unclear why stones needed to be erected at all. There is, however, this passage: "When building a garden to the south, you must leave a space of six or seven *jō* [one *jō* is about three meters] between the pillars at the outer edge of the canopy over the stairs and the edge of the pond, or eight or nine *jō* if palace ceremonies will be held because accommodations must be made for worship and the like." The idea is that a garden on the south side of a *shinden-zukuri* style aristocratic residence will be used for the performance of ceremonies so a space of between six or seven, or eight or nine, *jō* must be left open between the building and the pond. In other words, it would be impossible to perform the requisite ceremonies unless an open space of between just under twenty to just under thirty meters were left before the pond. Here the notion of garden encompasses the pond, islands, and plantings that lie beyond this open space, but to our sensibilities the notion of garden covers the whole, including the open space. A garden was not just a space to be gazed upon; it was a place where events were held. Garden parties were held beginning in the Meiji period and there came to be a need to consider people walking through the garden and having conversations. Is the need for a place to hold such events enough to explain the building of gardens? Gardens were built not just because they were necessary but also because those who had the land and money to build them seem to have taken enormous pleasure in doing so.

Takahashi Yoshio, who introduced the gardens of Yamagata Aritomo, spoke as follows about his own enjoyment of gardens:

Among the many pastimes in this world, surely few are so enjoyable as building a garden. Architecture, too, is interesting, and they say that nothing is so delightful as the constant din of the hammer and the axe, but things are generally set once a building's plans are fixed and, though modest changes may be made before its completion, there is no thrill of the unexpected. The plan of a garden, however, changes constantly with the addition of each rock or tree as the position of this stone influences the placement of that one and the placement of that one requires changing the pattern of undergrowth. Just as a person playing the game of go may adjust in unlikely ways in re-

sponse to an opponent's move, this constant moment-to-moment shifting of situation is the ineffable pleasure of those who make gardens. [From *Garakuta kago* (Basket of odds and ends)]

The pleasures of garden-making described here are the pleasures of the bourgeois class beginning in the Meiji period. They combine an appreciation for traditional gardens with a taste for those of a new age. Here the joy of gardens is found in their making, in their sense of motion, and in the way they shift like a game of go.

Gardens with water like those favored by Yamagata Aritomo, then, surely displayed the most motion of all. There is motion in the swaying of treetops in the breeze, in the shifting play of sunlight, and in the constant flow of water. This is what Yamagata meant when he said, "it seems different every time I look. I never grow tired of watching."

It may be said that the joy of gardens was found in their making and in motion as far back as the Edo period, but the balance shifted toward motion beginning in the Meiji period. This was a change that got to the very essence of the garden. *Sakuteiki* placed such emphasis on erecting stones due to the significance that such stones had as symbols. Many traditional groupings of stones—triad stones, Mt. Sumeru stones, Mt. Hōrai stones, crane islands, tortoise islands—are symbolic. Dry landscape gardens represented the elegance of waterfalls and the flow of water through groupings of motionless rocks, eliminating actual water to better express its spirit symbolically. Gardens for the tea ceremony were replete with conventional symbolism. The introduction of actual motion into the garden replaced the symbolic elements of earlier gardens with real, natural ones.

Even when incorporating actual water, ponds in Japanese gardens have long symbolized the sea, full to the brim and suggestive of an infinite expanse. This is also why ponds were designed so that they could not be seen in their entirety from any one location, with the water always stretching off into the shadows and out of sight (as with *shinji-ike* ponds shaped like the ideograph for "heart"). Laying small stones along part of the pond to create a pebbled beach was also done to suggest the feeling of the seashore. By contrast, the pond at Murin-an was not the sea but a stream. The water at Murin-an, shallow and smoothly flowing, actively drew motion into the garden. This, too, is an aspect of garden aesthetics created by modernity.

Takahashi Yoshio also wrote, "The essence of garden-making is when the entire scene within view becomes one with nature, with nothing that appears unnatural, and before you know it you have become part of it, too." This, then, is the essence of a garden that favors motion. When Yamagata Aritomo spoke of his own garden Murin-an to Kuroda Tengai, saying, "I can see plainly enough by looking at what's before me that the focal point of the garden will be the soaring green Higashiyama mountains. And because the garden sits at a point where the foothills protrude, the mountains will also supply water for a waterfall. If so, then surely the placement of the stones and the arrangement of the trees must be calculated on this basis," it was no doubt because he felt the same way.

In other words, gardens during the Meiji and Taisho period transformed from the symbolistic to the naturalistic. Those of Yamagata and his peers lacked superfluous symbolism and did without analogous portrayals or recreations of famous scenic places. They were grounded in nature as it is, incorporating the natural flow of water and the swaying of treetops. Bearing no relation to the gardens of Zen temples, this form of garden may have been chosen through ignorance. Or perhaps, having spent their impoverished childhoods amid nature, when these men had the ability to display their wealth by building massive gardens they simply sought to recreate the formative landscapes of their youth. It was in naturalistic gardens that they were able to find peace of mind.

Ueji and Yamagata Aritomo

For Ogawa Jihei, to take on the garden of Yamagata Aritomo was a matter of enormous significance, one that can be seen to have laid the foundation for his subsequent activities. Kuhara Shōzaburō is said to have brought Yamagata and Ueji together, but the source of the connection between Kuhara and Ueji remains unclear. One thing we can look at is where Ueji lived.

Ogawa Jihei lived in Kyoto just off the approach to the Heian Jingū shrine, in a spot adjacent to the home of cloisonné artist Namikawa Yasuyuki at Shimogyō-ku, Sanjō Shirakawa-suji, Higashi-iru 1-chōme, Horiike-chō. We saw earlier that Namikawa was the first to draw water from the Shirakawa River for use in his own garden, and there is little doubt that his neighbor would have been fully aware of this application of the waters of the canal. The 1894 edition of *Kyōto annai miyako hyakushu zen* (Kyoto guidebook: 100 aspects of the capital, complete edition) lists "Ogawa Jihei, purveyor of garden plants and stones, Sanjō Shirakawa-bashi, Kitaura, Horiike-chō," so we know that he had a residence next to Namikawa's at that time, but it is unclear whether Namikawa adopted a suggestion by Ueji to use water from the canal for his garden or if Ueji was helping Namikawa pursue his own efforts at garden building and then adopted the technique as his own.

It is evident, though, that Namikawa Yasuyuki came to live on the banks of the Shirakawa in Sanjō long before Ogawa Jihei did. The 1883 guidebook *Miyako no sakigake* (Pioneers of the capital) already lists "Namikawa Yasuyuki of Shimogyō, Daihachikumi, Horiike-chō" while the 1887 *Kyōto meisho annai zue* (Guide map of famous sites in Kyoto) lists "Namikawa Yasuyuki of Sanjō Shirakawa-bashi, Horiike-chō." Namikawa's success with cloisonné would lead many to practice the same industry in Kyoto; according to Nakahara Tessen in *Kyō shippō mon'yōshū* (A collection of Kyoto cloisonné designs), "the area from Sanjō Ōhashi bridge to Sanjō Shirakawa-bashi bridge came to be lined with more than twenty businesses involved with the cloisonné industry." It may be no more than conjecture to imagine that Ogawa Jihei, living in such a neighborhood, would be awakened to the possibilities of a "garden with streams" that made use of waters from the Shirakawa, as seen in Namikawa's garden, but the idea does seem compelling.

Cloisonné was a new technology for Kyoto, a craft virtually designed to play a part in modernization. If the gardens of Ueji began with the canal as their mother and the cloisonné industry's location as their father, then this was fertile ground for "Japanese spirit and Western learning" indeed.

In 1910, in an interview with Kuroda Tengai, Ogawa Jihei recalled the following:

In the beginning of my training in gardening I studied the concepts of heaven, earth, and man and the five elements, and through the age of 34 or 35 I was climbing up in trees and snipping with shears. When Mr. Yamagata decided to build Murin-an, though, I was asked to plant 50 firs measuring about 5 shaku [1.5 meters] *each. Firs were not used in gardens at the time, though, so I had none at hand and struggled to gather them together from various places. Now, of course, firs are used in gardens everywhere, as are holly and nandin, but Mr. Yamagata was the first.*

Later, when it came time to landscape the gardens at Heian Jingū shrine, the call went out to send for Mr. Yamagata's gardener, and I was asked to take on the project. There was no way to do a garden of 3,000 tsubo [10,000 square meters] *with just 1,000 or 1,500 yen and I really struggled but managed to get through it. Then I was asked to do a garden for a museum and transformed an open field of 10,000* tsubo [33,000 meters] *in just a month or a month and a half. It was around that time that my name started to get around.* [From *Zoku zoku kōko kaishin roku* (A record of pleasant scenes in and around the capital, Vol. 3)]

That Kuhara Shōzaburō, who was assisting Yamagata Aritomo in the construction of his garden, might have happened to hear of a gardener who was building gardens for the cloisonné artisans along the Shirakawa and asked him to renovate the garden at Murin-an is a plausible-sounding narrative.

Takahashi Yoshio relates an episode from when Ogawa Jihei was building the garden at Murin-an. In *Sankō iretsu* (Distinguished deeds of the late Prince Yamagata), Takahashi says that Ogawa went to visit Ijūin Kanetsune, who was from Kagoshima and knowledgeable about gardens, to ask for his advice. Ijūin, however, declined to offer an opinion. The reason was that it would have been presumptuous to advise, even if indirectly, someone such as Yamagata Aritomo who already knew about gardens, and because doing so would only call into question Yamagata's authorship of the garden. Takahashi also noted that, "Ijūin was a tea aficionado with quirks" but it was actually Yamagata who could be difficult to deal with. Surely Ijūin, knowing of Yamagata's obstinate character, simply decided it was wisest to remain silent. Ogawa Jihei was known for his flexibility, which no doubt equipped him well to work with Yamagata.

Prior to creating his two versions of Murin-an in Kyoto, Yamagata created an enormous garden at Chinzan-sō in the Mejiro area in Tokyo. Now a hotel, Chinzan-sō was Yamagata's primary residence. Yamagata seems to have had confidence in the landscape gardener he commissioned to produce it, Iwamoto Katsugorō, and when Iwamoto suggested, during the construction of Murin-an, that one of the stones in the waterfall should be reset at a different height, Yamagata adopted the advice. Such improvements were apparently permitted as long as they were done under Yamagata's leadership.

After creating Murin-an for Yamagata, Ogawa Jihei did not go on to serve Yamagata by tending the gardens at his various residences outside of Kyoto but instead followed his own path. He created countless gardens in the Kyoto area before expanding beyond the city to work nationwide.

Yamagata Aritomo created many gardens other than Murin-an, leaving an indelible mark on the history of Japanese-style gardens during the Meiji and Taisho periods, but never summoned Ogawa Jihei to work on them and instead used other gardeners for each.

Yamagata set up many homes in his later years:

- Chinzan-sō (primary residence in Mejiro)
  Acquired after the Satsuma Rebellion. Gardener: Iwamoto Katsugorō
  1918: Transferred to Fujita Heitarō (son of Denzaburō).
- Murin-an III (villa near Nanzen-ji temple in Kyoto)
  1894: Kuhara Shōzaburō ordered to begin constructing a villa.
  1896: Completed in December. (Massive stone pulled by 20 oxen

from the mountains of Daigo.)

- Koyurugi-an (villa in Ōiso)
  Built around 1887. Garden of 5,000 *tsubo* [16,500 square meters].
  1907: Given to the family of Baron Mitsui.
- Sarasara-tei (mistress's house in Koishikawa Suidō-chō)
  Built around 1892. Garden of 500 *tsubo* [1,650 square meters].
  After Yamagata's death, became the residence of his mistress Sadako.
- Koki-an (villa in Shōnan, Odawara)
  1907: Built to replace Koyurugi-an. Garden of 6,000 *tsubo* [19,800 square meters]. Gardener: Iwamoto Katsugorō.
  1916: New garden of 500 *tsubo* [1,650 square meters] added at the front of the property.
  1918: Main residence after transfer of Chinzan-sō. Yamagata dies here in 1922.
- Kaishun-sō (villa in Odawara)
  Built on the heights behind Koki-an.
  1913: Taken over from Kiyoura Keigo when he moved to Ōmori.
- Shin Chinzan-sō (Kōji-machi Goban-chō)
  Built in 1917. Western- and Japanese-style buildings. More than 700 *tsubo* [23,100 square meters].
  Tokyo residence after Chinzan-sō.
- Nasu Yamagata Farm (Nasu)
  An expression of the lifestyle of the landed aristocracy.
  The Western-style building (designed by Itō Chūta) from Koki-an is moved here in 1924 after Yamagata's death.

Each of these residences was a place where Yamagata could put into practice one of the different lifestyles available to him.

The gardens of Ogawa Jihei, meanwhile, like many streams diverging from a single source, would broaden and establish a new tradition in Japanese-style gardens originating in Murin-an. The world of Ogawa's gardens, however, never again intersected with the world of Yamagata Aritomo.

The Expansion of Ueji's World

When comparing the world of gardens that Ogawa Jihei created with the composition of gardens from other times or created by other landscape gardeners, what are the differences and what was truly new? With respect to individual techniques, Ogawa Jihei is often said to have demonstrated nothing especially unusual. Contemporary garden designers are particularly prone to saying such things, to the point where one cannot help but sense a measure of envy. What sets Ogawa apart may not be any specific technique but rather the way he rearranged the Japanese-style garden to fit modern Japan.

Ogawa Jihei is often noted for his use of firs and other new varieties of tree, of low-trimmed topiary, and stones set on their sides, but he is also notable for introducing expansive lawns in the foregrounds of his gardens. Each of these characteristics, however, is in evidence at Murin-an. Was his style of garden simply based on the suggestions of Yamagata? Did he ever actually rise above the level of a gardener-for-hire?

Fig. 2-4: The gardens at Heian Jingū shrine

Yet Ogawa Jihei went on to make a name for himself with work on gardens such as those at Okazaki Park, the Heian Jingū shrine, and the Imperial Museum of Kyoto. The trees he planted would take root and survive without withering, so he gained a reputation as a man of good fortune.

Ogawa Jihei famously used stone pilings from Kyoto's old Sanjō Ōhashi and Gojō Ōhashi bridges as stepping stones in a pond in the gardens of the Heian Jingū shrine (Fig. 2-4). The use of these columnar stones that once supported bridges linked the pond to a world of motion. The use of bridge pilings defined the atmosphere of the pond as not of the sea but of a flowing river. Like the egg of Columbus, so simple once revealed, the design was extremely clear and immediately understood by all. The bridge pilings set in the pond instantly gave visitors an impression of the garden's gentle immediacy and delightfulness. Such was the naturalism of Ogawa Jihei.

Ogawa Jihei was contracted to do the gardens of the Heian Jingū shrine on 11 December 1894, but construction seems to have been underway since the beginning of that year. Ogawa's contract for the construction work was for 1,603 yen and 56 sen, and in it he named Nakagawa Tomejirō of Shimogyō-ku Sanjō-dōri Shirakawa-bashi Agaru Horiike-chō as his representative. The contracted fee was later raised as adjustments were made such as the addition of more trees.

The gardens of the Heian Jingū shrine are some of Kyoto's most celebrated and continue to captivate many visitors. Surrounding the main shrine building, they include the south garden, west garden, middle garden, and east garden. The west and middle gardens were finished in 1913. Construction continued on the east garden, which was completed in 1926, while the south garden was completed later. The west garden pond incorporates water lilies, *hanashōbu* irises, and Japanese spatterdock, while the middle garden uses *kakitsubata* irises. It is the middle garden whose pond has the "crouching dragon bridge" made of recycled bridge pilings. The east garden has an expansive pond spanned by a pavilion-like structure called the Taihei-kaku ("bridge of peace"). The Taihei-kaku and the Japanese-style Shōbi-kan guesthouse that stands nearby were moved to the Heian Jingū shrine after being used at the Kyoto National Industrial Exposition held at the Kyoto Imperial Palace. Among Ogawa Jihei's gardens, this one stands out for its grand scale and gorgeousness. The shrine gardens include many weeping cherry trees whose beauty captivates visitors every year.

The stone pilings from the Sanjō and Gojō bridges and the weeping cherries were popular highlights that are unusual for Ueji, who generally did not emphasize famous stones and trees. In *Sasameyuki* (*The Makioka Sisters*), Tanizaki Jun'ichirō appealingly describes a visit to shrine by members of the Makioka family, the novel's protagonists, to enjoy the weeping cherries, even writing, "what was left to stand for the Kyoto spring if not the cherries in the Heian Shrine?"

Ogawa Jihei often created vast private gardens for the wealthy. The gardens of the Heian Jingū shrine, however, were one of his few projects to be viewed by the masses, and perhaps he was conscious of this when he incorporated accessible showiness such as the bridge pilings and weeping cherries. The result is that the gardens of the Heian Jingū shrine are bright and expansive.

In the same way, in another appealing technique frequently seen in Ogawa Jihei's gardens, azaleas and other low topiary that grow close to the ground both make the garden look larger and lead the eye to borrowed landscapes far beyond it. Large topiary plantings had been used in various ways since ancient times in gardens such as the one at the Shūgakuin Imperial Villa. If Ogawa added anything new, it was perhaps the use of large topiary in flat gardens. Large topiary were originally used to compensate for topographical changes in places where the ground rose up sharply or suddenly dropped off like a cliff. Ueji, however, created depth by bringing such techniques into the middle ground of flat gardens. Where did this idea come from? The garden at Murin-an is famous for being made up of very low-cut azaleas and other plants. This was probably an idea implemented at Yamagata's direction. If so, then maybe Yamagata should get credit for bringing large topiary into flat gardens. Maybe.

On this point, I would like to return to Ijūin Kanetsune, the "tea aficionado with quirks" mentioned above. Ijūin was from Satsuma, and Satsuma had a tradition of martial landscape gardening known as *bugaku-ryū*. The town of Chiran in Kagoshima is famous for the many gardens of this type that can be found at the old homes of samurai families, gardens notable for their large topiary plantings. Isn't it possible that this technique of *bugaku-ryū* gardens was actually imparted to Ueji by Ijūin, a Satsuma native? This is, of course, merely speculation, and yet the broad-minded gardens of Ueji seem unlikely to have emerged from the gardens of Kyoto alone, whether those of Zen temples or tea practitioners.

In something perhaps related, Robert Fortune, a Scottish botanist and plant hunter who spent about a year and a half in Japan beginning in October 1860 during the Bakumatsu period, wrote the following in his book *Yedo and Peking*:

Japanese gentlemen in Nagasaki, whose wealth enables them to follow out their favorite pursuits more extensively, have another class of gardens. These, although small according to our ideas, are still considerably larger, than those of the working classes; many of them are about a quarter of an acre in extent. They are generally turfed over; and, like the smaller ones, they are laid out with an undulating surface, some parts being formed into little mounds, while others are converted into lakes. In several of these places I met with azaleas of extraordinary size—much larger than I have ever seen in China, or in any other part of the world, the London exhibitions not excepted. One I measured was no less than 40 feet in circumference! These plants are kept neatly nipped and clipped into a fine round form, perfectly flat upon the top, and look like dining room tables.

The garden Fortune describes seems uncannily reminiscent of the topiary of Ogawa Jihei. Although presumably reflecting the gardening traditions of Kyushu, it also suggests an affinity with Ueji's gardens.

Ogawa Jihei does not, however, seem to have gained renown for his gardens from the outset. Ozawa Keijirō's "Meiji teienki" (A record of Meiji gardens), contained in *Meiji engeishi* (A history of Meiji gardening), which was written in 1912 and published in 1915, fails to even mention Ogawa. When touching on the gardens of Kyoto, it emphasizes how "the gardens of Kyoto's various temples have suddenly come to ruin since the Restoration." When it mentions the commemoration of 1,100 years since the founding of the capital at Kyoto, Ogawa's efforts at the Heian Jingū shrine pass without mention.

The same publication contains an essay by Kajūji Tsuneo, "Kyōto no Meiji ishingo no hensen" (Changes in Kyoto after the Meiji Restoration), that mentions Maruyama Park, a project with which Ogawa Jihei was involved, but the commentary is generally unfavorable:

> *City parks in Kyoto include Maruyama Park, located in Shimogyō-ku Maruyama-chō. Opened in December 1886, it occupies a total area of 6,916 tsubo [22,823 square meters]. The Shōgun-zuka Mound is on its east while the west offers distant views of the city over Yasaka Jinja shrine. An ancient weeping cherry stands at its center and the park adjoins Makuzugahara to the south and Chion-in temple to the north. Greatly expanded in recent years, construction is mostly finished but the style, similar to a tea garden, has been criticized as marring the scenic beauty of the surroundings.*

Throughout, *Meiji engeishi* (A history of Meiji gardening) combines an attitude critical of the trend of casting aside the traditions of Edo with a point of view favoring Western-style gardens as a matter of civilization and enlightenment, and the activities of those like Ogawa Jihei seem to fall away in the gap between the two.

What distinguishes Ogawa Jihei's gardens, though, is that they went in a different direction, one suggested by Yamagata's comment when building Murin-an that, "the gardens of Kyoto…are…tea gardens…of very little interest." Ogawa's gardens were certainly not "similar to a tea garden." Indeed, Ueji's characteristic use of firs and other new varieties of tree, low-trimmed topiary, and horizontal stone settings were the secret to creating a new style of Japanese garden that left a brighter and more open impression.

I would like now to introduce some fascinating commentary pulled from the history of gardening in the form of the following passage from *Teien zakki* (Miscellaneous notes on gardens), written by landscape gardener Harigaya Kanekichi and published in 1938, long after *Meiji engeishi* (A history of Meiji gardening):

> By the mid-Meiji period someone had appeared with the skill to put Western-style gardening into practice. Regarded as probably the first to do so, this was Kodaira Yoshichika, who was active in designing gardens for the court. His method involved dispensing entirely with the stepping stones, groupings of stones, and stone lanterns that were standard in conventional Japanese gardens and instead creating winding paths that traced pleasant curves through peaceful lawns interrupted here and there by rounded topiary plantings that enhanced the effect of the paths. This was, in other words, the perfected form of the immature compromise seen in his garden for his Tsukiji Hotel and can be thought of as a Japanese adaptation of the French landscape garden. Factors in elevating this blended style to the height of popularity no doubt included how well it harmonized with both Japanese and Western architecture and how comparatively easily the turf and plantings required could be obtained in the Tokyo area. Much in demand by high society at the time, this eclectic style became known as the "lawn garden," came to rival the "hill and pond garden" in popularity, and deserves mention as a Meiji period blend of Japanese and Western styles.

The blended style is mentioned here in praise of Kodaira Yoshichika, who worked for the Imperial Household Agency, but its description could just as well be used to introduce the gardens of Ogawa Jihei, which tells us something about their modern aspect. Ogawa Jihei, by the way, would later be asked to work on the garden for the Momoyama Imperial Mausoleum, to serve at the new emperor's first ceremonial offering of rice, and to help maintain the gardens at the Katsura and Shūgakuin Imperial Villas. In other words, he came to be commissioned by the Imperial Household Agency as a landscape gardener worthy of being entrusted with renovations to the mausoleum of Emperor Meiji and other garden-related projects for the imperial family.

With respect to "lawn gardens," Ogawa offered the following comments to Kuroda Tengai:

> *The gardens of old took on a patina and grew better naturally. Even a single tree would be tossed about by the wind, struck by the rain, and lay down roots. Its branches would flourish and it improved on its own. But gardens must change with the times, and patina alone is not enough these days. You need to have a lawn that can accommodate garden parties for two or three hundred guests....*

In other words, Ogawa himself sought the kind of blending of styles that was noted by Harigaya Kanekichi. Still, unlike Imperial Household Agency gardener Kodaira Yoshichika, whose style was influenced by his studies of trends overseas, Ogawa arrived at a blended style of his own strictly by improving the techniques of the Japanese garden. The introduction of lawns and other elements that appear Western in style softened by way of naturalistic ideals the sense of tension that had until then been found in the symbolic gardens of Kyoto's temples.

Ogawa Jihei frequently used temple foundation stones called *garan ishi* in his gardens. Such stones are instantly recognizable as they typically have an elevated portion used to receive the standing pillar and a hole at their center to keep the pillar from slipping. Compared to conventional compositions made up of symbolic "key stones," this approach of using stones for their historical evocativeness was far more naturalistic or even romantic.

This character of Ueji's gardens seems to have marked not so much a change from Japanese gardens to those blending Japanese and Western styles as a shift from the symbolic gardens of tea and Zen toward naturalistic gardens. This also seems to be a characteristic that can be found in Japanese-style culture as a whole from the Meiji through early Showa periods.

In this, the rise of newly powerful figures such as Yamagata Aritomo during the Meiji period played a role in the background. They endeavored to make Japan as modern a state as possible and yet, as if to soften the tension of their public postures, in their private domains they pursued Japanese-style culture. This is the refracted shadow covering the whole history of Japan's modernization. The Japanese style they sought was something of their own, something not bound by the tea ceremony and Zen of the past. The systems of symbolic meaning that haunted tea and Zen were too heavy for them. They favored natural compositions attuned to an aesthetic of their own, something revealed in the naturalistic garden.

The Culture Ueji Encountered

Here I would like to suggest a sketch of the people who sustained Japanese culture from the Meiji through early Showa periods. We observe, of course, that Yamagata Aritomo occupies a central position within it, one reflecting exactly the words with which Oka Yoshitake described Yamagata's position in political history:

Imagine for a moment a kind of historical distribution map depicting the many figures that moved across the political stage during the Meiji and Taisho periods. Yamagata Aritomo would no doubt occupy the position of a central mountain range, both by virtue of the many roles he played during his long life and because of the extensive factional network at whose center he stood.

In other words, the stage described here was not just a political one but also that of Japanese-style culture. In fact, this is a critical truth that teaches us the character of Japan's modernization: the politics and Japanese-style culture of the Meiji to the early Showa periods are grounded in a common mentality.

Like ridges that diverge from a shared peak, Ogawa Jihei, too, went on to create a range of new Japanese-style gardens originating in the one at

Murin-an. The encounter between Yamagata and Ueji no doubt had a decisive influence on them both.

The people who sustained Japanese-style culture from the Meiji through early Showa periods overlap neatly with those who drove Japan's modernization during that same period. Since those who sustain culture in any given period of time are inevitably those who sustain the state, this may seem utterly unsurprising. The point I wish to make, though, is that the Japanese-style culture they sustained was a modern Japanese culture that functioned as a greatest common denominator, and that Ogawa Jihei was the landscape gardener who stood at its center.

Chapter Three

Gardens of the Bourgeoisie and the Aristocracy

The Gardens of the Sumitomo Family

Sumitomo Kichizaemon Tomoito (art name: Shunsui) was head of the Sumitomo family and one of the great peaks in the topography of the Japanese-style culture at the heart of modern Japan. In addition to being Ogawa Jihei's greatest patron, he would have enormous influence on the rise of modern Japanese-style culture generally. Originally named Takamaro, he was born the sixth child of the Tokudaiji, a family of court nobles of the *seigake* rank, second only to the highest-ranking *sekkanke*. His grandfather Sanemi and father Kin'ito had both taken an interest in the way of tea.

In terms of the modernization of the Sumitomo family, the arrival of Takamaro as its adoptive heir in 1892 and his subsequent transformation into Sumitomo Kichizaemon Tomoito, fifteenth head of the family, was an event of enormous significance. Born in 1864, the young man was 28 years old at the time and had already thoroughly mastered the ways of the aristocracy as practiced in the Tokudaiji family.

In its education, the Tokudaiji family followed the traditions of the Kogidō academy for the Chinese classics; the teachings of Fujiwara no Kinnari as received through Takenouchi Shikibu for the Japanese classics; and the Keien style of Kagawa Kageki for *waka* poetry. For the tea ceremony, Tomoito's grandfather Tokudaiji Sanemi and father Tokudaiji Kin'ito studied under Fukatsu Sōmi of the Urasenke school, and under their influence Takamaro had been initiated to the practice under Sen Genshitsu at an early age. His hobbies also included horseback riding and watching Noh performance, and he later showed himself to be fond of new things, taking an interest in both hunting and bicycles. He adopted the art name Shunsui and retained it unchanged throughout his life.

For the Sumitomo, taking in someone with such an aristocratic upbringing was naturally of great significance in elevating the family's standing, but this significance was even more pronounced because it had adopted an heir from the Tokudaiji, an aristocratic family that ranked just below the five regent houses. Tomoito's oldest brother Tokudaiji Sanetsune eventually served as grand chamberlain to the emperor while his brother Kinmochi became heir to the Saionji family and, as a *genrō* elder statesman, one of the most powerful liberal politicians of Japan's pre-war history. In providing financial support for such people, the Sumitomo perhaps benefitted from their protection in both tangible and intangible ways.

Sumitomo Shunsui began collecting ancient bronze ware and mirrors and took a particular interest in bonsai and green tea. Shunsui's collection reflected the Sumitomo family business of copper mining, and he set out to put together a collection of uncompromising quality and scale. The results were compiled in 1911 as *Senoku seishō* (The collection of old bronzes of Baron Sumitomo). Later, a storehouse for bronze ware was designed in 1925 for Shunsui's villa in the Shishigatani area of Kyoto; this was completed in 1928, after his death.

Although it may initially appear that Shunsui, despite having joined the Sumitomo family, merely indulged his hobbies and contributed nothing at all to the family business, he was the primary factor, and an extremely effective one, through which the Sumitomo family gained access to the aristocracy and, by extension, the world of politics. Conversely, the Sumitomo became patrons to the political world, which is why Saionji Kinmochi is said to have enjoyed their financial backing.

The first contact between the Sumitomo and Ogawa Jihei is said to have been around 1909 when the Sumitomo family began building a primary residence and garden in Osaka's Chausuyama area. Later, the Sumitomo also had gardens built at other properties such as their Shishigatani villa and Kinugasa-chō residence, both in Kyoto. The landscaping of all of these gardens was entrusted to Ogawa Jihei.

The Sumitomo family originated in Kyoto but moved its base for copper smelting to Osaka's Awaji-machi with the establishment of a refinery there in 1623. Eventually the head office of the family business was also transferred from Kyoto to Osaka and everything moved to Nagahori Mozaemon-chō. An estate had been maintained in the area since 1636, and it would eventually become the location of the family's primary residence. Also known as Unagidani-tei, this residence would come to serve as the strategic base for the modernization of the Sumitomo during the Meiji period.

The copper refinery that had been located at the primary Sumitomo residence in Unagidani was moved to Besshi in what is now Ehime Prefecture in 1869, with relocation not fully complete until 1876. Unagidani, meanwhile, saw the construction of Osaka's first privately-owned Western-style building in 1879.

The Sumitomo were one of Osaka's best-known wealthy merchant families. Osaka, though, also suffered a steep decline in the wake of the Restoration. In order to turn things around, the city put together a plan to rebuild the port and worked to develop infrastructure centered on commerce and industry.

Thanks in part to such efforts to build a new port, the city of Osaka gradually began to recover. As if to further nudge economic conditions forward, the Fifth National Industrial Exposition was scheduled to be held in Osaka over five months between 1 March and 31 July 1903, only the second time, following the fourth exposition in Kyoto, that the event was held outside Tokyo. Although Osaka was playing runner-up to Kyoto, the Meiji government's final National Industrial Exposition was the largest of all, held at venues around what is now Tennōji Park and Ōhama Park in Sakai.

At the time, the Sumitomo family provided exposition organizers with land at Chausuyama—which the family had obtained after the Restoration—that led to the Tennōji venue. The Sumitomo family had begun acquiring land in the area in 1895 and continued to make additional purchases in 1897, 1898, 1900, and 1902. Notably, the final parcel was acquired through transfer from Iwasaki Hisaya. The *Mitsubishi shashi* (Mitsubishi company journal) of the day records the following:

12 May 1902
Chausuyama Property Transfer
We transferred a woodland lot measuring 1 chō, 6 tan, 1 se, and 20 bu [16,005 square meters] *located in the city of Osaka at Minami-ku Tennōji Chausuyama-chō 92 and nine other lots to Sumitomo Kichizaemon for 45,000 yen. Conditions include honoring the commitment that we made to preserve the site's historic remains when we took it over from the Department of the Army.*

According to this account, when the Sumitomo family obtained the Chausuyama land from Mitsubishi it accepted the requirement not to damage its value as a historic site. Chausuyama is a small hill about eight meters high located in what is now Tennōji Park and is thought to have been a burial mound. Tokugawa Ieyasu and his son Hidetada used this hill to observe Osaka Castle during the Osaka Winter Campaign in 1614–1615, and Ieyasu eventually relocated his field headquarters there. During the Summer Campaign in 1615, Sanada Yukimura from the Osaka side made his field headquarters at Chausuyama, later the site of ferocious fighting known as the Battle of Chausuyama. Ultimately victorious in the Summer Campaign, Tokugawa Ieyasu gathered the various generals under his command on the hill to celebrate, earning it the nickname *okachiyama* ("victory mountain"). It was because the location had such a storied past that the Sumitomo were willing to preserve it.

The Sumitomo began construction of a residence on the site in earnest following the exposition. A groundbreaking ceremony was held on 1 March 1912 and a ceremony marking the completion of the framework on 29 May the following year. Completed in 1915, the residence was designed by Sumitomo architects Noguchi Magoichi and Hidaka Yutaka and built by master carpenter Yagi Jinbei II. Landscaping of the garden was initiated in advance of the residence in 1908. The scale of the garden was said to recall the massive construction works of Toyotomi Hideyoshi. This Sumitomo family garden at Chausuyama came to be named Keitaku-en.

It was Ogawa Jihei who undertook the landscaping at Keitaku-en. In fact, on 5 October 1911, the year before construction began on the main residence at Chausuyama, Sumitomo Shunsui took Ogawa Jihei to Kanazawa where they saw the Kenroku-en garden and are said to have paid particular attention to the stone bridge. Shunsui also visited Kōraku-en in Okayama the following year and probably referred to such daimyo gardens in thinking about how to compose the landscape at Keitaku-en.

Keitaku-en is a massive garden where Ogawa Jihei was able to give full play to his abilities. It has a large pond at its center and a hill to the pond's northeast made from the earth and rock excavated in its creation. A waterfall flows over massive rocks placed at the base of this hill, generating a sense of motion in the garden as a whole. The boldness of the waterfall's composition seems to set the tone for the character of the entire garden. Large stones placed here and there—said to have been brought to the site over great distances from across the Seto Inland Sea—add further atmosphere. Such ambitious scale is why the garden was compared to the construction projects of Toyotomi Hideyoshi. Still, the areas surrounding the pond are provided with a number of beaches that also create more calming views. While there may be a row of natural stones arranged as stepping stones over a stream, there is also a long bridge made of sharply cut stones that bends in a dogleg; in this way, a great many landscaping techniques are employed throughout. This is just the kind of massive project that would be a landscaper's dream. Ogawa Jihei himself described his early days of involvement with the garden as follows:

Mr. Sumitomo is now building a villa at Chausuyama, devoting about half of the property's 40,000 tsubo [132,000 square meters] to the garden. It's like something Hideyoshi would have built in the old days. I've been involved since last year and, having been entrusted with the whole thing, figure it will take at least three years. After all, it takes up roughly as much space as Osaka Castle, and hundreds of massive stones weighing 5,000 or even 7,000 kan [18,750 or even 26,250 kilograms] *have been brought in from Shikoku for use in the garden. When it is complete it will be number one in the Kansai region, even beyond the reach of Okayama Park!* [From *Zoku zoku kōko kaishin roku* (A record of pleasant scenes in and around the capital, Vol. 3)]

Here we have the beginning of Ogawa Jihei's work under Sumitomo Shunsui. Nevertheless, it remains unclear what specific ties brought them together. Ueji probably already had a good reputation as someone who could be called upon when building a large garden, and it is perhaps natural to assume that his work on the gardens of the Heian Jingū shrine is what brought him to Shunsui's attention. Indeed, Shunsui had been involved in the construction of the shrine since 1893 when he became a member of the sponsors association for the commemoration of the 1,100th anniversary of the transfer of the capital to Kyoto.

This association, under Chairman Konoe Atsumaro and Deputy Chairman Sano Tsunetami, constructed a memorial hall to serve as a venue for commemorative events, added a main sanctuary building to turn the whole into a shrine, and constructed the gardens to beautify the area around the shrine buildings. Shunsui was impressed with the results of the construction and came to think highly of Ueji, who had been responsible for the gardens. The biography *Sumitomo Shunsui* describes the relationship between the two as follows:

When Ueji was asked by Shunsui to take on the landscaping of the garden at Chausuyama in 1909, he was fifty years old and mature in his technique. In addition to being resourceful, Ueji was also straightforward in saying what he felt without hesitation, something that appealed to Shunsui. Ueji was slightly older than Shunsui and despite the great discrepancy in their social standing the two seem also to have found common ground as both had been adopted.

While the suggestion that the two empathized with one another because both had been adopted seems far-fetched, Ueji dose seem to have had a talent for getting along with people. His reputation for flexibility served him well when constructing the gardens of the Heian Jingū shrine, a task he completed smoothly while working under the direction of Naiki Jinzaburō—later the first mayor of the city of Kyoto—and the many other fussy members of the gardens committee. This was probably one reason Ueji was able to interact so naturally even with Shunsui, who had gone from a family of aristocrats to heading a family of capitalists.

Later it was said that Yamagata Aritomo and Sumitomo Shunsui were the only ones who could address Ueji without using an honorific, but this conversely also suggests that Shunsui and Ueji were, in a way, very close. In any case, Ueji had met the man who would become his greatest patron.

Construction of the Western-style building at Chausuyama began in 1916. From the early Meiji period through the early Showa period, many large estates were designed with both Japanese-style and Western-style buildings to be used in parallel. At the Chausuyama property, the Sumitomo family followed this pattern in building residences that were both massive and grand. At the time, architects trained at Imperial Universities were beginning to make inroads into the world of *sukisha* connoisseurs. Notable among them were Hidaka Yutaka and Noguchi Magoichi, both graduates of Tokyo Imperial University who were employed by Sumitomo Eizen Design Office. (Hidaka designed the Western-style building at Chausuyama, which was completed in 1920.) In addition to designing various buildings for the Sumitomo family as industrialists, they also saw it as their mission to build their employer's private world and devoted themselves to the task to the limits of their expertise. Their legacy can be seen today at sites such as the Sumitomo family's primary residence at Shishigatani in Kyoto. Such buildings were created as architects trained in Western architecture turned their talents toward the maturation of private worlds, something possible because Japan's modern society had finally come into its prime.

Previously, the primary residence of the Sumitomo family had been located at Unagidani, a mercantile neighborhood in central Osaka. The family had owned land there since 1636 and maintained its primary residence there since 1685. During the Meiji period, master carpenter Yagi Jinbei built a Western-style building there in 1879 while his successor Yagi Jinbei II remodeled the eastern wing of the Japanese-style building in 1905.

Establishing a residence at Chausuyama meant leaving the carefully maintained Unagidani residence for a new site. In transferring the primary residence from a downtown location, the family no doubt sought a new lifestyle. In 1915, the remodeled *shoin*-style formal reception area of the eastern wing of the Japanese-style building at Unagidani was relocated to the family's villa in Suma. In 1917, two years after the completion of the Japanese-style residence at Chausuyama, the Kōjitsu-an tea ceremony room was relocated from Unagidani to Chausuyama and it was decided that the Unagidani residence would be placed under the administration of the Sumitomo general head office.

No sooner had the primary residence been transferred from Unagidani to Chausuyama, and its Western-style building completed, than something very strange occurred. In 1921, the year after the Western-style building was finished and everything at the new residence had been put in good order, the Sumitomo family donated the residential property and its gardens in their entirety to Osaka City for use in the establishment of an art museum. The biography *Sumitomo Shunsui* describes this as follows:

> *On the morning of 6 December, Directors Tanaka and Ogura visited Mayor Ikegami Shirō at the Osaka City Office and proposed donating Chausuyama and the Sumitomo family residence there to the city of Osaka, delivering to him the following letter: [Omitted] The proposal happened suddenly but had deep origins.*

The reasons given were that Osaka City had been planning since about 1920 to build an art museum but had been unable to find a suitable site while, on the Sumitomo side, the environment surrounding Chausuyama had deteriorated since the Fifth National Industrial Exposition in 1903. The exposition had been held in part on land adjacent to the Chausuyama property, and although the Sumitomo family had cooperated by providing that land, the exposition had transformed the area surrounding the residence. As described in *Sumitomo Shunsui*:

In the beginning, the area was a wild expanse with very few houses other than two or three villas and felt far removed from the troubles of human society, but it underwent a remarkable transformation beginning with the exposition. A park was created, to the west of which emerged an area filled with the hustle and bustle of the Shinsekai neighborhood, which in turn opened up on its south to the squalid back alleys of Tobita. What is more, trains running frequently to and from Tennōji Station rained soot on the hills and were particularly loud at night.

Although the Sumitomo had contributed to the exposition, it led to development of the surrounding area that made it less desirable as a location for the family's primary residence. Earlier we saw that, in the year the exposition was held, Katsura Tarō, the prime minister; Itō Hirobumi, president of the Seiyūkai political party; and Komura Jutarō, the minister of foreign affairs, had visited Yamagata Aritomo at Murin-an in Kyoto, whose garden Ogawa Jihei had landscaped, to consult about the Russo-Japanese War in what would come to be known as the Murin-an Conference. In this we caught a glimpse of Ueji's garden as a stage for making political decisions. In Osaka, meanwhile, Ueji's garden would leave the hands of the Sumitomo to become the grounds of an art museum in what was also a kind of garden-related political decision.

The Fifth National Industrial Exposition was the largest exposition held during the Meiji period. Visitors reached 5.3 million people, ten times the number that had visited the previous exposition in Kyoto's Okazaki neighborhood, and there were a great variety of exhibition halls. Unlike previous industrial expositions that were like trade fairs, the Osaka exposition had a strong emphasis on entertainment and amusements. Pavilions included the Educational Building, Foreign Samples Building, Fine Arts Building, and Anthropology Building. There were also attractions such as a panorama building, an around-the-world building, a hall of wonders, a circus, a newly-built tower outfitted with Osaka's first elevator, a water chute, and a merry-go-round, making the whole rather like an amusement park.

The National Industrial Exposition was, as its name suggests, an important part of an industrial promotion policy that furthered modernization in Meiji Japan. The First National Industrial Exposition was held in Tokyo's Ueno Park in 1877, followed by the second in 1881 and the third in 1890, both of which were also held in Ueno. Because these expositions were designed to promote industry with a mind to exports, they were similar to what we would today describe as trade fairs. At the time, exports were centered on craft objects, ceramics, and other works of art. The concept of expositions, museums, and exposition secretariats spread widely across industry and the arts without differentiation between these realms. The exposition venue, therefore, was less an industrial trade fair than a mecca for the arts. Construction of the museum at Ueno was followed by provision of a zoo and further improvements to the area as a park. The National Industrial Exposition played a decisive role in establishing Ueno as a place of culture.

For the Fourth National Industrial Exposition in 1895, the event left Tokyo and was held in Kyoto. Holding the exposition in Kyoto was an opportunity to turn the Okazaki Park area into a focal point for culture and the arts. New facilities that were built included a zoo, the Heian Jingū shrine, and the Butokuden martial arts hall. With its rows of museums, the scene was a fair match for Tokyo's Ueno. Here, too, we see how the industrial exposition gave birth to a cultural district. Incidentally, the painting *Chōshō* [Morning Toilette] by Kuroda Seiki that was exhibited at the Fourth National Industrial Exposition in Okazaki caused a scandal for its depiction of the naked female form, a famous episode in the establishment of the arts in Japan.

Of course, the Lake Biwa Canal runs through Okazaki, which is adjacent to Murin-an, and since Ogawa Jihei had made his name through improvements to the area, the shift of Okazaki toward culture is inextricably linked with Ueji's origins. Just as the Lake Biwa Canal, a product of industrial policy, was transformed into something cultural through Ueji's gardens, the National Industrial Exposition, also the product of industrial policy, cultivated the area and made Ueji's gardens possible.

By contrast, the Fifth National Industrial Exposition in Osaka would deliver the neighborhood of Shinsekai. The Osaka Land Co., Ltd. was established in 1911 to administer Shinsekai and roads were constructed (ostensibly with reference to Parisian city blocks), a tower called Tsūtenkaku was built, and the brightly illuminated Luna Park took shape. This entertainment area for the masses and Tennōji Park were the offspring of the exposition. Although perhaps envisioned as a means of infusing the area with culture, in fact the result was to create an area teeming with entertainment for the masses. This was not to the liking of the Sumitomo family.

Here, then, I would like to try and arrange the steps related to the construction of the Sumitomo family residence at Chausuyama and the land development after the Fifth National Industrial Exposition in a single timeline:

1895 The Sumitomo family begins acquiring land in Chausuyama.

1902 The Sumitomo family acquires land from the Iwasaki family.

1903 The Fifth National Industrial Exposition is held.

1908 Ogawa Jihei begins work on the garden of the residence at Chausuyama.

1909 The eastern portion of Tennōji Park opens on the former site of the exposition.

The Sumitomo family begins construction on the residence at Chausuyama.

1912 A groundbreaking ceremony is held for the Chausuyama residence.

The western portion of Tennōji Park opens.

Shinsekai begins operation, and Tsūtenkaku and Luna Park are built.

The Great Minami Fire (Loss of the red-light district prompts a search for a new location.)

1913 A ceremony marks the completion of the framework at the Chausuyama residence.

1915 The Chausuyama residence is completed.

A privately run zoo opens within Tennōji Park.

1916 The adjacent Tobita neighborhood is selected as the site of the new red-light district.

1917 The Tobita red-light district opens.

1921 The Sumitomo family donates the Chausuyama residential property for use as the grounds for an art museum.

1925 The Sumitomo family has the Chausuyama residence dismantled and moved to Sumiyoshi.

Was the Sumitomo's offer to donate their Chausuyama residential property and gardens to Osaka City for use in establishing an art museum an expression of the family's desire to turn the site of the exposition into a cultural district for the city, as had been done in Tokyo and Kyoto? No one knows the truth. The Sumitomo family itself was probably unable to settle on a vision for Chausuyama's future. Still, it must have felt unbearable for the family to watch the center of Osaka's deep culture of the common people take shape immediately to the west of its Chausuyama residence in the form of Shinsekai, Luna Park, and Tsūtenkaku, followed by the opening of the red-light district in Tobita to its south. Before donating the Chausuyama property to Osaka City, the Sumitomo had previously donated a library on the downtown island of Nakanoshima to Osaka Prefecture. In this way the family contributed to the enculturation of Osaka, but ended up pulling out of Chausuyama and relocating its primary residence first to Sumiyoshi in Hyōgo and then to Shishigatani in Kyoto. The process by which the cities of Kyoto, Osaka, and Kobe came to constitute a region segregated by character—with tradition in Kyoto, business in Osaka, and lifestyle in Kobe—seems to be symbolically expressed in the movement of the Sumitomo family primary residence. It is impossible to determine whether the Sumitomo escaped from Osaka or Osaka drove the Sumitomo out; all one can say of the particulars is, "Well, that's Osaka for you."

In any case, the largest of Ogawa Jihei's landscape gardens—Keitaku-en at Chausuyama—left the hands of his patron and became a public park. It seems unlikely that this could have been consistent with Ueji's original vision for the garden.

In 1925, the Sumitomo family's Japanese-style residence at Chausuyama was dismantled, transported to the Tantakabayashi area of Sumiyoshi village in Hyōgo Prefecture, and rebuilt. This residence at Sumiyoshi was completed on 2 May of that year. The Sumitomo had left only the garden behind in Osaka.

The property in the Tantakabayashi area of Sumiyoshi village was now the Sumitomo family's new primary residence, but it had originally been the estate of Tanabe Sadakichi, who had worked in positions including manager of the Sumitomo Bank head office. In 1909, Tanabe registered the property in the name of his son. Registration appears to have occurred post-construction, however, and renovations to the garden—undertaken by Ogawa Jihei—had been completed by 1 June of the previous year. With respect to buildings completed in advance of the gardens, Sumitomo family architect Noguchi Magoichi designed the Western-style building while Yagi Jinbei II served as master carpenter for the Japanese-style residence. As a Sumitomo executive, Tanabe used people who were frequently employed by the Sumitomo to build his own residence. He had purchased the land upon his retirement from Sumitomo in 1904 and seems to have intended it as a place to live out his old age in seclusion.

The Sumitomo acquired the Tanabe residence prior to vacating their primary residence in Chausuyama. Upon the marriage of Tomoito's daughter Taka to Tadateru, the third son of Viscount Torii, on 11 July 1914, Tanabe Sadakichi transferred his own home, completed only a short time earlier, to the Sumitomo family for use as the couple's new residence. This was an act of gratitude by Tanabe toward the Sumitomo.

The new couple, Taka and Tadateru, left Unagidani in Osaka to move into the estate on 15 July and lived there as a branch of the Sumitomo family. Then came the Sumitomo's withdrawal from the primary residence at Chausuyama, when the family concluded that the property in Sumiyoshi was suitable as a new primary residence. The Japanese-style building at Chausuyama was transferred to the site while the location of the Western-style building that Tanabe Sadakichi had built was shifted slightly to facilitate its use as part of the new primary residence. This completed the Sumitomo family's move of its primary residence to Tantakabayashi in Sumiyoshi.

When Tanabe Sadakichi bought his property in Sumiyoshi, the area had still exuded the sort of rural atmosphere where one expects foxes and badgers to appear. The only prominent residence nearby was the large estate of Murayama Ryōhei, founder of the Asahi Shimbun newspaper. Later, however, the area would be transformed into an exclusive residential district with numerous estates owned by the bourgeoisie of the Kansai region.

On 1 June 1900, the Sumitomo family set up a provisional construction department with architects such as Noguchi Magoichi and Hidaka Yutaka that aimed to construct buildings such as the company's head office, banks, the library on Nakanoshima, and the villa in Suma. The main building at the Suma villa was completed in 1903. From the end of the Meiji period through the Taisho period the Sumitomo assembled a remarkable collection of residential properties. The remodeling of the eastern wing at the Unagidani primary residence in 1905 suggests that it was still in use at that time, but then, in addition to the residence at Chausuyama and the villa at Suma, the Sumitomo also purchased property in Tokyo at Azabu Toriizaka from Ōtori Keisuke, expanding it and turning it into their Azabu villa. The family also acquired a 3,400 *tsubo* [11,220 square meters] property in Azabu's Ichibei-chō to create a second villa in the area (Table 3-1, Table 3-2).

In 1913, the Sumitomo purchased property in Shishigatani Miyanomae-chō near Nanzen-ji temple in Kyoto at the recommendation of Ogawa Jihei, then later added to the property and turned it into the Shishigatani villa. It was around this time, too, that the Sumitomo purchased the residence at Sumiyoshi for the branch family of Sumitomo Tadateru. The Sumitomo also prepared a residence in the Kinugasa foothills for Tomoito's son Kan'ichi. In addition, the family purchased land at Takada-machi in

Tokyo's Kitatoshima-gun and established the Mejiro villa there for son Atsushi to use while commuting to school at the Peers' School. The family also purchased the Maiko villa of Prince Arisugawa and renovated it in a half-Western style, and appears also to have owned villas at the hot springs in Arima and in Atami, though it remains somewhat difficult to gain a complete picture of their vast holdings. Meanwhile, the *shoin*-style reception area from the eastern wing of the primary residence at Unagidani was moved to the villa in Suma, and the residence placed under the administration of the company's general head office since the Sumitomo family's primary residence had shifted to Chausuyama in 1915.

Ogawa Jihei was responsible for the garden at the Chausuyama residence and also landscaped the gardens at most of the other Sumitomo residences, too. Let's look at the lineup of major Sumitomo residences from about the time when Keitaku-en at Chausuyama became the family's primary residence during the early Taisho period:

Residence at Unagidani	Former primary residence (Administered by the company's general head office from 1917)
Residence at Chausuyama	Primary residence (Donated to Osaka City for use as the site of an art museum in 1921)
Residence at Shishigatani	Villa in Kyoto (Completed in 1920; later made the primary residence)
Villa at Suma	(Framework for new eastern residence completed in 1915)
Residence at Sumiyoshi	Residence of Tanabe Sadakichi → Residence of the Sumitomo Tadateru branch family → Primary residence (later shifted to Kyoto)
Residence at Azabu Ichibei-chō	Villa in Azabu (Now redeveloped as the Izumi Garden tower complex)

I mentioned above that there were many other villas, too, and Ogawa Jihei—that is, Ueji—was involved to a greater or lesser degree in landscaping most of them.

Keitaku-en was by far the largest in scale, but the garden at the Shishi-gatani villa in Kyoto should be seen as best representing the characteristics of the Ogawa Jihei style. Situated to make use of the waters of the Lake Biwa Canal, the garden was originally developed by Ueji himself, and acquired by Sumitomo Shunsui upon his recommendation. Ueji's specialty was using the waters of the canal to create gardens that flowed, and the location of the Shishigatani residence was an ideal place to display his talents. The Sumitomo family's garden there was named Yūhō-en.

The gardens of Ogawa Jihei are known for their use of water not in the form of still ponds but as running streams, for stones laid flat, for azaleas trimmed close and low, and for wide-open grassy areas. The refreshing, vibrant atmosphere of these modern gardens is especially well suited not only to viewing from the inside but also to garden parties.

With respect to the trees within the garden, however, Ogawa avoided the use of magnificent trees. The use of firs and bayberries and other varieties rarely used before to conceal garden borders was well suited to gardens that were expansive but urban.

At the Sumitomo villa in Shishigatani, however, Ueji planted countless red pines, pruned in the spare Kyoto style, to create a garden that blended seamlessly with the "borrowed landscape" of the Higashiyama hills visible beyond their tops. Gardens with many pines are considered extravagant because they demand so much time and trouble to maintain. The garden at Shishigatani was a world created without concern for cost, one that would have been impossible had Ogawa Jihei and the Sumitomo never met.

The water for the Sumitomo family's Shishigatani villa is drawn from the Lake Biwa Canal's branch canal, feeds into the pond, and winds throughout the garden as a stream before ultimately emptying into the Shirakawa River running along the property's south side. The garden of the Shishigatani villa creates water in motion by applying Ueji's preferred technique of using water from the Lake Biwa Canal (Fig. 3-1). The canal bringing water to the garden was originally intended to serve as an upper canal to the lower canal of the Shirakawa River, into which the water of the gar-

Fig. 3-1: Yūhō-en garden at the Sumitomo family villa in Shishigatani

den empties. Were it not for the practical realization of hydroelectric power, the waters of the canal would have been used to drive industry and the site of Yūhō-en itself would likely have been home to factories. This garden was born from the transformation of energy infrastructure for modern industry into infrastructure for modern Japanese-style culture.

The garden contains a magnificent "copper bridge." Not ostentatious, of course, it has low railings and might even be crossed without noticing it. It represents, however, the source of the wealth that established the Sumitomo as modern capitalists. For Shunsui, who collected ancient bronze ware and mirrors and in 1897 donated the bronze sculpture of Kusunoki Masashige on horseback that stands before the Imperial Palace, the copper bridge at the Shishigatani villa was an expression of his own identity as head of the Sumitomo family.

Reflecting the stability emphasized in the Sumitomo family precepts, the copper bridge has always been located at the primary residence as a symbol of the modernizing family. That is, although originally situated at the Unagidani residence, the bridge has been moved each time the primary residence was relocated. That it fits so well in the garden of red pines at the villa in Shishigatani is testament to Ueji's skill (Fig. 3-2).

Fig. 3-2: The "copper bridge" at Yūhō-en

From the Gardens of the Sumitomo to Those of Saionji

Among those who had many gardens by Ogawa Jihei, Saionji Kinmochi deserves to be counted together with Sumitomo Kichizaemon Tomoito (Shunsui).

Ogawa Jihei carried out the landscaping for the gardens at the Saionji family's primary residence in Tokyo's Surugadai area, its Zagyo-sō villa at Okitsu in Shizuoka, and its Seifū-sō villa in Kyoto. Born in 1849 as the second son of Minister of the Right Tokudaiji Kin'ito, Saionji was adopted by Middle Captain of the Right Division of the Inner Palace Guards Saionji Morosue in 1851. The following year he succeeded to the Saionji estate upon the death of his foster father and in 1853, despite his young age, was appointed chamberlain. Firmly rooted in the aristocracy, Saionji Kinmochi was sent to France to study in 1870 after the Restoration, returning to Japan after spending an enjoyable decade there.

With the promulgation of the Peerage Act in 1884 Saionji was given the title of marquis. After serving in posts such as ambassador to Austria-Hungary, minister of education, and president of the Privy Council, Saionji went on to form two cabinets as prime minister. In 1919, at the age of 70, he attended the signing of the Treaty of Versailles ending the First World War.

He received the title of prince the following year. During the Showa period, he was responsible for providing the emperor with advice as the last surviving *genrō* elder statesman. He passed away at his Zagyo-sō villa in Okitsu in 1940.

Saionji Kinmochi entrusted the landscaping at his various residences to Ogawa Jihei because Saionji's younger brother had become head of the Sumitomo family. Of the three Tokudaiji brothers, the eldest took over the Tokudaiji family, the second joined the Saionji, and the third was taken in by the Sumitomo. This Tokudaiji-Saionji-Sumitomo triangle not only served a variety of politico-economic purposes but also, in the creation of its gardens, provided the territory for the activities of Ogawa Jihei. From their foundation in this triangle, the gardens of Ogawa Jihei would undergo a rapid expansion.

After returning from France in 1880, Saionji Kinmochi first took up residence at Kobiki-chō in Kyōbashi in what was said to be a smart house in the style of a *machiai* house of assignation. He then moved to Ōmori, where he built the first house of his own. Saionji named it Bōryoku Sansō ("mountain villa with verdant views") and enjoyed living on the outskirts of the city. The house is said to have later passed into the hands of Uchida Kakichi.

Saionji's third residence was in Surugadai and had been built by the Sumitomo family. A Western-style building designed by Sumitomo architects, the residence had Japanese-style rooms in its interior. The structure had aged, however, and was extensively remodeled two years prior to the Great Kanto Earthquake. This time, too, Sumitomo architects handled the design, which resulted in a Western-style building whose interior rooms were also primarily Western in style. This structure, however, was reduced to ashes during the Great Kanto Earthquake in 1923. For the third time, then, a residence was built on the property at Surugadai, with construction once again undertaken by the Sumitomo. This time, part of the Sumitomo family villa at Kinugasa in Kyoto was transported to the site, resulting in a two-story building with both Western- and Japanese-style rooms. Con-

Fig. 3-3: Saionji Kinmochi's primary residence in Surugadai

structed for Sumitomo Tomoito's son Kan'ichi, the Kinugasa villa had only just been completed in 1920. After the earthquake, Saionji Kinmochi lived temporarily at the Tokyo Station Hotel until the relocation was completed. Shortly after that, Saionji added a single-story Western-style annex, having found it troublesome to go up and down the stairs, and apparently enjoyed devising the layout himself.

Exactly when Ogawa Jihei began landscaping the garden at the main residence in Surugadai is unknown. According to the timeline of gardens contained in *Ogawa Jihei*, edited by Yamane Tokutarō, Ueji began work on the Saionji residence in Tokyo in 1918, suggesting that his involvement with the garden at Surugadai began prior to the earthquake. If so, then he would probably have taken part in the pre-earthquake construction as well as the post-earthquake reconstruction that was achieved through relocation of the Kinugasa villa (whose garden, incidentally, Ueji had also landscaped).

A sketch that appears to be a bird's-eye plan of the third, post-earthquake primary residence and estate at Surugadai can be found in *Saionji kō tsuioku* (Remembering Prince Saionji), published by Chūō University, which took over the property following Saionji's death (Fig. 3-3). Regrettably, the gardens so important for our purposes are omitted. The description indicates that the property covered an area of 812.21 *tsubo* [2,685 square meters] and the buildings a total floor area of 255.28 *tsubo* [844 square meters]. The illustration appears to show all of the estate's buildings as Japanese in style with tiled roofs, but the accompanying text indicates that "the buildings with lightning rods are Western in style." The building at the back left, therefore, is probably the single-story Western-style building that Saionji devised himself.

Seifū-sō, the Saionji villa in Kyoto, was originally a Tokudaiji family retreat named Seifū-kan. It was built in 1832 by Saionji's grandfather Tokudaiji Sanemi in what was then a remote location in the village of Tanaka on the outskirts of the capital, and a place where Sanemi enjoyed hobbies such as producing *rakuyaki* pottery. Both Saionji Kinmochi and Sumitomo Shunsui would have remembered playing there as young lords of the Tokudaiji family. Their father, Tokudaiji Kin'ito, is said to have walked around the garden with young Kinmochi perched on horseback. The Tokudaiji sold the estate to the Sumitomo in 1907. Enlarged through the addition of neighboring property, the new estate was completed in 1913 and used as the Kyoto villa of Saionji Kinmochi. Sumitomo master carpenter Yagi Jinbei II was responsible for construction and Ogawa Jihei for landscaping the gardens.

The relaxed garden exhibited many of the distinctive traits of Ogawa Jihei's landscaping. With low-trimmed plantings and a gently expansive lawn, the garden was a modern one in line with the tastes of Saionji Kinmochi, who loved the culture of the West. The garden was centered, of course, on a constantly changing pond and stream. Said to suggest Lake Biwa, the pond even included an island modeled on Chikubushima Island at the real Lake Biwa. Water was drawn from the Shirakawa River when the Tokudaiji owned the villa, but beginning with Ueji's landscaping water was drawn from the branch canal of the Lake Biwa Canal. Among the gardens that draw water from the branch canal, Seifū-sō is the one located furthest to the west. In an unobtrusive application of modern technology, a motor was used to draw water for the garden. Although the garden is relaxed and expansive, it is also filled with a variety of atmospheric details such as the washbasin and the Oribe-style stone lantern at its Hoshinsai tea ceremony house.

As a politician and aristocrat, it was extremely important for Saionji Kinmochi to maintain a villa in Kyoto as an expression of his political style. Even after the capital was moved from Kyoto to Tokyo in the Meiji period, maintaining an estate in Kyoto remained an important status symbol, one that was of great significance to industrialists as well. Given his aristocratic origins, it would have been unthinkable, then, for Saionji not to have a suitable residence in Kyoto.

Even with a primary residence in Surugadai, having a villa in Kyoto was a critical demonstration of Saionji's identity. Continuing to use a villa once owned by the Tokudaiji—his birth family—as his own no doubt made for a lifestyle much to Saionji's liking. Saionji is said to have been indifferent to politicians while at the estate, spending much of his time instead with people like historian Naitō Konan or ikebana master Nishikawa Issōtei. Whether in Kyoto or Tokyo, a garden by Ogawa Jihei combined tradition and modernity in a way that was appropriate as a status symbol.

Saionji Kinmochi apparently also took quite a liking to Ogawa Jihei. The biography *Ogawa Jihei* includes the following reminiscence by the head priest of Kōun-ji temple:

When it came to Ueji, though, he would say, "Ah, I see Ueji is here to-day. Call him over," and invite him into the house. He seems to have fully approved of Ueji's landscaping, referring to him in correspondence as "Brother Ogawa."

After Saionji Kinmochi's death, the Sumitomo family donated the house and garden at Seifū-sō to Kyoto Imperial University, which Saionji had loved. From 1944 through the present day, Seifū-sō has been maintained as a guesthouse for Kyoto University. There Ueji was able to display his abilities to their fullest on his home turf in a garden whose style suited

Saionji's mix of modernity and aristocratic taste. The scholarly lifestyle for which the garden was used, too, has been carried on by the people of Kyoto University.

Saionji Kinmochi also maintained the Zagyo-sō villa in Okitsu, a residence that made the Saionji lifestyle complete.

Powerful people in Japan since the Meiji period favored maintaining primary residences in Tokyo and villas not only in Kyoto but also in Shōnan. Those in Shōnan were places to get away from the secular world and enjoy time in quiet solitude, reflecting in part an aspiration for the lifestyle of a Western-style "country gentleman."

To have a villa in Kamakura, in Odawara, in Ōiso, Yugawara, or Atami, in Numazu, in Shimoda, in Iwabuchi, or in Okitsu—such was the lifestyle that developed beginning in the Meiji period. The villas and second homes grouped along the Shōnan belt stretching from Kamakura into Shizuoka represented a new lifestyle made possible by Japan's modernization. Many imperial villas were maintained throughout this belt region, followed by the groups of villas that formed around them.

Even among the Shōnan villas, however, those too far away were considered less convenient given that people still spent their everyday lives in Tokyo. A second home as far away as Kamakura was ideal for balancing the needs of everyday life. If there was no need for such concerns, however, one could maintain a villa a little further out. Okitsu, where Saionji Kinmochi had his villa, was particularly far from Tokyo.

Okitsu is located way beyond Kamakura and further out even than Ōiso, where Itō Hirobumi maintained his Sōrō-kaku villa, or Odawara, where Yamagata Aritomo maintained his Koki-an villa, or even Iwabuchi, where Tanaka Mitsuaki maintained his Kokei-sō villa. Saionji Kinmochi had first established a villa in Ōiso—located on land adjacent to what would later become the villa of Mitsui's Ikeda Shigeaki—but did away with it and moved to Okitsu.

In establishing Zagyo-sō in Okitsu in 1920, Saionji is said to have chosen the name (literally "cottage of sitting and fishing") in the hope of fishing nearby, or perhaps as a reflection of the written similarity between his own first name Kinmochi (公望) and a nickname for a fisherman drawn from the name of a Chinese sage (*taikōbō*, 太公望). Nevertheless, people soon began making the "pilgrimage to Okitsu" to seek his political judgment.

Saionji also established a villa in Gotenba in 1922. Developed by relocating and renovating a historic farmhouse from the Kamado area in the nearby village of Fujioka, the Gotenba villa was used together with Zagyo-sō in Okitsu as a place to escape the summer heat. Alone among his residences, this villa was not named and functioned purely as a rustic cottage. Behind the cottage were rice paddies covering nearly six *tan* [5,952 square meters] that produced thirteen sacks of rice per year and kept Saionji fed. The site offered an enjoyable view of Mt. Fuji, and there Saionji is said to have risen at seven-thirty in the morning, gone to bed at nine-thirty at night, and spent his days absorbed in reading. Fresh fish, however, was unavailable so he apparently ate Western-style food during his stays. At his other residences he ate Japanese-style food prepared by a chef who accompanied him from Okitsu, even when at Seifū-sō in Kyoto. In this way, Saionji spent the latter half of his life moving among multiple residences: the primary residence in Surugadai, the Seifū-sō villa in Kyoto, and the Zagyo-sō and Gotenba villas in Shōnan.

In *Enkō hiwa* (The secrets of Saionji Kinmochi), published in 1938, Andō Tokuki writes, "the situation suggests that Saionji lived mainly in Okitsu, used Kyoto as a villa, stayed temporarily in Tokyo as needed, and utilized Gotenba as a detached annex of his Okitsu home." In Saionji's later years, he spent most of his time in Okitsu.

At each location, Saionji pursued a lifestyle and maintained personal relationships appropriate to the setting. This he shared with Yamagata Aritomo, who also maintained many residences.

Zagyo-sō offered enjoyable panoramic views of the sea from the Japanese-style rooms on the second floor while concealing the identity of guests from those outside, something said to have irritated the reporters who gathered there to collect information. The garden at the villa was, of course, landscaped by Ogawa Jihei. Ueji's method of employing low, closely

Fig. 3-4: Zagyo-sō, Saionji Kinmochi's villa in Okitsu (relocated to Museum Meiji-mura)

trimmed plantings no doubt resulted in a garden that was well suited to Okitsu's location overlooking the sea. Backed by the financial power of the Sumitomo, Saionji was able to give full play here to his steady, relaxed political methods.

Following Saionji's death, Zagyo-sō remained in Okitsu even as it underwent a variety of changes. In 1968, however, it was decided that the building would be relocated to Museum Meiji-mura in the city of Inuyama in Aichi Prefecture, where it was opened to the public in 1970. The building is now a registered cultural property (Fig. 3-4).

At Zagyo-sō's original site, meanwhile, a movement to recreate the structure took shape and this reconstruction was accomplished in 2003. The appeal of Saionji Kinmochi's life spent looking calmly out over the sea in Okitsu, far removed from Tokyo, no doubt spoke to people once again.

In fact, the Shōnan villa lifestyle that peaked with Saionji Kinmochi was carried on by the politicians of the post-war period. Yoshida Shigeru, who maintained a villa in Ōiso and seemed to enjoy receiving those who took the "pilgrimage to Ōiso" in his retirement, was clearly emulating the lifestyle of pre-war politicians in the way he staged his later years, while Kishi Nobusuke surely placed himself within the same lineage with his residence in Gotenba.

Ogawa Jihei made no effort to single-handedly undertake all the gardens at the villas of politicians in Shōnan, but he did landscape the expansive garden at Yōwadō, the villa in Atami maintained by Iwasaki Koyata. Iwasaki also entrusted the garden at his primary residence in Tokyo's Azabu Toriizaka neighborhood to Ogawa Jihei, but Ueji's first forays into Tokyo probably came with the primary residence of Saionji Kinmochi in Surugadai and the garden at the Sumitomo villa in Azabu Ichibei-chō, which was completed in 1917. The Tokudaiji-Saionji-Sumitomo triangle was extremely significant, too, in expanding the scope of Ogawa Jihei's work.

In *Enkō hiwa* (The secrets of Saionji Kinmochi), referenced above, Andō Tokuki described the relationship between Saionji and the Sumitomo as follows:

> *Even if rather cramped and casual, Surugadai serves as his primary*
> *residence while Tanaka [Seifū-sō in Kyoto] serves as his villa, but his*
> *relationship to both of these locations, neither rented nor given to*
> *him, remains ambiguous. Although this ambiguity is no doubt full of*
> *brotherly affection, to put the facts coldly the properties at Minami-*
> *kōga-chō in Kanda-ku [the location of the Surugadai residence] and*
> *at Tanaka Sekiden-chō in Sakyō-ku [the location of Seifū-sō] still*
> *clearly belong to the Sumitomo. Moreover, ordinary miscellaneous*
> *costs associated with the grounds and houses and even the salaries of*
> *their caretakers are all paid by the Sumitomo company; Prince*
> *Saionji merely uses the houses when and how he pleases in the con-*
> *duct of his public business. The only difference between Prince Saion-*
> *ji and an ordinary renter is that he is a tenant to be respected and*
> *need pay no rent. For someone to lend a home to a relative at no cost*
> *is common enough in normal society and only merits mention here*
> *because it is the Sumitomo and Saionji. There are those who see the*
> *fact that the prince is accompanied by three to five housemaids and*
> *cooks as he moves east and west between his residences as pompous*
> *traveling in luxury, but when the prince is away from Surugadai or*
> *Tanaka (and the same is true of Gotenba) the houses may as well be*

empty, with books and furnishings and even writing materials put away in storage and not a single member of the prince's household in residence other than a Sumitomo caretaker who cleans in the mornings and evenings. Once you know the inside story that he has no choice but to leave Okitsu empty and take his everyday servants with him, you can surely see that far from being extravagant his travel is actually quite frugal.

Given this relationship between the Sumitomo and Saionji, it seems only natural that Ueji, who had become a Sumitomo regular, would have been involved in the gardens of Saionji. Andō Tokuki had the following to say about Seifū-sō, though I have no idea whether or not the story is true:

Every tree and blade of grass that Ueji took such pains to place followed not only Prince Saionji's general aesthetic but also the natural alignment of every stone and grain of sand. Ueji is said to have landscaped the garden in exchange for calligraphy by the prince, but when construction was finished the prince, as one might expect, gave him 20,000 yen wrapped in paper.

If I may relay a personal experience, as director since 2010 of Museum Meiji-mura where Zagyo-sō had been relocated, I naturally had the opportunity to observe the building carefully. What I was impressed by, in addition to the building's magnificent design and overall atmosphere, was the quality of workmanship in details such as its copper rain gutters. Looking upon such copper work I was struck by the way it emanated the power and pride of the Sumitomo family, which got its start in copper smelting.

Table 3-1: Sumitomo Residences Including Those of Sumitomo Kichizaemon Tomoito (1864–1926)

Unagidani Residence	1636	Land procured.
	1685	Primary residence established, with eastern wing (north-facing entrance, three 8-mat tatami rooms, 41-mat room, 7-mat room, 8-mat room) and western wing (16-room first floor, 8-room second floor).
	1879	Construction of Western-style building completed (Yagi Jinbei). Garden created by Matsui of Kōzu around 1894.
	1905	Framework completed for remodeled eastern wing on 11 February (Yagi Jinbei II).
	1915	Formal *shoin*-style reception area from eastern wing moved to villa at Suma.
	1917	Unagidani residence placed under the administration of the company's general head office. Tea ceremony room Kōjitsu-an moved to the residence at Chausuyama.
Chausuyama Residence	1895	Purchase of villa properties begins. (Roughly 7 *tan* [6,944 square meters] purchased around 1897 and an additional roughly 4 *tan* [3,968 square meters] purchased to east and west in 1898.)
	1900	Approximately 3,300 *tsubo* [10,890 square meters]purchased to expand the garden.
	1902	Chausuyama and other properties purchased from Iwasaki Hisaya.
	1903	Fifth National Industrial Exposition held on land adjacent to Chausuyama.
	1912	Groundbreaking ceremony for Chausuyama residence held on 1 March.
	1913	Framework completed on 29 May.
	1915	Chausuyama residence completed (Noguchi Magoichi, Hidaka Yutaka, Yagi Jinbei II). Keitaku-en garden. Living space for Shunsui and his wife: 114 *tsubo* [376 square meters]. Reception rooms and entrance: 126 *tsubo* [416 square meters]. *Shoin*-style formal reception area and servery: 152 *tsubo* [502 square meters]. Children's rooms: 37 *tsubo* [122 square meters]. Kitchen and workspace: 200+ *tsubo* [660+ square meters]. Wardrobe and furnishings storage (earthen storehouses). Brick storehouse.
	1916	Framework of Western-style building completed.
	1917	Tea ceremony room Kōjitsu-an moved from Unagidani to Chausuyama.
	1920	Western-style building completed (Hidaka Yutaka).
	1921	Donated to the city of Osaka for use as the site of an art museum.
	1925	Japanese-style residence moved to site of Sumiyoshi residence.

Suma Villa	1895	Purchase of an additional 2 *tan* [1,984 square meters] to the north to complement existing site.
	1900	Construction of villa begins (Noguchi Magoichi, Hidaka Yutaka).
	1901	Framework completed 1 October.
	1903	Completed late April. Western-style building (1 basement floor, 2 above-ground floors): 161 *tsubo* [531 square meters]. Detached annex (children's rooms): 67 *tsubo* [221 square meters].
	1915	Framework for new eastern residence completed 1 August. Formal *shoin*-style reception area from the eastern wing of the residence at Unagidani moved to the Suma villa.
Maiko Villa	1917	Former residence of Prince Arisugawa at Kashiwayama in Tarumi-chō purchased in July. The existing 1893 building is renovated in a half-Western style.
Shishigatani Villa	1913	730 *tsubo* [2,409 square meters] purchased in Miyanomae-chō in addition to 1 *chō* and 3 *tan* [10,890 square meters].
	1914	*Sukiya*-style building completed at year's end (2 floors, 32 *tsubo* [106 square meters]).
	1920	Residence completed following further expansion of the property (Hidaka Yutaka, Yagi Jinbei II). Yūhō-en garden.
	1925	Storehouse for bronze ware designed.
	1928	Storehouse for bronze ware completed.
Sumiyoshi Residence	1914	Purchased the former home of Tanabe Sadakichi (designed by Noguchi Magoichi) for use by the branch family of Sumitomo Tadateru.
	1922	Purchased the property at 23 Ushigamimae in Sumiyoshi for the branch family of Sumitomo Tadateru.
	1925	Residence completed on 2 May (moved from Chausuyama).
Kinugasa Foothills Villa	1918	Framework completed on 23 April.
	1920	Completed on 10 August. After the Great Kanto Earthquake, moved to Saionji Kinmochi's Surugadai villa and rebuilt.
Tokyo Secondary Residence		*The previous secondary residence at Jinbō-chō was let go.
	1898	Purchased at Kanda-ku Surugadai Minamikōga-chō in March. Land: 850 *tsubo* [2,805 square meters]. Total floor area: 200 *tsubo* [660 square meters].
Higashi Toriizaka Residence	1906	Purchased the top of the Higashi Toriizaka slope in Azabu-ku in July (the former residence of Ōtori Keisuke). Land: 850 *tsubo* [2,805 square meters]. Cliff: 200 *tsubo* [660 square meters]. Japanese- and Western-style building: 2 floors, 148 *tsubo* [488 square meters].

Azabu Villa	1912	Purchased Azabu-ku Ichibei-chō 1-chōme (the former residence of Marquis Ikeda Nakahiro of the former Inaba province). Land: 3,400 *tsubo* [11,220 square meters].
	1917	Western-style building completed (Hidaka Yutaka). Japanese-style building: 165 *tsubo* [545 square meters]. Western-style building: 64 *tsubo* [211 square meters]. Subordinate buildings: 70 *tsubo* [231 square meters]. Total floor area: 452 *tsubo* [1,492 square meters].
Mejiro Villa	1921	Land purchased at Takada-machi in Kitatoshima-gun. Wood-frame Western-style building: 2 floors. Japanese-style building: 1 floor, 51 *tsubo* [168 square meters].
Kamakura Villa	1925	Purchased.
Arima Villa		
Izu Atami Villa		
Ōiso Villa		
Nasu Villa	1937	Completed (Satō Hidezō). Wood-frame Western-style building: 2 floors.
Matano Villa	1939	Completed (Satō Hidezō).
	2009	Lost to fire.
Saionji Kinmochi's Kyoto Villa Seifū-sō	1907	Seifū-kan passed from the Tokudaiji family to the Sumitomo. Nearby land was added and the property turned into a villa for the Saionji.
	1911	Construction began in August with the framework completed in December.
	1913	Completed (Yagi Jinbei II). 2 floors, 80 *tsubo* [264 square meters]. Single-story building: 22 *tsubo* [73 square meters].
	1944	Donated to Kyoto Imperial University (Now Kyoto University).

Table 3-2: Sumitomo Construction Organizations

1900	Establishment of provisional construction department at Sumitomo head office (Noguchi Magoichi and Hidaka Yutaka).
1911	Reorganized as construction section at Sumitomo general head office.
1918	Establishment of provisional civil engineering section at Sumitomo general head office.
1921	Reorganized as works department at Sumitomo Gōshi Kaisha (Head engineer: Hidaka Yutaka; Engineers: Hasebe Eikichi, Takekoshi Kenzō).
1933	Above works department abolished. Establishment of the stock company Hasebe and Takekoshi Architectural Office.
1936	Above reorganized under private management (1938 Tokyo office, 1940 Manchuria office, 1942 Nagoya office).
1944	Establishment of the Sumitomo Land Co., Ltd.
1945	Establishment of Nippon Kensetsu Sangyo Co., Ltd.
1950	Nikken Sekkei Kōmu Co., Ltd.
1970	Renamed Nikken Sekkei Ltd.

CHAPTER FOUR

Bringing the Lake Biwa Canal to Gardens

A Kingdom Along the Canal

As many have noted, Ogawa Jihei's deft command of water from the Lake Biwa Canal defines him and was the secret of his success. His artistry in this regard is most evident in the cluster of gardens he created across a realm that extends from Keage, where the Lake Biwa Canal enters the Kyoto Basin, to just beyond Nanzen-ji temple.

Once acquired by Ijūin Kanetsune, who began building a garden there, the residence known today as Tairyū Sansō later passed into the hands of Kyoto kimono merchant Ichida Yaichirō. Said to have once been part of the grounds of Konchi-in, a sub-temple of Nanzen-ji, before being made private, the property was turned into a villa by Ijūin Kanetsune in 1896. Ichida Yaichirō took over the property in 1901 and began renovations the following year that were completed in 1905. It was Ogawa Jihei who renovated the garden.

Long from north to south, the property has a number of streams starting on its south side that feed into a large pond situated at the north. The south side is an open and airy expanse of lawn and streams that eloquently expresses Ogawa's skilled use of flowing water (Fig. 4-1). Of particular note is the *tsukubai* stone basin placed directly into the stream. Someone crouching down to use the low basin is drawn closer to the water's surface, bringing an unexpected realization of the breadth of Ogawa's garden as the shallow stream seems to assume the proportions of a great river. Ogawa Ji-

Fig. 4-1: The garden at Tairyū Sansō, the villa of Ichida Yaichirō

hei also used this technique of placing *tsukubai* in flowing water at other gardens such as the one at Hekiun-sō, the villa near Nanzen-ji that belonged to Nomura Tokushichi II.

The north side, meanwhile, is centered on a great pond featuring an island and a large waterfall that even has a waterwheel positioned behind it. The tranquil abundance of water in the pond provides a counterpoint to the flow of the streams, a contrast that was undoubtedly intentional. This north side with its great pond is thought to be the portion originally landscaped by Ijūin, and reflects the orthodox structure of traditional Japanese gardens. In contrast, the south side, with its multiple streams, offers just the kind of dynamic representation of changing waters that typifies Ueji's work.

The Tairyū Sansō villa extends for a considerable length along the north-south axis of the property. It was built under the supervision of Shimada Tōkichi, a master carpenter from the Kanto region. Shimada made lavish use of timber from the hemlock fir, which was frequently employed in high-class Kanto buildings. On its north side, the villa extends out over the pond to powerful effect. The name Shimada brings to mind Shimada Tō who graduated from the faculty of architecture at Tokyo Imperial University in 1913 and later established the Shimatō Corporation. As it happens, Shimada Tōkichi was his father.

According to research conducted by Yagasaki Zentarō of the Kyoto Institute of Technology, Shimada Tōkichi was born in 1848 and made his way to Edo in 1867. While working in Edo, he undertook the restoration of the Enomoto house in Nihonbashi, which Ichida Yaichirō had acquired in order to expand his business. The resulting acquaintance between Shimada and Ichida is thought to have led to the construction project in Kyoto. Shimada Tōkichi passed on his craft to his son, Shimada Tō, who established the Shimatō Corporation in 1932. The company changed its name to Shimatō Construction in 1946, Shimatō Construction Industries in 1956, and finally merged with the Toda Corporation in 1987.

The name Tairyū Sansō (对龍山荘) is said to play on Nanzen-ji temple's "mountain name," Zuiryūsan (瑞龍山), with the "tai" (对) reflecting the villa's position "facing" the temple. Similarly, the main *shoin* reception room on which the building is centered is named Tairyūdai (对龍台). The name suggests a direct challenge to Kyoto's famed Nanzen-ji, and the villa as a whole has a scale and breadth befitting the boldness of its name.

Born the third son of a merchant in Hikone, Ichida Yaichirō was adopted by the Ichida family, which anticipated his talent for business. He started out as a traveling peddler of kimono fabric. By 1874, not long after the Meiji Restoration (and the change of the capital's name from Edo to Tokyo), Ichida had risen high enough to set up a Kyoto kimono fabric wholesale business in the Nihonbashi district. A self-made man, he might be described as an entrepreneur who succeeded in modernizing the traditional kimono business of Kyoto.

Tairyū Sansō was Ichida Yaichirō's personal villa, but it must also have functioned as a stage for showing off his kimono fabrics in a way that would leave a deep impression on his clientele. Ogawa Jihei's great garden with its aura of modernity was tied to this business strategy. Ogawa was more than just a gardener. He composed his gardens with the eye of an impresario to ensure they could be used to best effect. Because he understood the qualities that made for a garden truly suited to the times, he sought to create naturalistic gardens that were spacious, open, and lively rather than wast-

Fig. 4-2: Waraku-an, the villa of Inabata Katsutarō

ing effort by adhering to symbolism.

His skill as a producer made Ueji much sought after by a variety of clients who were pursuing Japan's modernization. With a reputation for being able to converse easily with clients, Ueji had a flexible personality born of a keen understanding of the changing winds of the times.

The north side of the Tairyū Sansō garden centered on the great pond and the south side with its streams are fed by different systems. Given the property's long north-south orientation, it is perhaps to be expected that it would have several water intakes. The different intake systems reflect different ways of drawing water from the canal.

Tairyū Sansō is located closest to the point where the Lake Biwa Canal arrives in the Kyoto Basin and is thought to have had the first intake systems for drawing water from the canal for garden use. Ogawa Jihei would build a series of large gardens, starting with Tairyū Sansō, in the area below Nanzen-ji, with each incorporating a system for drawing water from the Lake Biwa Canal that would then flow through the garden and drain into the Shirakawa River. The orderly way in which the canal water was used demonstrates his talent and knowledge of the Lake Biwa Canal system.

Here we can see how he built a veritable kingdom along the basin of the Lake Biwa Canal.

Another major villa adjacent to Tairyū Sansō is Inabata Katsutarō's Waraku-an (Fig. 4-2), sometimes also referred to as Waraku-en. After Inabata's death, Ōmiya Kurakichi, a sake brewer in Fushimi known as the owner of Takara Shuzo, acquired the villa and changed its name to Kaiu-sō. It has since had a succession of owners but remains generally known by this name. Here, however, I would like to look at the context in which the villa took shape, so I will be referring to it as Waraku-an, the Inabata villa.

Inabata Katsutarō was a new type of entrepreneur, a product of post-Restoration Kyoto. He went to France at the age of 16 and studied at the La Martinière technical school in Lyon. After this he studied dyeing techniques at a Lyon dyeing factory operated by Jean-Aimé Marnas and audited classes on applied chemistry at the University of Lyon.

In this way, Inabata mastered modern industrial dyeing techniques and successfully introduced them into Japan. He is notable in particular for bringing to Japan the dyeing techniques required to produce the khaki color essential for the Japanese army's field uniforms. Although Inabata's business was textiles, he was not so much a traditional Kyoto kimono fabric merchant as an entrepreneur in a leading industry. In this regard, Inabata's Waraku-an and Ichida Yaichirō's Tairyū Sansō can be seen as villas maintained by men representing opposite poles of innovation and tradition.

Inabata Katsutarō is said to have acquired his property in 1905. As was the case with the neighboring Tairyū Sansō, the land had once been part of a Nanzen-ji sub-temple. Landscaping of the property continued into the Taisho period, but a traditional Japanese structure in the *shoin* style was built there in early 1912, at the very end of the Meiji period, and a Western-style structure designed by architect Takeda Goichi was built in 1916.

As noted earlier, Waraku-an was owned by Ōmiya Kurakichi after Inabata's death. It is thought that renovations were made during the transition, so it is unclear whether the current Western-style structure completely adheres to its original design. Nevertheless, it is most elegant and stylish, likely reflecting both the design sensibility of Takeda Goichi, a leader of the

Fig. 4-3: Stained glass window in the
Western-style building at Waraku-an

Arts and Crafts movement in Japan, and the tastes of Inabata, one of the Meiji period's most international industrialists.

The technique of locating a traditional folding screen, an alcove-like shelf for displaying hanging scrolls, and stained-glass windows with Japanese motifs (Fig. 4-3) in a carpeted drawing room filled with Western-style furniture represents a style attributable to either Takeda Goichi or Inabata Katsutarō.

With ties to France that were unusual among Japanese industrialists, Inabata Katsutarō was deeply involved in furthering cultural and academic exchange between Japan and France, and instrumental in establishing the Institut Franco-Japon du Kansai. His Waraku-an was used as a venue for international exchange and non-governmental diplomatic events. In 1916, for example, Ernest Roume, the governor-general of French Indochina, was invited to Waraku-an and is said to have responded to Inabata's welcome address by saying, "I was told in advance that Kyoto was a beautiful city, and have arrived today to a grand welcome at Mr. Inabata's villa amid the rich scenery of its quiet and peaceful garden…."

In 1920, Crown Prince Carol II of Romania visited Waraku-an and gave the name Gishi-kutsu [Loyal Retainers' Cave] to a tunnel some dozens of meters long that Inabata had built in the villa's gardens to provide shelter in the event of air attack in some future war. The name, a reference to a Romanian legend, is said to have been chosen to reflect the tunnel's intended purpose. A plate explaining these origins in Romanian is said to have been installed at the tunnel entrance, and may still be there.

In May of that year, Inabata Katsutarō had his friend Shibata Tadakatsu include the story of the Romanian crown prince and the tunnel in a history of the villa titled *Warakuen ki* (An account of Waraku-en).

The tunnel at Waraku-an still exists, but today more closely resembles the kind of grotto often found in baroque European gardens (Fig. 4-4). Waraku-an was frequently used for events that fostered international goodwill, and eclectic features like the expansive lawn for Western-style garden parties seem designed to that end. Pathways offering varied scenery wind through the garden, which also incorporates a number of accent structures (Fig. 4-5). Grottos or caves are rarely incorporated in traditional Japanese gardens, but the open-minded spirit evinced by the inclusion of the grotto-like cave at Waraku-an is probably one reason for the villa's longevity.

Another episode concerning Waraku-an involves Saionji Kinmochi. Invited to the villa in November 1916, Saionji was asked to name the waterfall in the garden. He initially christened it Waraku no Bakufu [Waraku Cascade], but then thought better of it and suggested Zuiryū no Taki [Waterfall of the Auspicious Dragon], no doubt a nod to Nanzen-ji temple's mountain name, Zuiryūsan.

Through their respective gardens, Inabata Katsutarō is known to have been friendly with Yamagata Aritomo, whose Murin-an villa was just a short distance from Waraku-an. This suggests that those of influence with villas near Nanzen-ji formed a social circle. Inabata used Waraku-an as a site for upscale social gatherings and invited many guests.

In 1909, Fujita Kotarō set up a residence of his own in the area, drawing water from the canal. Fujita Kotarō was the nephew of both Fujita Den-

Fig. 4-4: Entrance to the tunnel at Waraku-an

Fig. 4-5: The garden at Waraku-an

zaburō and Kuhara Shōzaburō, industrialists within the Fujita and Kuhara zaibatsu who also provided funds in support of the business ventures of Ayukawa Yoshisuke. Fujita Denzaburō was deeply involved with the Lake Biwa Canal as a contractor, while Kuhara assisted in the construction of Yamagata Aritomo's Murin-an. Given that the brothers Denzaburō and Shōzaburō were businessmen politically connected to Yamagata, it is perhaps only natural that their nephew Fujita Kotarō should also build a villa that drew water from the canal. And only natural, too, that Ogawa Jihei would be entrusted with the landscaping of its garden.

Ueji provided Fujita Kotarō's garden with a pond modeled on Lake Biwa. The canal supplies the garden with four liters of water per second. Because of the location of the water inlet and the garden's topography, the pond is not oriented exactly as the real lake, but its shape is very similar. There is even a bridge over the pond resembling Lake Biwa's Seta no Karahashi bridge and an islet analogous to Lake Biwa's Chikubushima Island. Ueji is said to have referred to a recently published map of Shiga Prefecture when determining the shape of the pond. In this respect, this garden can be seen to blend the traditional technique of incorporating features analogous to famous views with a modern application of scientifically based geographic information.

Deep in the garden there is a small Chinese-style pavilion called Gasen-dō ("Hall of Immortal Painters") with a pyramidal roof topped by a phoenix with folded wings. This phoenix forms a pair with the "crouching dragon bridge" at the center of the pond. The crossing is made up of a combination of rectangular cut stone and millstones in a clear reference to the "crouching dragon bridge" that spans Sōryū-ike pond in the Heian Jingū shrine's middle garden. The stone pilings from the old Sanjō and Gojō bridges that were used there are substituted here with millstones incised with radiating grooves. At Heian Jingū, the crossing resonates with the phoenix that stands on the roof of the covered bridge over Seihō-ike pond in the shrine's east garden.

At Fujita Kotarō's garden, the experiments of the Heian Jingū shrine are recreated in a composition modeled on the actual scenery at Lake Biwa.

143

The concept was probably inspired by the decision to place the phoenix-topped, Chinese-style Gasen-dō in the garden. This pavilion, like Shisen-dō ("Hall of Immortal Poets") at the villa of Ishikawa Jōzan and Kasen-dō ("Hall of Immortal Singers") at Kōdai-ji temple, imbues the garden with a poetic atmosphere. However, positioning this pavilion as akin to these others, and the use of landscaping that replicates Lake Biwa almost too faithfully, may be one reason Ogawa Jihei's gardens are sometimes criticized for being too explanatory, lacking depth or philosophy.

Adjacent to Gasen-dō stand tall fir trees. When one looks up at them and sees the sunlight striking their tops, the garden seems to expand beyond its boundaries with the breadth of a vast plateau. We can see here how Ueji has made skillful use of firs in the manner he seems to have mastered at Murin-an. Such features illustrate how Ueji escaped from the symbolism of Zen gardens to create a more magnanimous, natural style. Ueji's characteristic use of trees, however, is actually best seen in the towering broadleaf cedar, a variety resembling the fir, that stands at the southwest corner of the Fujita garden near a gorgeous gate called Akezu-no-mon that is believed to have come from Fushimi Castle. Such trees were typically planted near the unlucky northeastern corner of an estate or building.

After the Second World War, the villa and its garden passed from Fujita Kotarō's hands and became a facility for the Ministry of Posts and Telecommunications mutual aid association. Later owned by Nihon Chouzai, a pharmaceutical company, the garden has since been maintained under the name Rakusui. The residence facing the garden was torn down and replaced with a reinforced concrete structure when the property was owned by the Ministry of Posts and Telecommunications, but the composition of the garden itself can be considered to remain mostly as it was.

A number of large gardens landscaped by Ueji can be found in the area surrounding Rakusui. Shinshin-an, which for a time was owned by Matsushita Kōnosuke, is right next door while I-en, former villa of the Hosokawa family, and Shokuhō-en, owned by the Tatsumura Textile Company, are nearby. The world of Ogawa Jihei's gardens spread throughout the Lake Biwa Canal basin to form a veritable kingdom for the elite of the day. That so many of these gardens have been maintained to the present day despite changes in ownership is to be highly commended. Surely this is because the appeal of Ueji's gardens has not faded and they have continued to speak to people across the ages. Even as gardens have changed owners, they have remained in the hands of those with the means to maintain them, with the result that this cluster of large gardens has remained a feature of the landscape of modern Kyoto.

The Showa Emperor's Enthronement Ceremony

In the same way that the 1964 Olympic Games in Tokyo and the Expo '70 world exposition held in Osaka six years later were major national events in post-war Japan, the enthronement of a new emperor was a major national event in pre-war Japan, even though only the highest ranked could participate directly in the pomp and ceremony. Given that state ceremonies of all kinds in pre-war Japan were limited to the world of the ruling elite, the emperor's enthronement was the only one that could be called a truly national event.

The Daijō-sai enthronement ceremony—also sometimes referred to as the Tairei or Taiten—was especially important when the Taisho and Showa emperors ascended to the throne because it reaffirmed the imperial nature of the modern Japanese state. Many people gathered in Kyoto for these enthronement ceremonies. The list of those scheduled to attend the ceremony for Emperor Taisho grew to 1,800 people, and finding lodgings in Kyoto became a real problem. Members of the imperial family who did not have their own estates or villas in Kyoto were assigned to the estates of prominent local families, and many of these residences had gardens landscaped by Ogawa Jihei. Prince Higashifushimi, for example, was lodged at Ichida Yaichirō's villa Tairyū Sansō.

There were also cases where residences and gardens underwent major renovations in preparation for the imperial dignitaries and other elites who would be arriving in Kyoto for the ceremonies. This can be said to follow a Japanese tradition dating back to pre-modern times of palatial buildings being constructed specifically to accommodate the shogun or other powerful personages on their travels. Beginning in the Meiji period, building such majestic structures was often also intended to impress upon the people the progress being made in Japan's modernization. For example, the Public Hall of Hakodate Ward was thoroughly renovated, and given the form visible today, to welcome a visit by the crown prince. In fact, excursions and visits by the emperor and members of the imperial family constituted a campaign to bring a real sense of the Meiji government to outlying areas. Taking these opportunities to establish official guesthouses around the country, the government reinforced the Meiji system in a way that left a tangible impression on the people. Such guesthouses served in outlying areas much as Rokumei-kan did in Tokyo—as visible symbols of Japan's civilization and enlightenment.

The early modern tradition of building majestic accommodations for traveling dignitaries, then, transformed to take on a new role in the age of civilization and enlightenment; imperial excursions around the country were calculated to demonstrate Japan's civilization and enlightenment in provincial areas. In this context, the enthronement ceremonies for the Taisho and Showa emperors held in the old capital of Kyoto confirmed and asserted the staying power of the Meiji government. They were also an opportunity to build or refurbish guesthouses for the nobility and dignitaries who flocked to Kyoto for the enthronements. Although the direction of movement was different, this building phenomenon was qualitatively the same as the construction of Western-style guesthouses—regional Rokumei-kan, if you will—for imperial family visits to outlying regions. While Imperial visits to outlying areas demonstrated that the Meiji government had been firmly established, the enthronement ceremonies in Kyoto asserted that the new government's position as a unifying force continued to grow even in the old capital.

At the time of the Showa emperor's enthronement ceremony, many private estates were once again offered as lodging for imperial family members. Some of these estates had gardens by Ogawa Jihei, including the Sumitomo family's Shishigatani villa that was given over as lodging for Prince Chichi-bu. Another is the villa of Nomura Tokushichi II, which was provided as lodging for the Kuni branch of the imperial line, the family of the Showa emperor's consort. The Nomura villa, named Hekiun-sō, is the classic example of a property whose renovation was undertaken and completed to meet the requirements of the enthronement ceremony. Its massive garden should be considered the culmination of Ogawa Jihei's landscaping efforts in the Nanzen-ji area, and remains his pinnacle achievement.

Nomura Tokushichi II, who maintained Hekiun-sō, was an industrialist who, in a single generation, founded a modern finance and securities company and successfully expanded it to become what is now the Nomura Securities Group. Under the art name Tokuan he was also an art collector and a connoisseur with broad interests in traditions such as the tea ceremony and Noh performance.

According to Nomura's biography, he registered the land for Hekiun-sō in 1917 but had been watching the property for two or three years before then. At the time, cultivated fields occupied much of the site, but Nomura turned to Ogawa Jihei to transform these into a large garden. The entire estate covers around 7,000 *tsubo* [23,100 square meters], with roughly 3,000 *tsubo* [99,000 square meters] given over to the garden. Of all the great gardens in the Nanzen-ji area, this was to be the largest and most expansive. Construction continued for many years, and was finally completed in 1928. As explained in Nomura's biography, there was a reason the garden was completed in that year:

The special circumstances requiring that the garden be completed in 1928 were related to the enthronement ceremonies for the Showa emperor that were to take place at the Imperial Palace in Kyoto that year. The estate had been selected to provide accommodation during the ceremonies for the late Prince Kuni Kuniyoshi. Needless to say, Tokuan may have been a business tycoon, but he was deeply moved by the honor. Once such an honor had been bestowed, he was naturally not going to let the wonderful opportunity slip by. Tokuan pushed to get the construction done, increased the number of workers, and finally managed to get the estate completed in 1928.

Ogawa Jihei is believed to have collaborated on the garden at Heki-un-sō with his son Yasutarō (Hakuyō). There is a story that Jihei stepped aside after an altercation with Nomura Tokuan, moving Hakuyō to the fore in an effort to further his son's career, but the finished garden is typical of Ueji in its spaciousness and grand views. Tokuan followed the Yabunouchi school of tea under the master Setsuan, and Yabunouchi aesthetics permeate the garden.

Invested with various hopes and expectations, work on the garden and villa progressed in preparation for the Showa emperor's enthronement. A main entrance (Fig. 4-6), Noh stage, and grand *shoin* reception hall were completed in quick succession, with construction undertaken by Kitamura Sutejirō, a master of the *sukiya* architectural style. The Noh stage was built back-to-back with the main entranceway, with audiences enjoying performances from the adjacent *shoin* reception hall. Nomura Tokuan studied Noh under Kanze Sakon and the stage, naturally, was intended to provide a setting for his own performances. To this day a wooden carving of Nomura Tokushichi II performing the Kanjinchō dance from the Noh play *Ataku* can be found on this private Noh stage.

The vast property extends east-to-west and there is a magnificent front gate with a door made from a single piece of wood on the east side of the property along the road to Eikan-dō temple. The west gate on the opposite side is also exquisite and fronted by a well-ordered garden. The centerpiece of the garden is its large pond. Viewed from Taigetsuken, a gazebo on its west side, the pond appears as a broad and deep expanse brimming with water (Fig. 4-7). The mountains of Higashiyama are visible off in the distance while the pagoda at Eikan-dō can be glimpsed on the left. One of Hekiun-sō's charms, this incorporation of "borrowed views" invests the expansive garden with even greater depth.

A boat is moored within a structure that stands along the edge of the pond. The boat itself is a tea ceremony room named Royōshū (Fig. 4-8) and

Fig. 4-6: The main entrance at Hekiun-sō, the villa of Nomura Tokushichi II

Fig. 4-7: The garden at Hekiun-sō

Fig. 4-8: The Royōshū tea ceremony room at Hekiun-sō

can actually be floated out into the middle of the pond with guests aboard. This perhaps combines the dragon and phoenix boats enjoyed by Heian aristocrats with the *wabi* refinement of the tea ceremony. A tea ceremony enjoyed on this gently rocking boat would surely sweep away all worldly cares.

Looking at the Royōshū, however, one cannot help but imagine that it must have been an ideal place to discuss important business without anyone listening in. The center of the pond, in a sense, is a sanctuary no one can approach. Is it the elegance of dragon and phoenix boats, the understated refinement of the tea ceremony, or some manifestation of hardboiled business acumen? The garden has an air of complexity that is difficult to define.

In another business-related episode, the Geisen-kyō stone bridge spanning the pond is said to have been an ideal spot for secretive conversations because the sound of the neighboring waterfall would prevent voices from being overheard. It certainly seems a plausible story. Ueji and Nomura are said to have had different opinions about the stone bridge, with Ueji stating that such a solid structure was ill suited for a *sukiya* garden. If Tokuan did indeed insist on the stone bridge, this suggests a confrontation between a client who needed a place to do business and a gardener who preferred to preserve a *wabi* atmosphere. This reading seems too convenient, however, so it might be best to think of it as nothing more than another legend relating to the garden. Carved on the Geisen-kyō bridge are geometric motifs related to *genjikō*, an elegant game involving the comparison of incense. Such ingenuous combinations of elegance and practicality are found throughout this garden, with *genjikō* motifs also appearing on the villa's main entrance.

In addition to the many tea ceremony rooms in this garden, there are also a number of stone objects of archeological significance, such as an Asuka period stone that may have been used in the making of sake. One has to wonder how such curious stones found their way to this garden. The *tsukubai* washbasin set in the stream is said to have come from the Korean Peninsula and has a beautiful whitish surface. Here, too, crouching to use the basin brings one's eyes close to the flowing water, which suddenly comes to seem like a great river, and the pond in the distance a vast ocean.

Completed in time for the Showa emperor's enthronement ceremony, the Hekiun-sō incorporates stunning Showa period design, particularly in the grand *shoin* reception hall built expressly to welcome Prince Kuni. The lighting fixtures, the paintings on the sliding door panels, and other appointments have a supple, fluid beauty unlike the rigid style of the Meiji period. The work of Takeda Goichi, who designed Inabata Katsutarō's Waraku-an, had lovely flowing curves suggesting the influence of Art Nouveau, but the decorative appointments at the Hekiun-sō *shoin* reception hall indicate that this design sensibility had come to be adopted more broadly for Japanese-style mansions.

Rather than opting for traditional symbolism, Ogawa Jihei, working through his son, Hakuyō, created a garden that was not only grand and majestic but also met the practical social requirements of its businessman owner. There are obvious elements that border dangerously on the mundane, such as an arrangement of disk-shaped stones perhaps symbolizing the sun and moon that may have been Hakuyō's idea, but the Hekiun-sō garden still presents water as flow and breadth in a way that captures the celebratory mood that shaped the time surrounding the Showa emperor's enthronement. Here we see the pinnacle of the open naturalism that defines Ueji's gardens.

Ogawa Jihei had complete mastery over the waters of the Lake Biwa Canal, and the series of gardens he built along the canal through the point where it emptied into the Shirakawa created an entirely new landscape for modern Kyoto. Of these gardens, Hekiun-sō was the nearest to Nanzen-ji. Next to it, along the same water system, came the Sumitomo family's Shishigatani villa, Yūhō-en; Shimogō Denpei's Seiryū-tei; the Hosokawa family's I-en; Shokuhō-en; and then the Rakusui garden. The furthest out is Saionji Kinmochi's Seifū-sō.

Nomura Tokushichi II's Hekiun-sō marked the finale of the string of gardens that Ogawa Jihei built one after the other near Nanzen-ji. Although the capital had been moved to Tokyo, holding an important event like the Showa emperor's enthronement in the old capital of Kyoto was significant for the Japanese people. The people of Kyoto took pride in the fact that its identity as Japan's "thousand-year capital" continued even into the Showa period, and this pride was reflected in the magnificent gardens crafted by Ueji at his peak. Although Ueji is said to have left completion of the Hekiun-sō garden to his son Hakuyō due to a difference of opinion about the Geisen-kyō bridge, the overall composition of the splendid garden can surely be considered the work of a mature Ogawa Jihei VII. After all, unlike the work of a painter or sculptor, gardens are created by groups of skilled craftsmen working as one under the direction of a leader.

The Road to the Imperial Mausoleum

Ogawa Jihei's participation in the work on the Fushimi Momoyama Mausoleum (Fig. 4-9) was a proud moment in his career. A timeline of Ogawa Jihei's activities around the time the Meiji period changed to the Taisho is recorded in *Ogawa Jihei*, edited by Yamane Tokutarō, as follows:

Fig. 4-9: Fushimi Momoyama Mausoleum

1912　In preparation for the enthronement ceremonies, appointed to work on renovations to the gardens at the Imperial Palace in Kyoto and to the Katsura, Shūgakuin, and Nijō Imperial Villas, beginning an ongoing position working on gardens of the Imperial Household Ministry.

1913　Appointed to work on the Fushimi Momoyama Mausoleum.

1914　Appointed to build the brushwood fence and other landscaping around the Yukiden and Sukiden buildings used for the enthronement ceremonies.

1915　Appointed to work on the construction of the Fushimi Momoyama Higashi Mausoleum.

By way of explanation, the Fushimi Momoyama Mausoleum is the tomb of Emperor Meiji and the Fushimi Momoyama Higashi Mausoleum is the tomb of his wife, Empress Shōken. In working on these projects, Ueji literally put the finishing touches on the design of the Meiji state.

This does not mean Ueji was responsible for creating the aesthetics of the imperial household, which presents its own distinctive sensibility. The contrast of trees and gravel, for example, seen in graveled paths winding gently through stands of trees creates a clean, solemn design. The elegance of sparse groves of pine also frequently appears in imperial household de-

153

Fig. 4-10: Approach to the Fushimi Momoyama Mausoleum

sign. Gravel, stands of trees, and sparse groves of pine are design elements seen in the grounds before the imperial palace, at the garden path leading to Ise Jingū shrine, and along the road to the Fushimi Momoyama Mausoleum (Fig. 4-10). They have also been adopted when making improvements to other smaller imperial tombs that remain in various places.

Is it not amazing, though, to find such a modern aesthetic sensibility in this clean and solemn imperial design? Perhaps this is because such imperial design is more a product of modernity than of some archaic piety.

The mausoleum of Emperor Kōmei, the last emperor of the Edo period, is known as the Nochinotsukinowa no Higashiyama Mausoleum. It is located in Higashiyama-ku Sennyū-ji Yamanouchi-chō, that is, adjacent to Sennyū-ji temple in southeastern Kyoto (Fig. 4-11). Commonly called Mi-tera, Sennyū-ji is known as a mortuary temple for emperors of the Edo period. The mausoleum of Emperor Kōmei is larger than those of his predecessors and takes the form of a freestanding, double-stacked circular mound. The movement toward reverence for the emperor that grew at the end of the Edo period resulted in revival of past practices regarding imperial mausoleums. Until then, imperial tombs erected on the grounds of Sennyū-ji were nothing like ancient *kofun* burial mounds. Instead, most took the form of more modest early modern structures: small mausoleums, ash

Fig. 4-11: The mausoleum of Emperor Kōmei

mounds, or nine-tiered stone pagodas for emperors; egg-shaped *muhōtō* stone pagodas for empresses; and rectangular *hōkyōintō* stone pagodas for imperial princes.

Sennyū-ji had long been chosen as the site for imperial tombs. Emperor Kōmei is said to have issued an imperial edict in 1865 stating that "because [Sennyū-ji] has protected imperial tombs for generations since Emperor Shijō, out of respect for our imperial ancestors it shall for all sects occupy the highest place," and the temple has been referred to by the honorific name Mi-tera ever since. This perhaps gives a sense of where Emperor Kōmei's life fell during the transitional period from renewed reverence for the emperor to the revival movement and eventual restoration of imperial rule.

One can visually experience this tumultuous period of historical change by visiting Emperor Kōmei's Nochinotsukinowa no Higashiyama Mausoleum. As noted above, the mausoleum takes the shape of a double-stacked circular mound, but since it juts out of the mountainside rather than standing completely free, it is difficult to clearly distinguish its shape. Following the approach to the mausoleum, one is able to glimpse only the tip of the mound. Although standing alone, the mausoleum seems rather small in both scale and form compared to the great *kofun* of the ancient emperors or even the mausoleums of subsequent emperors from the modern period. Still, the fact that it was an independent mausoleum, unlike the heavily Buddhist-influenced imperial burial grounds of the early modern period, can be called a major development. Emperor Kōmei's Nochino-tsukinowa no Higashiyama Mausoleum truly symbolizes the transitional times in which it was built.

As one follows the path to the imperial mausoleums, one notices an approach along the way that is decorated with fine workmanship. This leads to the Nochinotsukinowa no Higashi Kita Mausoleum, the tomb of Empress Dowager Eishō, empress consort of Emperor Kōmei. The drainage gutters alongside both sides of the approach are made using beautifully worked stone that remains impressive to this day despite the many years that have passed since they were installed.

Rapid progress was made in stone masonry beginning in the early modern period, but the stonework of the Meiji period has a unique look all its own. The finely crafted stone walls surrounding aristocratic estates from the Meiji period have a delicate, precise softness not unlike a pile of *chirimen* silk crepe cushions. The stone masonry along the approach to the Nochinotsukinowa no Higashi Kita Mausoleum exudes the aroma of a technique that developed beginning in the Meiji period.

Emperor Kōmei died at the end of the Edo period, but Empress Dowager Eishō lived until 11 January 1897. Born to Kujō Hisatada in 1835, Eishō was married to Emperor Kōmei and later became the lawful mother of Emperor Meiji. She was invested with the rank of Empress Dowager with the start of the Meiji era and lived in Tokyo beginning in 1872. Her residence was located in the southwest portion of the Akasaka imperial grounds, near what is now the Aoyama 1-chōme intersection, and was called the Aoyama Gosho or Ōmiya Gosho. Back when the former Tokyo residence of the Kishū Tokugawa clan—located on the northeast portion of the grounds—was being used as a temporary imperial residence, Emperor Meiji is said to have often used the roads within the grounds to visit the Ōmiya Gosho.

After her death, Emperor Kōmei's empress consort was given the posthumous title of Empress Dowager Eishō. By the time her mausoleum was built adjacent to that of Emperor Kōmei at Sennyū-ji, the Meiji regime was well established and ample funds and technology were available for the construction and maintenance of imperial mausoleums. The walk from Emperor Kōmei's Nochinotsukinowa no Higashiyama Mausoleum to Empress Dowager Eishō's Nochinotsukinowa no Higashi Kita Mausoleum offers a way to visually experience the improving fortunes of the Meiji regime.

Money paid to Sennyū-ji by the imperial household during this time gradually increased. In 1876, the imperial household paid an annual amount of 1,200 yen for grave tablets and protection. By September 1879 this had increased to 1,800 yen, and by May 1912 to 4,200 yen.

Concealed in the time between the building of Emperor Kōmei's mausoleum and that of Empress Dowager Eishō lies the development of a new imperial design born of revived imperial power. As historian Takagi Hiroshi notes, "The 1897 funeral of Empress Dowager Eishō set the standard for the Shinto-style funerals of the modern imperial household," in the process developing the clean and solemn elements of modern imperial design. In fact, Prince Yamashina Akira, who died in 1898, the year after Empress Dowager Eishō, was given a Shinto funeral even though he had specifically requested a Buddhist service in the manner of those held at the Shingon sect Kajū-ji temple. Upon his death, Imperial Household Minister Tanaka Mitsuaki consulted the Privy Council, an advisory body to the emperor, as to what should be done and was told that post-Restoration imperial funerals should revert to the practices of old.

Prince Yamashina Akira was born into the Fushimi branch of the imperial family. Prior to the Restoration, he had been a Buddhist priest, serving as abbot at Kajū-ji temple. Despite reverting to secular life after the Restoration and being designated head of the newly established Yamashina branch of the imperial household, he may have wished at the time of his death to return to being a Buddhist priest. The Japanese government, however, had decreed that imperial funerals would be carried out in the Shinto style. Already, in 1868, a Shinto ceremony had been held in the Shishinden to commemorate the second anniversary of Emperor Kōmei's death, and in 1871, Buddhism and Shinto were officially separated within the imperial household, with the Buddhist altar in the Kurodo building at the Imperial Palace in Kyoto replaced by an altar dedicated to the imperial ancestors in the Kōreiden, one of the three palace sanctuaries at the imperial grounds in Tokyo.

Nevertheless, although the official position demanded Shinto ceremonies for modern imperial funerals, Buddhist rites were not in fact done away with, and certainly not in private practice. Prince Yamashina, for example, is said to have also had a private Buddhist funeral. The clean and solemn designs of the modern imperial household were fostered primarily for public consumption as the designs of a modern state. The people charged with implementing them were the craftsmen and engineers of the Takumi-ryō, Goryō-kyoku, and Naien-kyoku bureaus of the Imperial Household Agency. Kodaira Yoshichika, considered a pioneer who established imperial household landscape design, was born in 1845, joined the Imperial Household Ministry in 1869, became an engineer in the Naien-kyoku in 1904, and retired in 1911. He is credited with introducing landscape design that blended Japanese and Western styles in sweeping open lawns.

Ichikawa Yukio joined the Imperial Household Ministry Goryō-kyoku in 1893 and worked on numerous imperial household-related gardens and improvements under Kodaira. He became an assistant engineer in 1896, transferred to the Takumi-ryō in 1898, traveled to France in 1899 to study European gardens, and became a full-fledged engineer with the Naien-kyoku in 1904. Throughout his long career, Ichikawa carefully preserved the substance of Meiji imperial household design.

Others besides Kodaira Yoshichika and Ichikawa Yukio who served in the Imperial Household Ministry during the mid-Meiji period included Fukuba Hayato, who helped to maintain the Shinjuku Gyoen garden, and is known for improving garden varietals such as the Fukuba strawberry, and the young Orishimo Yoshinobu. During the Taisho era, there was Okami Yoshio, who studied at the Royal Botanic Gardens in Kew in the United Kingdom, as well as Fukuba Hatsuzō, Shiihara Hyōichi, and Kimura Yasushi. In fact, the Imperial Household Ministry was at the forefront of gardening and garden landscaping in Japan at the time. These people were well acquainted with western landscaping concepts and had the talent and motivation to develop new designs that saved the imperial designs of the day from the confusion of the early modern period's synthesis of Shinto and Buddhism. They enabled the establishment of a clean and solemn style of imperial household design suited to the ideology of the separation of Shinto and Buddhism. Their advanced knowledge of western techniques and their modern sensibilities made it possible to realize the difficult task of incorporating a revivalist imperial style within the framework of a nation-state that was striving to modernize. It was precisely because the engineers and craftsmen of the Imperial Household Ministry Goryō-kyoku and Naien-kyoku bureaus were so well versed in western styles and techniques that they were able to achieve an ambivalent balance of revivalist design in a modern context.

During the Meiji years, the engineers of the Naien-kyoku carried out a number of projects related to the Ise Jingū shrine:

1891 The Jingū Nōgyōkan Agriculture Museum
1901 Expansion of the Agriculture Museum
1909 Jingū Chōkokan Museum

Attached to the Ise Jingū shrine, these two Meiji period Western-style facilities offer an intriguing look at modern Ise. The Western-style gardens attached to these buildings are considered the forerunners of Western-style landscape design in Japan.

The approaches within Ise Jingū were also redesigned on modern principles. The approach to the Inner Shrine, roughly 750 meters long, and that to the Outer Shrine, which is about half as long, are both paved with gravel, as are the rear approaches and the pathways to the other shrines in the vicinity. The essence of these shrines seems to reverberate with the feel and sound of every step taken on the gravel. The gravel used, we are told, comes from the river that runs through the shrine; such attention to detail was the

Fig. 4-12: Approach to the Inner Shrine at Ise Jingū shrine

work of the engineers of the Imperial Household Ministry. The approaches to the Inner and Outer Shrines and their associated purification halls are built using Western composition and an almost baroque layout (Fig. 4-12). By applying within the precincts of Ise Jingū, a place thought to be quintessentially Japanese, the latest techniques of Western gardens, Kodaira Yoshichika, Ichikawa Yukio, and their co-workers achieved a clean and solemn design.

These same people were also involved in landscaping the imperial mausoleums. Although the head of the Takumi-ryō was nominally in charge, it was to them that the actual landscaping was entrusted. Applying their knowledge of techniques from overseas, they created a clean and solemn atmosphere through the use of gravel and stands of trees.

The following imperial mausoleums have been constructed and maintained by the Imperial Household Ministry or the later Imperial Household Agency:

1897 (Dec)   Nochinotsukinowa no Higashi Kita Mausoleum
             (Empress Dowager Eishō)
1913 (Jul)   Fushimi Momoyama Mausoleum (Emperor Meiji)
1915 (May)   Fushimi Momoyama Higashi Mausoleum
             (Empress Shōken)

1927 (Dec)   Tama Mausoleum (Emperor Taisho)
1952 (May)   Tama Higashi Mausoleum (Empress Teimei)
1990 (Jan)   Musashino Mausoleum (Emperor Showa)
2001 (Jun)   Musashino Higashi Mausoleum (Empress Kōjun)

Construction only occurred on special occasions and required meticulous attention to design. The jump from the Nochinotsukinowa no Higashi Kita Mausoleum to the Fushimi Momoyama Mausoleum also meant perfecting the elements of modern imperial household design.

The shift from the circular mounds of Emperor Kōmei's mausoleum to the square base and round top of the Fushimi Momoyama Mausoleum was one result, and all imperial mausoleums built since have followed this precedent. Construction of the Fushimi Momoyama Mausoleum was overseen by architect Katayama Tōkuma, head of the Takumi-ryō, who designed the former Tōgū Palace (now the Akasaka Palace), the Jingū Chōkokan Museum, and the imperial museums in Nara and Kyoto. Ichikawa Yukio and numerous other landscape engineers were also involved.

Subsequently, an edict was issued in 1926 that defined and systematized how all imperial tombs were to be built thereafter. Another edict issued at the same time concerned imperial funerals. Just two months later, Emperor Taisho passed away. Article 5 of the edict on imperial funerals specified that the imperial mausoleum must have a square base and round top or take the shape of a mound. Article 21 stated that mausoleums must be built on imperial grounds in the Tokyo area or in a nearby prefecture. As a result, the mausoleums of emperors and empresses thereafter have been fixed in Tama and Musashino. The Fushimi Momoyama Mausoleum was the last imperial mausoleum to be built in the traditional Kyoto and Nara region. In a sense, then, it is perhaps not unexpected that it would reflect the turbulent transition from the early modern to the modern.

Ogawa Jihei most likely took part in this national project that perfected the design of a modernizing imperial household by working on site as a contractor under the supervision of the state landscape gardeners who oversaw construction of the Fushimi Momoyama Mausoleum, and is not likely

Fig. 4-13: Pines at the Fushimi Momoyama Mausoleum

to have been in a position to suggest revival designs. Nevertheless, when one visits the Fushimi Momoyama Mausoleum and sees the vast expanse of pine trees surrounding the square-based, round-topped mound, it nevertheless recalls the distinctive landscaping style of Ogawa Jihei (Fig. 4-13).

When Yamagata Aritomo later visited the Fushimi Momoyama Mausoleum, he composed the following *waka* poem:

How are you, great emperor?
In the mountains of Fushimi
There is only the sound of wind in the pines.

In this verse we see Yamagata moved by a sparse forest of pines so very like those of Ogawa Jihei. The work of breathing life into the details of state design was a task that could only be left to a master of his craft like Ueji.

CHAPTER FIVE

The World of Ueji's Gardens Expands

Gentlemen and Their Gardens

In 1925, Shimogō Denpei II purchased the eastern portion of an estate at
Nanzen-ji Shimokawa-chō 43-1 that had been developed by Tsukamoto
Yosaji using water drawn from the Lake Biwa Canal. Born in 1872, Shimogō
was an entrepreneur based in the city of Nagahama on the shores of Lake
Biwa who took his father's name. Shimogō's villa is said to have been named
Seiryū-tei by Admiral of the Fleet Tōgō Heihachirō in 1915, when it still
belonged to Tsukamoto. The western portion of Tsukamoto's estate, inci-
dentally, was purchased by Mitsubishi's Iwasaki Koyata.

Shimogō Denpei II's motivation for acquiring Seiryū-tei is unknown,
but one senses that an Ogawa Jihei garden was an attractive status symbol
for the wealthy merchants of Shiga and Kyoto. Both the first and second
Shimogō Denpei left their mark on the business world. During the period
of transition around the Meiji Restoration, the elder Shimogō profited from
real estate trading and market speculation. He eventually became a major
figure in business and was involved in numerous companies including
Osaka Paper, Nagahama Bank, Shimogō Paper, Ohmi Spinning, Japan Silk
Spinning, and the Ohmi Railway. He was also a philanthropist, providing
funds for education, welfare, and the construction of temples and shrines.

In one interesting episode, in 1889 the elder Shimogō offered to donate
3,000 yen for the construction of a new Nagahama Elementary School in
his hometown. People protested, however, that to erect the school with

money from only one person could give the donor unwarranted influence on its operations, and the project never got off the ground. Such objections were probably tied to an early-modern Japanese tradition of avoiding single donors when constructing temples and shrines in order to prevent excessive subsequent influence.

Later, however, in 1937 a splendid new elementary school was constructed in the town of Toyosato in the nearby Inukami district. Everything at the school—land, building, fixtures and furnishings, and even maintenance costs and teacher housing—had been donated by a local entrepreneur named Furukawa Tetsujirō. Born in Toyosato, Furukawa went on to become a senior managing director of the Itochu Corporation. In the Heisei period (1989–), there was a much-publicized movement to preserve the Toyosato school building, which had been designed by the Ōmi Hachiman-based architect William Merrell Vories.

It is interesting to imagine what the result might have been had the elder Shimogō Denpei's offer been accepted and a new Nagahama Elementary School been built in the early Meiji period, but all that remains are the tantalizing possibilities.

The elder Shimogō Denpei was a sympathetic supporter of the project to build the Lake Biwa Canal, and at the time of its completion hosted Sanjō Sanetomi at his residence in Ōtsu. As the story goes, Koteda Yasusada, then the governor of Shiga Prefecture, was adamantly against the canal. To secure permission for building it, the governor of Kyoto Prefecture, Kitagaki Kunimichi, arranged to have Koteda replaced by Nakai Hiroshi, with Koteda instead being made governor of Shimane Prefecture.

Given that the waters of the Lake Biwa Canal were an indispensable element of Ogawa Jihei's gardens, it may seem inevitable that Shimogō Denpei II and Nakai Hiroshi, both supporters of the canal, would come to own villas that had them. After a rich and colorful life, the elder Shimogō Denpei died at his Kyoto villa in 1898 at the age of 56. (This was, of course, not the villa called Seiryū-tei later acquired by his son.)

The elder Shimogō's villa had previously been the residence of Ijūin Kanetsune, who, as noted earlier, joined Yamagata Aritomo and Nakai

Hiroshi among the three benefactors to whom Ueji attributed his success when speaking with Kuroda Tengai. Located on the southwest corner of the intersection of Oshikōji and Kiyamachi streets, just to the south of the Takase River's Ichinofunairi docking inlet, the residence had been acquired by Ijūin sometime around 1892. At the time, Yamagata Aritomo's second Murin-an was located nearby. By around 1896, Ijūin had sold the villa to move closer to Nanzen-ji (where Yamagata would establish the third and current Murin-an). Ijūin's new property would later become Tairyū Sansō, now known for the massive garden so representative of Ogawa Jihei's work.

When Ijūin Kanetsune moved out of the villa near the Takase River, it was acquired by the elder Shimogō Denpei, who used it until his death. Here I would like to pause to look briefly at what happened to this villa thereafter. In 1902, it passed from the Shimogō family to Hirose Mitsumasa, son of Sumitomo executive Hirose Saihei. After Mitsumasa's death, the villa became the Buddhist temple Kōsei-in, which still exists today and whose garden is said to have been built by Ijūin. The philanthropic traditions of the Shimogō family were passed on with the family business to Shimogō Denpei II. He established a foundation called the Shimogō Kyōsaikai to carry on his father's activities in welfare, education, and culture, and also constructed the Shōshū-kan museum to display the family's collection of artwork. It was no doubt because Shimogō Denpei II was such a man of culture that he purchased Seiryū-tei and its garden by Ogawa Jihei from Tsukamoto Yosaji.

Incidentally, the second son of Shimogō II, Shimogō Torajirō, married the oldest daughter of Ogawa Chikanosuke, a physician who lived behind the Sumitomo villa in Shishigatani. In 1922, Ogawa Chikanosuke had Ogawa Jihei build a garden. Here, again, is another connection to Jihei that suggests the extent to which his gardens had permeated a certain social class.

There was another Nagahama entrepreneur whose stature rivaled that of Shimogō Denpei: Asami Matazō. Journalist Oshitani Moritoshi wrote about the two men as follows:

Among the many Ōmi merchants active in Kyoto and Osaka during the Meiji period, two were referred to in Kansai business circles as the "Nagahama lords." One was Shimogō Denpei and the other Asami Matazō. They say it is impossible for two great rivals to coexist, but these two lords of Nagahama both made major contributions to social welfare and industry, and their generosity extended beyond Nagahama not only to the rest of the northern Lake Biwa area but also throughout the prefecture.

Shimogō died in 1898 at the age of 56, followed just two years later in 1900 by Asami at the age of 61. Later critics likened Shimogō to Uesugi Kenshin and Asami to Takeda Shingen. [From *Ōmi shōnin to Nagahama shōnin* (Ōmi merchants and Nagahama merchants)]

Asami Matazō was born in 1839, the third son of an apothecary in the city of Nagahama, and adopted into the Asami family at the age of 22. The Asamis were producers of the famed Nagahama *chirimen* silk crepe. Matazō, however, would became a major investor in modern industry, expanding the family business through interests in banks, railroads, and shipping to become one of Nagahama's leading merchants.

Hearing that Emperor Meiji would be visiting Nagahama in 1887, Asami financed the construction of a magnificent official guesthouse. In 1935 the guesthouse was designated a national historic site called the Meiji Emperor's Temporary Palace in Nagahama, and the following year it was donated to the town (later the city) of Nagahama. This pre-war designation as a historic site was revoked in 1948, but in 2006 the garden was named a national place of scenic beauty (Fig. 5-1).

The garden, as it turns out, underwent a major renovation in 1912—directed by Asami Matazō's successor Asami Matazō II—to commemorate the twenty-fifth anniversary of the emperor's visit in 1887. Ogawa Jihei undertook this renovation, so it was his garden that was designated a national place of scenic beauty. The garden includes a front section between the front gate and the middle gate, and a main section leading from the middle

Fig. 5-1: The garden at Asami Matazō's Keiun-kan villa

gate to the expansive area before the main guesthouse. As a whole, the garden is noted for its large undulations, massive rocks, and the incorporation of views of Lake Biwa. Ogawa Jihei's eldest son, Yasutarō (Hakuyō), is said to have been involved in the landscaping, and indeed, he compiled an album of photographs of the garden.

The guesthouse is called Keiun-kan, a name attributed to Itō Hirobumi. Here we see another point suggesting rivalry, with Shimogō Denpei's Seiryū-tei being named by Tōgō Heihachirō and Asami Matazō's Keiun-kan being named by Itō Hirobumi.

The Keiun-kan garden was not the only Ogawa Jihei garden owned by Asami Matazō. The biography *Ogawa Jihei* notes that he landscaped a garden in May 1921 for the Asami Matazō villa at Shogoin-chō in Kyoto. I had the opportunity to hear an interesting story about this garden from Ogawa Jihei's nephew, landscape gardener Iwaki Sentarō. When I interviewed Iwaki in 1980, he said, "I don't think the garden is there anymore, but its *kaya* tree was moved to the Ōhara villa in Kurashiki."

Ogawa Jihei's gardens had become popular with gentlemen of means throughout the country.

The Ōhara villa mentioned here is named Yūrin-sō and located across

the street from the Ōhara Museum of Art in the city of Kurashiki in Okayama Prefecture. Ogawa Jihei is known to have worked on the villa's garden, but it was not his first commission from the Ōhara family. In 1916 the
family had entrusted to him the creation of the Shinkei-en garden just behind the Ōhara Museum of Art, and between 1917 and 1927 he was working regularly on renovations to the garden at their primary Kurashiki
residence. From 1922 through the following year, the family also commissioned him to restore and renovate the garden of the Amase villa in the city
of Okayama. In 1932, he was commissioned to landscape the garden of the
Ōhara villa at Sumiyoshi in Kobe. The Amase villa in Okayama no longer
exists and is believed to have been destroyed during the war. Another
Ōhara villa located in the Tantakabayashi area of Sumiyoshi also no longer
exists, having been damaged in the Great Hanshin Floods of 1938 (described in Tanizaki Jun'ichirō's novel *Sasameyuki* (*The Makioka Sisters*)),
and then again during the war.

The Ōhara villa built by Ōhara Magosaburō in Kyoto's Kitashirakawa
area between 1936 and 1937, however, is still quietly maintained by the
Ōhara family.* Passing through the gate, you are welcomed by cryptomeria
and Japanese cypress standing so still and quiet that it is difficult to imagine
you are in the middle of Kyoto. A gently winding walkway leads to the entrance of a refined *sukiya*-style house. The ground before the entrance is
paved with fist-sized black stones arranged in a magnificent *ararekoboshi*
("scattered hail") pattern. This important point of connection between the
garden and the residence would have been the work of the garden's designer.

The building is a multi-storied structure in the *sukiya* style with an upper floor topped by a pyramidal *hōgyō*-style thatched roof. The lower floor
has a cambered roof covered in ceramic tiles, with wooden-shingled eaves
that wrap around the building in a manner reminiscent of *rōkaku* towers.
The deep eaves soften the light filtering in from the garden, letting us know
that the villa was intended as a place for quiet relaxation. There is a pond,
but given the site's location it draws water from a source other than the
Lake Biwa Canal. Following a typical Ueji design, the water flows from the
pond toward the west end of the property. Centered on the pond, the gar-

* The author presents the garden of this villa as the work of Ogawa Jihei VII,
    but it was actually created by Ogawa Jihei IX.

Fig. 5-2: The Ōhara villa at Kitashirakawa

den is given depth through the off-center placement of a stone bridge. A lone stone pagoda standing directly across the pond also imparts a sense of depth to the whole. The view back toward the residence from the tea ceremony room on the far side of the pond is another key point in the overall design (Fig. 5-2).

After the Second World War, having inherited this villa from his father Magosaburō, Ōhara Sōichirō enjoyed looking out over the garden while leaning against the main residence's alcove post or watching the moon rise from the second floor. Ogawa Jihei's gardens reward such viewing from high ground; even as far back as the garden at Murin-an that he landscaped for Yamagata Aritomo, all of his gardens look beautiful when seen from above. This was his answer to the growing number of two-storied mansions being built at the advent of the modern period. Stones placed flat and topiaries trimmed low not only helped open up a garden but also took into account the view from a second floor. Ōhara Sōichirō was purposeful in his enjoyment of the garden, and at one time is said to have hung a small painting by Paul Cézanne in a first-floor room of the main house so that he could appreciate it while comparing it with its surroundings. He must have enjoyed the way Cézanne's colorful overlapping brushstrokes echoed the sense of depth generated in the garden by layers of multicolored trees.

As the area around his villa urbanized, Ōhara had a low *tsuiji* pounded mud wall constructed along the south side of the garden to cut out the noise from outside. The wall passes behind a number of stone lanterns, but rather than being a visual distraction it expands the garden much like the wall that surrounds the stone garden at Ryōan-ji temple.

The villa of the Shimazu family, complete with a roundabout driveway and a Western-style residence, apparently once stood next door to the Ōhara villa at Kitashirakawa, but that property is long gone and the Ōhara villa now stands alone. After the death of Ueji VII, the villa's gardens were tended first by his subordinate Maeda Yoshijirō, then by successive generations of the family, and are now maintained by Ueji XI.

The history of Kurashiki's modernization owes much to the abilities of Ōhara Magosaburō. As the head of the Ōhara family, Magosaburō was made president of Kurabo Industries at an early age. He worked to expand the company's business while also becoming involved in numerous cultural and social undertakings, including building hospitals and schools and founding both an agricultural research center and a research institute for the study of social issues. A patron of Western-style painter Kojima Torajirō, he also had Kojima purchase paintings and assemble an art collection for him. The collection became one of Japan's finest, including paintings by Monet, Matisse, El Greco, and other great artists.

Meanwhile, the garden at Yūrin-sō in Kurashiki took shape under Ueji's direction between 1928 and 1931. Actual work on the garden appears to have been handled by Ueji's nephew, Ogawa Kazuo. Ōhara Magosaburō originally intended Yūrin-sō, which adjoined the primary Ōhara residence in Kurashiki, as a place to live with his wife Sueko. When the crown prince visited Kurabo Industries and other sites in Kurashiki in 1926, however, Magosaburō realized there was a need for an official guesthouse in Kurashiki and resolved to apply sufficient funds toward construction to meet

Fig. 5-3: Yūrin-sō, the residence of Ōhara Magosaburō

this need. The walls surrounding the property use thick planks of teak, a high-grade material that stands up well to water and is often used for the decks of ships. These walls alone are enough to tell us that Yūrin-sō as a whole employed the finest materials (Fig. 5-3).

The interior has both Western-style and Japanese-style rooms, with the unstinting consistency of design throughout the interior so typical of residences from the early Showa period. The Western-style appointments exhibit an art deco style also reflective of the trends of the times. Choice materials are used throughout, including interior pillars made of cypress from Alishan in Taiwan and ceilings made using cryptomeria from the island of Yakushima. The magnificent green-glazed roof tiles fired in Osaka left such an impression that Yūrin-sō also came to be known as the "green palace." In a successful blending of Japanese, Chinese, and Western designs, these same green-glazed tiles are also used atop the walls surrounding the estate.

After Yūrin-sō, Ōhara Magosaburō established the Ōhara Museum of Art in 1930 to display his personal art collection. Construction of the museum cost just over 55,000 yen, while Yūrin-sō is said to have cost as much as 260,000 yen to build. This suggests how strongly Magosaburō felt about his official guesthouse, feelings no doubt similar to those of Asami Matazō

Fig. 5-4: The garden at Yūrin-sō

toward his own Keiun-kan.

Collecting art and building residences worthy of being used as official guesthouses follows a pattern of behavior shared by successful industrial capitalists from the Meiji period through the pre-war Showa years. What set Ōhara Magosaburō apart from the *sukisha* connoisseurs who preceded him were his collection's focus on Western art and the incorporation at his guesthouse of a new style of architecture that blended the Japanese and the Western. Both the museum and Yūrin-sō were designed by local Kurashiki architect Yakushiji Kazue. A graduate of Tokyo Imperial University, Yakushiji worked as a construction engineer for the army in his youth, but designed buildings and facilities for the Ōhara family in Kurashiki during the latter half of his life. He is said to have had his mentor Itō Chūta supervise the design of the Japanese rooms at Yūrin-sō, while the Western-style rooms were his own work and demonstrate the art deco elements at which he excelled.

We can see, then, that the architectural environment for the garden at Yūrin-sō (Fig. 5-4) was very different from the traditional Japanese buildings Ueji worked with in Kyoto. According to Suzuki Makoto, who led a group investigating the Yūrin-sō garden, Ueji undertook a major renovation subsequent to its initial completion. After the residence at Yūrin-sō was finished in 1928, the death of Magosaburō's wife Sueko and the opening of the museum, both in 1930, probably led to an emphasis on its use as an official guesthouse, and therefore also to the garden's renovation. Changes included the relocation of two pieces of Aji granite and the complete removal of a thirteen-tiered pagoda, a well, and four stone lanterns. We can surmise that these changes transformed a more traditional Japanese garden into one that adopted a freer style. Although it is unclear when the *kaya* tree from Asami Matazō's Keiun-kan in Kyoto was brought to Yūrin-sō, it is fun to imagine that this occurred at the time of this renovation, and that it speaks to Ueji's determination to completely redo the garden.

Ōhara Magosaburō had Ogawa Jihei create gardens in Kurashiki at his primary residence, Shinkei-en, and Yūrin-sō; in Okayama at the Amase villa; in Kobe at the Sumiyoshi villa; and in Kyoto at the Kitashirakawa villa. He was not only one of Ogawa's most important patrons, but also played a significant role in greatly expanding the scope of his work.

The Gardens of Iwasaki Koyata

Ogawa Jihei's encounter with Yamagata Aritomo was his starting point for gaining expertise in drawing water from the Lake Biwa Canal for gardens and developing his landscaping style, so it is only natural that Kyoto should remain the center of his activities thereafter. Gradually, his reach expanded beyond Kyoto to places like Osaka and Sumiyoshi through his work for the Sumitomo family, then further afield to Okitsu in Shizuoka and to Tokyo through his work for Saionji. As his circle of patrons grew, so did the range of the gardens on which he worked. Because gardens are ultimately private worlds, this expansion of gardens represents the widening private worlds of their owners.

Another person who expanded the world of Ogawa Jihei was Iwasaki Koyata, Mitsubishi's fourth president and the head of the Mitsubishi zaibatsu. In 1925, Koyata purchased the western portion of the estate at

Nanzen-ji Shimokawara-chō 43-1 that had previously belonged to Tsuka-moto Yosaji. Since around 1912, Tsukamoto had been purchasing land in the area in his own name as well as that of Kakuboshi Gōshikaisha, a limit-ed partnership company he had founded, and developing it into one of Kyoto's grander neighborhoods. Tsukamoto built *sukiya*-style mansions, had Ogawa Jihei landscape the gardens, and then sold the properties to var-ious influential people. Some have called it the finest ready-built housing in Japanese history. The lot that Iwasaki purchased was one of two that result-ed from the division of a larger piece of land. As noted earlier, the other lot had been sold to Shimogō Denpei II, the Nagahama entrepreneur. Looking ahead, the two lots would later change hands; Iwasaki's villa came to be known as Shokuhō-en and is now owned by a religious organization. Shimogō's villa is known as Seiryū-tei.

Iwasaki Koyata's reasons for acquiring the Shimokawara-chō property are unclear, but having a villa in Kyoto was considered a desirable lifestyle for powerful Japanese at the time and he may simply have been following the fashion of the day. Iwasaki's property contained a two-storied wooden *sukiya*-style building. Later named Kotō-an, this villa no doubt proved use-ful a few years later as accommodation for guests at the time of the en-thronement ceremony for Emperor Showa. Iwasaki added a reception room and had Ueji make improvements to the stream that ran through the estate. At the start of 1928, Iwasaki sent New Year's greetings to Iwasaki Hisaya, his cousin and predecessor as Mitsubishi president: "I celebrate your good health / the Kyoto spring is mild / Koyata." Infused with the calm of a tranquil New Year spent in Kyoto, these brief words also suggest Iwasa-ki's satisfaction with his new Kyoto villa. In 1933, Iwasaki asked Ueji to un-dertake a major renovation of the villa's garden.

During the same year in which Iwasaki Koyata enjoyed such a peaceful New Year's in Kyoto, he was planning to build a new primary residence in Tokyo at Toriizaka in Azabu, on land that had held the Kuni-no-miya Pal-ace before being acquired by entrepreneur Akaboshi Tetsuma. Iwasaki had Ōe Shintarō design the residence and Ogawa Jihei the garden.

For Iwasaki Koyata, the Tokyo residence was a kind of state guesthouse intended to showcase the stylishness of Japanese culture and art to dignitaries from overseas. Ōe Shintarō placed a Japanese-style structure with a dash of the broader Orient atop a concrete terrace. He had graduated from the Faculty of Architecture at Tokyo Imperial University in 1904 and worked for a long time on repairs of the Nikkō Tōshōgū shrine. He also succeeded Itō Chūta and Andō Tokizō as the supervisor of construction at the Meiji Jingū shrine, also designing its Hōmotsu-den treasure museum. He was, in other words, the leading architect of the day for Japanese-style buildings. In selecting Ōe, Iwasaki showed his eagerness to demonstrate the best of traditional Japanese architecture. Nakamura Junpei worked on the interior of the residence, as did the lacquer artist Matsuda Gonroku. Because the building sat atop a large concrete terrace, the garden could be viewed from above. It was not very large, though, and would not have accommodated the expansive style in which Ogawa Jihei usually worked.

Still, a trademark Ueji stream cuts across the garden and a luxurious lawn stretches out beneath the concrete terrace. Although the garden is not large, tall trees around the perimeter block neighboring sightlines to create a world apart from its urban setting. Bringing light and a sense of breadth to a garden that is actually not so large creates a space that feels typical of Ueji. Intended to be seen from the concrete terrace above, the garden probably put little weight on providing a place for an enjoyable stroll, and gains its sense of openness by emphasizing elements best savored when standing on the terrace above.

The stream starts at the southwest corner of the property and flows to the southeast. Near the beginning of the stream is the opening to a small tunnel that leads to a cliff on the west side of the property. Although this could be seen as a charming walkway, it can clearly also be seen as an evacuation route providing a means of escape in case of an attack. Similar tunnels are found in other Ueji gardens around Nanzen-ji temple in Kyoto as well as in his later gardens such as Iwasaki Koyata's Atami Yōwadō villa and Nagao Kin'ya's Senko Sansō villa in Kamakura. Such tunnels take advantage of the terrain to reduce vulnerability to attack, and while Ogawa Jihei specialized in landscaping spacious lawns, he must also have enjoyed working

Fig. 5-5: Iwasaki Koyata's Atami Yōwadō villa

with such varied configurations.

The luxurious mansion that paid such careful attention to defense was reduced to ashes during the air raids of May 1945, just 16 years after its completion in 1929, leaving behind only a few earthen storehouses and the garden. The primary residence of Iwasaki Koyata, no doubt one of the finest guesthouses of the early Showa period, disappeared in a moment as if it had been but a vision.

Iwasaki Koyata, however, had also built a new villa in Atami in 1935 (Fig. 5-5). Designed by the Sone-Chūjō Architectural Firm, it was a magnificent half-timbered construction in the Tudor style. While the primary residence in Toriizaka had a Japanese-style structure intended to display Japan's finest craftsmanship to foreign guests, the private villa in Atami appears to have reflected Iwasaki's personal preferences. Having travelled and studied in Britain, the medieval Tudor style of England suited him. While Josiah Conder, the British architect who excelled in this style, had passed away, his legacy lived on in the architectural office established by his favorite pupil, Sone Tatsuzō, and Sone's junior partner, Chūjō Seiichirō, who had studied in the UK.

The Sone-Chūjō Architectural Firm erected a massive half-timbered structure that retained a strong woody feel despite being made primarily of reinforced concrete. What appear to be stout wooden beams over the vaulted grand hall, for example, are actually concrete formed with molds made using zelkova wood, whose grain, raised in relief, has transferred to its surface. A pre-Raphaelite painting adorns the wall of the built-in inglenook recess by the fireplace. The interior is appointed with exquisite taste, including a library with richly grained wooden wainscoting, a conservatory with Islamic-style tiling, and an airy French-styled room once used by Iwasaki's wife. The bathroom, which draws waters from the Atami hot springs, has a magnificent bathtub carved from granite. To this day, the mansion remains the finest Western-style structure in all of Japan.

This mansion's name, Yōwadō, is the same one that had been given to a villa built in Kamakura by Koyata's father, Iwasaki Yanosuke. In Kamakura the name (whose last character means "cavern" or "cave mouth") referred to a tunnel that cut across the estate. In Atami it is the name of a tunnel along the road leading to the villa. Visitors approaching the villa first pass through a lush bamboo grove and then through the tunnel (the name is engraved on a plate above the entrance) before finally arriving at their destination.

The Iwasaki family, of course, had numerous villas. Kennan Sansō, a villa on the shores of Lake Ashinoko in Hakone, was originally a small hunting lodge, but Iwasaki expanded the property with the addition of Western- and Japanese-style buildings, gardens, and even a golf course as he transformed it into one of his favorite villas. Iwasaki is said to have gone to considerable trouble searching for just the right spot for his villa in Atami. *Iwasaki Koyata den* (A biography of Iwasaki Koyata) relates how, after an arduous climb through the mountains of Atami, he came upon a place with sweeping views of the ocean and shouted, "This is it! This is it!"

The garden at Yōwadō was entrusted to Ogawa Jihei, with actual work handled by his nephew Iwaki Sentarō. The property follows a downward slope leading south toward the ocean at Izu. A wide lawn spreads out before the Western-style building with an almost stubborn spaciousness and brightness. In the middle of this expansive lawn is set an impressive *garan ishi*, a temple foundation stone. Such foundation stones were frequently

Fig. 5-6: The *garan ishi* at the garden at Yōwadō

employed in gardens at the time, and Ogawa Jihei had used them in a number of his own, including at Yamagata Aritomo's Murin-an.

The foundation stone at the center of the Yōwadō garden (Fig. 5-6) was transported from An'yō-ji temple in Kyoto, and intended by Iwasaki as a memorial to his mother. The great lawn that opens up before the Western-style building has the atmosphere of a Western garden, but placing a temple foundation stone at its center generates the character of a Japanese one.

A bit further down the garden is a grove of plum trees that had been transplanted from Iwasaki's parents' villa in Kamakura. In this garden, however, there is no stream to play a leading role, although this is unsurprising given that its high ground offers views of the ocean. The focus, instead, is on providing a pleasant expanse. The garden is protected from the sounds of the town of Atami, and all that can be seen is the ocean through the trees, with no hint of the busy and boisterous hot springs area below. The Tanna train tunnel runs below the villa and, as one story has it, once the huge undertaking of the tunnel's excavation was complete, Iwasaki recruited the same laborers to build his villa. The grand scale of the Atami villa is enough to make the story, which seems also to reflect Iwasaki's character, almost seem credible.

One must pass through a tunnel to reach Yōwadō, but there is also another smaller tunnel that leads to the other side of the garden. This garden tunnel has a secretive, playful air, but probably also served a practical function as an evacuation or escape route. During the early years of the Showa period when the villa was built, the threat of terrorist acts against prominent figures was very real. Precautions were taken accordingly and at Yōwadō, in addition to the evacuation route, there was also a set of sturdy iron doors, like those of a safe, which could be used to barricade the corridor leading to the bedrooms on the second floor of the villa.

Iwasaki Koyata's father Yanosuke maintained a large residence at Goten'yama in Shinagawa, Tokyo that had been designed by the British architect Josiah Conder. Its Western-style garden was the work of Fukuba Hayato. In his plans for the building, Conder included an embroidery-like design for a formal garden, and Fukuba probably took Conder's idea into consideration when doing the landscaping. Conder had a keen interest in and knowledge of Japanese gardens, but designed Western-style gardens with well-regulated patterns. The garden that extends from the south of the property to the west is said to have originally been planned for peonies, but was later adapted for roses. Today it remains very much an English-style rose garden.

On the eastern side of the property there is a large wisteria arbor, from which a Japanese-style garden extends out along the southern slope. Many Western-style residences of the Meiji period also had separate Japanese-style buildings that were used in parallel. Similarly, there were instances where a Western-style garden was supplemented with a Japanese-style garden. Typically, a Western-style garden was provided around the Western-style building with a Japanese-style garden taking up the rest of the property or situated near the Japanese-style building. Many such dual-character estates were constructed in Tokyo where properties with south-facing slopes that offered good sunlight and good drainage were preferred for residences.

This preference for building large mansions on southern slopes, however, did not become pronounced until after the Meiji period. Many great residences of the earlier Edo period had gardens that extended to the water's edge along Edo Bay. Examples that still exist today include the Hama Rikyū gardens and Shiba Rikyū gardens that were built along the sea, and whose frontages changed with the rise and fall of the tides. The Kiyosumi villa, one of the earliest built by the Iwasaki family, and its garden also took advantage of the waterways in a low-lying part of the city.

The subsequent preference for building Western-style mansions on high ground where they would project proud silhouettes is said to have been influenced by foreigners such as Erwin Bälz, who served as a physician to the elite and insisted that dry, high ground and south-facing slopes were healthier than damp, marshy lowlands. In this way, cultural norms gradually evolved from the Edo period fondness for "low city" ambience to an affinity for "high city" stylishness.

Estates built on southern slopes were generally configured with the main Western-style residence at the top of the property surrounded by a Western-style garden, and a Japanese-style garden provided on the lower portion of the south-facing slope. The Shinagawa mansion built by Iwasaki Yanosuke is configured in this way, as is the Mitsui Club building in Mita Tsunamachi that was designed by Josiah Conder. At the Mitsui Club, stone steps lead from a Conder-designed Western-style fountain that stands before the Western-style building down to the Japanese-style garden below, whose design is attributed to a master of the Yabunouchi school of tea ceremony in Kyoto.

Iwasaki Yanosuke's mansion was built in 1908 at a time when Ogawa Jihei was not yet working in the Kanto region. While the Iwasaki family residences each have finely appointed gardens, it was not until the time of Iwasaki Koyata that Ogawa began working for the family.

Nevertheless, Ueji's first work in Tokyo—the garden at Saionji Kinmochi's primary residence in Surugadai—predated his involvement with the gardens of Iwasaki Koyata. Although it is unclear exactly when he began the Surugadai project, it was definitely prior to the Great Kanto Earthquake of 1923. According to Yamane Tokutarō's *Ogawa Jihei*, work on the primary Saionji residence began in 1918 and finished the following year. Other gardens mentioned as begun and completed during the same period include those of the Murai Kichibei and Furukawa Toranosuke residences, showing that Ogawa Jihei had expanded his garden work to Tokyo. Another Tokyo garden Ueji is said to have created was that at the residence of Ogura Masatsune, which was renovated in 1933. Ogura was president of the Sumitomo Group and, given his Sumitomo ties, it is no surprise that he would have an Ueji garden.

As we have already seen, in 1918 work began almost simultaneously on gardens at the residences of Saionji Kinmochi, Murai Kichibei, and Furukawa Toranosuke. The Saionji residence aside, the question arises as to how Ogawa Jihei came to be commissioned to do the gardens of the Murai and Furukawa residences, thereby expanding the world of his gardens to include Tokyo.

The Gardens of Murai Kichibei

Murai Kichibei was known as Japan's tobacco king. Before the tobacco industry was made a national monopoly, private companies engaged in the business of tobacco production. Two tobacco moguls, both based in Ginza, who became particularly famous were Iwaya Matsuhei, known for the Tengu brand, and Chiba Matsubei, known for the Botan brand. Instead of the pipe tobacco popular since the Edo period, these men manufactured cigarettes, which were first produced in Japan after Takeuchi Takeshi and Ishikawa Jihei brought back a cigarette-making machine from Europe in 1873 after attending the Vienna World Fair. In 1875, Takeuchi Takeshi is said to have presented Emperor Meiji with some prototype cigarettes he had made.

After this start, cigarette production eventually developed into a one-on-one competition between the Iwaya Shōkai company with its Tengu brand cigarettes and the Murai Shōkai company with its Sunrise, Hero, and other brands. The two companies engaged in a fierce advertising war as both continued to grow.

Murai Kichibei was from Kyoto and his company's main factory was located at Umamichi-dōri in the city's Higashiyama district. As the business grew, however, expansion into Tokyo became unavoidable. In July

1901, Murai moved his entire family to Tokyo to take up residence in Shiba-ku Mita Koyama-chō. In November of the following year the family moved again to a new residence in Kōji-machi Nagata-chō. This brought them to a higher-class neighborhood closer to the center of the city and, given that their only daughter Hisako was 11 years old at the time, was conveniently located next door to the Peers' School for Girls.

While continuing to produce tobacco, Murai Kichibei also diversified his business, setting up a number of companies in the textile and finance industries centered on the Murai Bank. Murai commissioned architect Yoshitake Chōichi, who is said to have studied architecture at Pennsylvania Technical College, to design both the bank's headquarters and its branches, which he did in an authentic classical style. In addition to designing the Murai Bank's buildings, Yoshitake also designed churches. Stately and dignified, the former Shichijō, Gojō, and Gion branches of the Murai Bank can still be seen in Kyoto. Among Yoshitake's churches, the Andō Memorial Church of the United Church of Christ in Japan in Tokyo also still exists.

The most famous Murai Kichibei building, though, is probably Chōraku-kan, which stands adjacent to Kyoto's Maruyama Park. An authentic Western-style mansion that served as the Murai family's residence in Kyoto, Chōraku-kan was built in 1909 following the design of American architect James McDonald Gardiner. Famously, the name Chōraku-kan was bestowed on the residence by Itō Hirobumi. Construction of this authentic Western-style mansion established tobacco king Murai Kichibei as a force to be reckoned with known far and wide. As his hiring of both Gardiner and Yoshitake suggests, Murai placed enormous importance on architecture and preferred architects who worked in orthodox styles. Within the tobacco industry, architecture must have been seen as an important means of establishing a corporate image.

Later, Murai Kichibei set about rebuilding in earnest the primary residence at Nagata-chō in Tokyo where he had been living since 1902. According to a book of photos of the residence titled *Sannōsō zushū* (Images of Sannō-sō), "Takeda Goichi, D. Eng., and Okada Shin'ichirō, B. Eng., served as advisors while Kobayashi Tomizō directed the entire project from start to finish as master carpenter. General plans are said to have been completed in the fall of 1915 and construction begun in January 1916, but the final date of completion is unclear." Meanwhile, the biography *Ogawa Jihei* notes that the garden was completed in 1919, so the building was probably finished around the same time. Although somewhat long, I would like to cite the following description of the residence from *Sannōsō zushū*.

The main part of the building from the entrance to the great drawing room largely reproduces the style of the Fujiwara period. The roof over the porte cochère has an undulating gable with cypress bark shingles whose design is said to combine aspects of similar gables at Ninna-ji and Hongan-ji temples.

The inner section beyond the moon-viewing platform that faces the garden has two stories with a cambered roof. The first story uses cypress, of course, but the second uses red pine in particular, a change in mood that must reflect the tastes of the master of the house. The first floor has rooms for the master and mistress of the house that open onto a courtyard to the north, beyond which stands a retreat.

The tea ceremony room is largely modeled on Konnichi-an and Yū-in. There is also another separate fifteen-mat tea ceremony room. The eaves in the section of this room with a raised floor have a bamboo understructure with an extremely time-consuming design said to have been made by carpenters from Kyoto.

Most of the pillars in the tea ceremony room and retreat use polished kitayama maruta *logs.*

The sliding fusuma *partitions in each room are generally decorated with paintings and have hand pulls modeled on those found at historic sites such as the Katsura Imperial Villa.*

As with the staggered shelves modeled on those at Daigo-ji temple and the Katsura Imperial Villa, the transoms and the like are also mostly modeled on famous examples, and I have generally included explanations of the various parts in the table of contents.

This rather muddled description seems to be based on hearsay, and there is a reason for this. The tobacco monopoly law had been enacted in 1904. Murai Shōkai's factories were taken over by the government, forcing the company to concentrate on its finance, textile and other businesses. Murai's wife Unoko then passed away in 1916. Murai Kichibei welcomed his second wife, Kaoru, from the household of Viscount Hinonishi the following year, which also brought the death of his only daughter Hisako. Kaoru got along poorly with Hisako's husband Yakichi, the fifth son of Viscount Mishima Michitsune, and drove him from the family. Throughout these developments the family continued to live at the primary residence of Sannō-sō, but its fate turned with the death of family head Murai Kichibei on 2 January 1926. The following year, buffeted by the Showa Financial Crisis, the Murai Bank was driven into bankruptcy.

The Sannō-sō estate was dismantled and the property transferred to Tokyo Prefecture. It later became the site of Tokyo First Middle School and is now the site of Tokyo Metropolitan Hibiya High School. While some of the buildings and documents from the Murai era still remain, there are no traces of the original garden. I would very much have liked to know what sort of garden Ueji created in the middle of Tokyo. Given that the photo book *Sannōsō zushū* was probably compiled in a great hurry amid the turmoil of dismantling and rebuilding Murai Kichibei's primary residence, it is perhaps unavoidable that its descriptions should sometimes seem muddled and second hand.

The Japanese-style mansion was dismantled and rebuilt at Enryaku-ji temple on Mt. Hiei in Kyoto, where it remains to this day and is used as a formal reception space. One of Takeda Goichi's most magnificent buildings, it is an overwhelming sight even for modern visitors. Not only is it a masterpiece of traditional *shoin* design, it is also surprising to see designs on the building's sliding *fusuma* partitions that appear to have been influenced by the Arts and Crafts movement. This interior design sensibility recalls Waraku-an, the villa belonging to Inabata Katsutarō that was also designed by Takeda Goichi and had an Ogawa Jihei garden. One can imagine that the design of the Sannō-sō garden, too, may have been influenced by such new trends. When Sannō-sō was dismantled, part of its tea ceremony room is said to have been taken by Nezu Kaichirō of Aoyama in Tokyo.

The Western-style building at Sannō-sō attributed to Yoshitake Chō-ichi was moved to Ochanomizu in Tokyo where it became the Maison Franco-Japonaise, but it no longer exists today. The Chōraku-kan villa in Kyoto still exists and is being used as a café and restaurant. Murai Kichibei had a keen interest in architecture, and it seems his various residences have all found appropriate caretakers.

Unfortunately, as a result of this dismantling of Murai Kichibei's prima-ry residence, there are few historical materials concerning the garden at Sannō-sō. The text of the *Sannōsō zushū* is muddled and confused because by the time it was published in 1927, the Murai Bank had failed and San-nō-sō had been disposed of. Indeed, the book of photographs was pub-lished only just in time. It opens by saying, "With regard to Sannō-sō, the grand residence in a corner of Sannō-dai that boasted a magnificent man-sion in a purely Japanese style and a tranquil garden, there must be much that would serve as a useful reference with regards to both architecture and landscaping, but here we can only provide an overview of the building that relies on our impressions based on what we have heard."

As far as we can tell from the photographs in the book, the garden had no significant stream or pond and it appears to have been largely governed by the style of traditional Japanese gardens. Still, we can see Ueji's hand in the expansive lawn and in the low-cut trees and shrubbery planted along-side the garden's stepping stones. The washbasin made from a granite piling taken from Gojō Bridge in Kyoto is clearly an example of a use of stone in keeping with the Ueji style.

What was the connection between Murai Kichibei and Ogawa Jihei? Murai was from Kyoto and must have been aware of Ueji's work. In particu-lar, given that the Chōraku-kan villa was immediately adjacent to Maruyama Park, whose gardens Ueji had designed, we can imagine that this brought Ueji's work to his attention. Murai's commissioning of Kyoto architect Takeda Goichi to design Sannō-sō also speaks to the importance he placed on Kyoto-style ambience. Murai seems to have chosen both architect and gardener based on their relationship to Kyoto, with the result that Ueji was able to expand the scope of his work to Tokyo.

Nevertheless, the great garden is long gone, as is that of the Saionji residence in Surugadai, and it must be said that to have lost such major gardens in the city center is a great pity. Of Ueji's gardens in Tokyo on which work commenced in 1918, the only ones that still survive are at the former primary residence of Iwasaki Koyata in Toriizaka—now the International House of Japan—and the residence of Furukawa Toranosuke.

The Gardens of Furukawa Toranosuke

The Furukawa family is a zaibatsu family that got its start when Furukawa Ichibei launched a mining business by purchasing the Ashio copper mine with funds provided by Shibusawa Eiichi's First National Bank. Ichibei adopted as his heir a man named Junkichi, the second son of Mutsu Munemitsu, a well-known diplomat of the Meiji period. This created a kinship tie between the Furukawa and Mutsu families that seems to have later benefitted the Furukawas in the form of tacit support provided by the Mutsu family when pollution at the Ashio copper mine became a problem. Mutsu Munemitsu died in 1897 at his Nishigahara residence in the north of Tokyo. Bequeathed to Junkichi, now a member of the Furukawa family, it became a Furukawa asset.

The Nishigahara residence is located between Komagome and Asukayama on the Iwatsuki Kaidō road that starts in Nihonbashi before passing through Hongō and Komagome on its way to Asukayama and Ōji. Seen from a broader perspective, it is located in northwestern Tokyo. Asukayama was already famous for its cherry blossoms during the Edo period, and beginning in the Meiji period the area from Ōji to Takinogawa became known as a popular destination for excursions by foreign residents; for a time, this scenic area was even sometimes referred to as "the Richmond of Japan." Indeed, the name Ōji itself is said to have been bestowed by Shogun Tokugawa Yoshimune—also credited with turning Asukayama into a famous spot— in reference to the ninety-nine Ōji shrines found along the

Kumano pilgrimage route in Kishū where he was born. The scenic area has both the hill at Asukayama as well as abundant water in the flow of the Shakujii River at Takinogawa.

In addition to being located in an area of splendid scenery, the Furu-kawa residence also had special meaning to the family because it was in close proximity to the residence that Shibusawa Eiichi maintained on Asukayama. The Furukawa family had benefitted greatly from Shibusawa's support for industry and respected him greatly. They must have felt most grateful to acquire the Nishigahara property so close to Shibusawa's residence.

Shibusawa Eiichi maintained a large estate on Asukayama. There are a number of reasons he may have chosen to live there, but one may be because his hometown of Fukaya in Saitama Prefecture was further out along the railroad line that passed from Ueno through Ōji. As time went by, more and more wealthy estates were established in Tokyo's western suburbs, which came to be called the Yamanote area, but few such large estates were found in the northern area of Asukayama and Nishigahara. Still, it was not uncommon for people to establish residences in areas with good access to their hometowns. During the Edo period, for example, the Edo estate of the Kaga domain's Maeda clan could be found on what is now the University of Tokyo's Hongō campus, a location that gave them immediate access to the Nakasendō road and would take them straight through Echigo to their home domain of Kaga. This also seems the most likely reason for the location of the Shibusawa estate. From this perspective it should also be noted that the Nishigahara residence acquired by the Furukawa family was conveniently located for traveling from Tokyo to the Ashio copper mine and to mines further afield in the Tōhoku region.

With Mutsu Munemitsu's death in 1897, the Nishigahara residence became the property of the Furukawa family. Furukawa Ichibei, head of the Furukawa family, passed away in 1903. Just two years later in 1905 he was followed in death by his adopted heir, Junkichi, formerly of the Mutsu family. With this, Furukawa Ichibei's biological son Toranosuke became the third head of the family. Toranosuke was born in 1887, married one of

Saigō Jūdō's daughters, and later had Josiah Conder build a Western-style mansion (and Ogawa Jihei landscape a garden) on the Nishigahara property that had come to his family through Junkichi.

The Nishigahara property sits on a south-facing slope suitable for such a large estate. The mansion of Mutsu Munemitsu that previously occupied the site was dismantled and turned over to the politician Nakajima Kumakichi, a member of the Furukawa zaibatsu, who relocated it to Aoyama to use as his residence. That building, however, was lost to fire during the Great Kanto Earthquake. Furukawa Toranosuke had a new vision for the Nishigahara site. He had a building designed by Josiah Conder erected toward the west on its northern, higher side, and a Japanese garden centered on a large pond built on its southern, lower side. It was this lower garden that Ogawa Jihei created. A formal rose garden—the only Conder-designed garden still in existence—was also prepared in front of Conder's building. Because of the difference in elevation, this Western-style garden and Ogawa's Japanese-style garden do not interfere with one another. A gentle slope leads people from the mansion to the rose garden, and as they continue further they reach the Japanese garden below.

This one clearly lacks the horizontal expanse of Ueji's gardens in Kyoto. No doubt this is a result of the shape of the site, but the garden nevertheless forms a world of its own centered on the pond. A large stone bridge spans the pond and a massive "snow-viewing" lantern is visible directly across it. Rather than conforming to the true Ueji style, this composition and use of stone seems more like a concession to reproducing the feel of an Edo period garden; the prominent use of large stone elements such as the bridge and the lantern is reminiscent of daimyo gardens.

Perhaps we should instead see this as a successful effort by Ueji to construct a Japanese-style garden on a Western-style estate, to create an independent world that was unflinching in the face of Josiah Conder's residence and garden. Indeed, this is all the more so because the Furukawa estate has no separate Japanese-style residence. The mansion has a roughly finished exterior of andesite volcanic rock, but its second story has a number of Japanese-style rooms including one for the family Buddhist altar. Conder's effort to incorporate tatami rooms—which he is believed also to have designed—within a building with a Western-style exterior is one of the distinguishing features of the Furukawa residence. Naturally, the rooms have sliding *shōji* doors, but the narrow corridors create a buffer zone to ensure that such Japanese-style fittings are not visible from the outside, achieving compatibility between the Japanese interior and the Western exterior.

The garden-side exterior of the Furukawa residence presents the gabled ends of two roof sections. Its distinctively designed, roughly finished walls are completely covered with andesite volcanic rock that appears to be Komatsu stone from Manazuru, and leaves an impression that some say reminds them of Scotland. Josiah Conder employed a similar exterior for Iwasaki Yanosuke's villa in Hakone-Yumoto. When the British crown prince (the future King Edward VIII, who abdicated to marry Wallis Simpson and became the Duke of Windsor) stayed at this villa in 1922, he is said to have exclaimed that he felt as if he were at Balmoral Castle in Scotland. The Furukawa mansion, too, must have given off the relaxing atmosphere of such a royal estate.

The dual gables facing the garden side of the mansion are a feature commonly seen in half-timbered houses, so at some point Furukawa Toranosuke may have envisioned building a half-timbered house in the style of an English mansion.

With respect to the mansion's relationship to the Japanese garden, a rear gate at the southeast corner of the property opens onto a road that follows its southern and western edges while winding toward the west side of the building. This may appear to be nothing more than a back entrance skirting the edge of the site, but the back gate at the southeast corner is the first point reached when approaching the estate from the city. The atmosphere of the route winding up and down along the property before arriving at the mansion may well have been an important design element intended to enhance the magnificence of the mansion. The Iwasaki Hisaya estate in Hongō Kaya-chō, designed by Josiah Conder, has its main gate at the southeast corner of the property and a road that winds around its east and north edges before arriving at the front of the mansion. It seems likely that the same dramatic approach to welcoming guests was also applied at the Furukawa estate. Providing as long an approach as possible between the main gate and the front entrance was a standard design element for such large estates.

At the Furukawa estate, the road leading from the back gate at the southeast corner passes through groves of trees that prevent the mansion and gardens from being seen, a feature also found at the Iwasaki Hisaya estate. The result is a layout that completely encloses and conceals the Japanese garden. This overall design may have been one reason Ueji opted to create a garden that stands alone rather than one that is more open and expansive. "Borrowed landscape" gardens in Kyoto that maintain continuity with the outside world always incorporate a visual axis that draws the eyes outward, but Edo gardens were both expansive and self-contained. The Japanese-style garden at the Furukawa estate probably aimed for the latter kind of garden, which had characterized those in Tokyo since the Edo period.

What led Ogawa Jihei to undertake the garden at the Furukawa estate is unclear. Toranosuke and his family had moved into the Nishigahara estate and made it their primary residence in 1917. It had been completed two years before then, but Toranosuke's mother had concerns related to Taoist directional divination so they first moved from their original primary residence in Tsukiji to Hongō Masago-chō for about two years before moving to Nishigahara. *Furukawa Toranosuke kun den* (A biography of Furukawa Toranosuke) describes the garden as follows:

Below and to the south of the European-style front garden is a tranquil, tree-enclosed strolling pond garden that incorporates a modern naturalism. A pond has been excavated at its center that is roughly shaped like the Chinese character for "heart" and covers more than 300 tsubo [990 square meters]. Islands built within the pond were provided with bridges, paths were built, vegetation planted, and stones set in place. The garden's design and construction were entrusted to Kyoto landscape gardener Ogawa Jihei, who brought trees and plants such as daisugi *cryptomeria and* sugikoke *moss from Kyoto's Kitayama area.*

Despite the completion of this great estate offering both Japanese and Western charms, in July 1926 the Furukawa family shifted the center of their life to Tokyo's Ushigome-ku Wakamiya-chō and the mansion of Kimura Chōshichi, a leading member of the Furukawa zaibatsu.

The Nishigahara estate came to be used as a kind of official guesthouse. Wang Jingwei lived there for a time, and the estate was also visited by executives from companies such as the Siemens conglomerate of Germany and the Chicago Daily News of the United States. In this way, Ueji's gardens took root in Tokyo, too. The mansion and gardens of the Furukawa estate are still well maintained and open to the public. The Tokyo metropolitan government is responsible for the gardens while the mansion is managed by the Ōtani Museum.

Returning to Iwasaki Koyata, as the last head of the Mitsubishi zaibatsu he was compelled to oversee its dismantling after the end of the Second World War. His primary residence in Toriizaka had been destroyed during the conflict, so he took up residence at the Atami Yōwadō villa and traveled from there to Tokyo by car.

On 21 October 1945, he left Yōwadō for Tokyo and set about his work with great energy. The task before him was addressing the dismantling of the zaibatsu. When busy in Tokyo, he used a storehouse at the Toriizaka estate that had survived the fires as his base and went about his business from there.

Iwasaki met with Kodama Kenji, the head of the Central Liaison Office, on 22 October, with Finance Minister Shibusawa Keizō on the 23rd, and once again with Kodama Kenji on the 24th. He fell ill that evening and took to bed at the Toriizaka storehouse. It was announced at the shareholders meeting that Mitsubishi corporate headquarters would soon be dissolved and that Iwasaki would be resigning as president and from all other managerial posts. A month later, on 2 December, Iwasaki breathed his last at the

Fig. 5-7: The garden of Iwasaki Koyata's primary residence in Toriizaka

University of Tokyo Hospital.

His widow continued to care for Atami Yōwadō and to this day it remains much as it did when it served as Iwasaki Koyata's villa. The primary residence at Toriizaka, on the other hand, after being destroyed by fire during the war, was taken over as state property. Eventually, it became the site of the International House of Japan, a foundation for the promotion of international cultural exchange that was established in 1952 with the support of the Rockefeller Foundation. The current building was erected in 1955, designed as a collaborative project by three architects who would play an important role in post-war Japanese architecture: Maekawa Kunio, Sakakura Junzō, and Yoshimura Junzō. The garden, however, was left just as it had been when part of Iwasaki Koyata's Toriizaka estate (Fig. 5-7). Intended to accompany a Japanese-style residence designed by Ōe Shintarō, the garden was reborn as one accompanying a building in the International Style. Although somewhat smaller than it had been originally, this stream garden with an open foreground continued to provide an attractive setting for the new structure. Gardens, perhaps, have longer lives than buildings.

With the passage of time and the advent of the twenty-first century, the building's age and inefficiency became an issue. After a great deal of debate about whether to remodel or rebuild, the building ultimately underwent major renovations in 2005. As work progressed it was discovered that the 1955 building had been designed to incorporate the concrete underground portion of Iwasaki Koyata's residence. Rather than demolishing this sturdy concrete structure, it had been reused. It seems that not only the garden but also an unseen portion of the original building had survived.

This led to the decision to ensure seismic resistance for the new building by reinforcing the original concrete structure rather than replacing it with a new seismically isolated structure. The new building was extended at the front, adding a large room named the Iwasaki Koyata Memorial Hall. In this way, Ueji's garden, the original building, and the memory of its former master have all been preserved for posterity.

CHAPTER SIX

On the Creativity of *Sukisha* Connoisseurs

The Design and Construction Organization of Ogawa Jihei VII

Although he seems to have been a dominant force in the realm of land-scape gardening in Japan, what kind of presence was Ogawa Jihei? It is difficult to imagine him as an individualistic, all-around genius, yet neither was he a tradesman who merely followed orders.

We can approach him, I think, both as an individual working in the realm of gardens, and as the leader of an organization during a period of transition between the early modern and the modern. In this chapter, I would like to discuss these aspects of Ogawa Jihei more fully.

Because Ogawa Jihei was involved in the most private worlds of his clients, even as a hired tradesman he played a role in staging and enabling their social styles. That he achieved so much was because he was liked by Yamagata Aritomo, Sumitomo Kichizaemon Tomoito, Saionji Kinmochi, Ōhara Magosaburō, and other powerful clients who built modern Japan.

As Niwa Keisuke recalled when describing Ogawa as "adaptable":

> *It sounds odd to say, but he was a man with a knack for associating with respectable people. Most gardeners scurry around in their livery coats but he had a friendly, heart-to-heart way of speaking and listening and a real ability to interact with Prince Saionji and with gentlemen like Yamagata and Iwasaki. And, well, not being especially vulgar of manner, he earned their confidence and became a success.* [From *Ogawa Jihei*]

The head priest of Kōun-ji temple said that Saionji Kinmochi, during his stays in Kyoto, really only let his guard down with Naitō Konan, Ueji, and Nishikawa Issōtei.

There were, between the Meiji period and the pre-war Showa years, a number of such partnerships between *sukisha* connoisseurs and their gardeners or the carpenters who constructed *sukiya* style buildings for them. For example, Shibusawa Eiichi, founder of institutions such as the First National Bank, had an enormous residence at Asukayama in Tokyo designed in the Japanese style by *sukiya* carpenter Kashiwagi Kaichirō (art name: Tankosai); the Mitsubishi zaibatsu's Iwasaki family employed Okamoto Harumichi, who might best be considered an instructor in the *sukiya* style; the Sumitomo had *sukiya* carpenter Yagi Jinbei; and, more recently, in addition to *sukiya* carpenter Ōgi Keiichirō (art name: Rodō), the Mitsui family also had Takahashi Yoshio (art name: Sōan) serve as a spokesman for Japanese culture in modern times. All of these men were capable of interacting on the same level with their connoisseur patrons and possessed the technical skills to actually construct *sukiya* buildings.

Backed by their literacy in the culture of early modern Japan, these men created expressions of Japanese style for the zaibatsu, capitalists, and politicians who were then growing in power as modern patrons. What enabled them to face their patrons as equals was that the expressions the modern patrons sought were Japanese in style and rooted in the early modern period or before. Put another way, it was because the patrons approached the world of *sukiya* carpenters fully prepared to entrust their own cultural expression to them. In this we see the essence of private cultural expression as sought by modern Japan.

Many of the powerful figures that became patrons of culture beginning in the Meiji period came to their positions by applying modern knowledge—that is, "Western learning"—within the systems of the modern nation state. With the exception of Sumitomo Tomoito and Saionji Kinmochi, most such patrons, judging by their origins, had nothing to boast of in terms of their knowledge of or fluency with the culture of early modern Japan or before.

Given that the ideology of "Japanese spirit and Western learning" was about the only means of dealing with the identity crisis into which both modern Japan and the powerful figures who sustained it were at risk of falling, it stands to reason that when they sought to establish their own cultural identity they would seek to grasp at something rooted in the culture of Japan from the early modern period and before. *Sukiya* carpenters, tea ceremony masters, landscape gardeners, and in some cases Noh performers were like gatekeepers who held the keys that would open the doors to the treasure house of cultural expression that the powerful needed. In the presence of these gatekeepers, they were able to set aside their roles as high-ranking officials in the Meiji government or as zaibatsu executives and carry themselves instead like feudal lords or patrons. It was a lifestyle perfectly in keeping with the way they dressed in Western clothing for their public roles but changed into Japanese clothing upon returning to their private residences.

For their part, in dealing with their patrons, did the *sukiya* carpenters, tea ceremony masters, and landscape gardeners, then, rely solely on their knowledge of and fluency with the culture of early modern Japan and before? Not at all; they were working through the process of modernization in their own domains even as they constructed a context for the cultural expression of their patrons. Conversely, it was only those individuals among the *sukiya* carpenters, tea ceremony masters, and landscape gardeners that were capable of such modernization who managed to survive. The course of landscape gardener Ogawa Jihei's style and work shows what a modern sensibility he possessed. In the same way, the *sukiya* carpenters offered the "tradition" demanded by the new "modern" age. With the authority to embody tradition, they could invest it with enough newness to make the traditional an expression of the modern.

"Ogawa Jihei" was both an individual and a team, a kind of creative collective; in Yamane Tokutarō's *Ogawa Jihei*, the head priest of Kōun-ji temple is quoted as saying that Ueji "oversaw a great number of eminent people, including masters of stone arrangement and experts in the planting of trees, who contributed greatly to the construction of Ueji's gardens." His team "at one time seems to have numbered about a hundred and fifty, including those with reputations of their own as landscape gardeners. To be able to manage such people well is a special skill; merely understanding gardens or being able to draft a plan is not enough."

As I have occasionally mentioned before, Ogawa Jihei's eldest son Yasutarō went by the name Hakuyō and was expected to carry on after his father. Niwa Keisuke described him as follows:

In collecting materials, I also learned about his son Ogawa Hakuyō. He was a bit of a hobbyist and had a taste for the archeological; in gathering old trees and stones from here and there and keeping them at hand in order to use them in appropriate spots, he behaved much like his father. In this way he was expanding beyond the style of those of old who pursued some typical Kyoto elegance. He was one of the first to employ old stone lanterns and standing stones in the creation of park-like gardens. Ogawa, then, was consulted about creating large gardens not only in Kyoto but also in Tokyo, Shikoku, and the Kansai area, enabling him to cultivate many men of strength and talent among his subordinates. [From Ogawa Jihei]

The current Ogawa Jihei XI—four generations removed from Ogawa Jihei VII—has noted the following points concerning Hakuyō: He liked photography and compiled *Keika rinsen-chō* (Notebook of gardens of Kyoto), a collection of photographs of celebrated gardens. He conducted research on items such as old roof tiles, stone lanterns, and illustrated hand scrolls. He founded Kansai Dōgu, a club made up of tool shops in Gion, and through it engaged in trade. He also enjoyed hobbies such as billiards and golf.

While the above conjures an image of a next-generation successor with a modern sensibility, Hakuyō would pre-decease his father, passing away in 1926 at the age of just 45 (Fig. 6-1). Even after losing its next-in-line, the band of landscape gardeners centered on Ogawa Jihei appears to have proudly maintained its cohesion as a group until his death.

Fig. 6-1: (L) The graves of Ogawa Jihei and Hakuyō (Bukkō-ji temple); (R) The graveyard's stone pillar was donated by Ogawa Jihei

Ogawa Jihei includes a description of Ueji's organization by Kotani Kiichi, who was responsible under Ueji for projects such as working at the home of Yamane Tokutarō, as it was around 1933, the final year of Ogawa's life. In essence, the organization consisted of three tiers of tradesmen:

- Nibiki-kai: An association of those who learned the trade from Ueji beginning at an early age as live-in apprentices and later struck out on their own.
- Shinboku-kai: An association of those in positions of responsibility who were permitted to visit clients wearing livery coats emblazoned with the trade name "Ueji."
- Shingi-kai: Members of this group could be selected by the Nibiki-kai to become members of the Shinboku-kai.

This introduction is followed by a list of eighty-nine "people who were active at the time (in no particular order)." Heading a group of nearly a hundred tradesmen in a landscape gardening enterprise with national scope during the early years of the Showa period, Ogawa Jihei VII occupied a transitional stage, or an intermediate organizational form, between the way of early modern *sukiya* carpenters, tea ceremony masters, or landscape gardeners and that of a modern group of skilled professionals.

199

Depending on the garden, Ogawa Jihei's son Hakuyō, nephew Ogawa Kazuo, or nephew Iwaki Sentarō might have actually made the trip, but all the projects done while Ogawa Jihei was alive should be seen as work for which he was responsible. I repeat myself, but the work of a landscape gardener, unlike that of a painter or sculptor, is the product of a collective, of a group of skilled tradesmen. To such work we attach the name Ogawa Jihei.

Nakahara Tessen drafted cloisonné designs for Namikawa Yasuyuki, who lived and maintained a workshop adjacent to Ogawa Jihei, and is also known to have provided drawings of gardens for Ueji, but this probably was not indicative of a move toward a modern system of integrated design and construction. Nakahara was an artisan who appears to have served as Namikawa's right-hand man, acting as a kind of concertmaster who managed Namikawa's workshop. Nakahara's designs took into account the silver outlines characteristic of wired cloisonné, and are said to have been ready to use in production just as they were. His drawings for Ueji were no doubt done on the same terms—that is, with some understanding of the technical limitations of landscape gardening—yet his involvement seems to have been based on an artisanal interest rather than a division of labor.

When Kyoto University carried out an architectural survey of Seifū-sō, the former villa of Saionji Kinmochi, they used related historical documents in the collection of the Sumitomo Historical Archives to analyze how the tradesmen working under Ogawa Jihei were involved in creating the villa's garden. At Seifū-sō, Ueji was responsible not only for the garden but also for construction of the inner gates (for this he introduced *sukiya* carpenter Kōsaka Asajirō, who worked regularly for the Tokudaiji family) and the relocation of existing structures.

For creation of the garden, workers specializing in planting, earthwork, and rockwork, as well as those hired to clean and weed, were permitted to come and go; all are thought to have been involved under Ueji's direction. From October to mid-December 1912 there were roughly six planting gardeners working on site per day performing both routine garden maintenance as well as landscaping improvements attendant to construction of the main residence. New planting and other garden renovations appear to have begun in earnest later, with the number of workers coming and going gradually increasing to a peak of 19 working on site on 22 March 1913. The number of gardeners then decreased, falling to about two per day by July of that year, so renovations to the garden had probably been completed by then. Through October of that year there were two to four gardeners on site, presumably the number needed for everyday tending of the garden.

As for workers specializing in earthwork, there were about five on site per day from mid-September through mid-December 1912, which then increased to about seven between mid-December and February of the following year, then decreased again to about one from late April through the end of the year. The number of earthwork specialists rose and fell roughly in line with the planting specialists, but peaked a little bit earlier.

Four rockwork specialists were on site per day from October through December 1912, which suggests that this is when garden rocks were moved and set.

There were also laborers hired to clean the garden (women) and pull weeds, with as many as six working on site per day. On average, though, there were usually only about two, probably engaged in everyday cleaning and tending of the garden.

It was Ogawa Jihei who had overall responsibility for procuring and managing these workers, who were not only engaged in landscaping but also in constructing *sukiya* structures and relocating buildings. Ueji is also known to have provided assistance in site acquisition and the managing of rentals, and to have been in a position to contact the main Sumitomo family directly. More than a specialized subcontractor, he made comprehensive arrangements related to the whole of *sukiya* construction. Nevertheless, this position appears to have been founded on his personal relationship with the head of the Sumitomo family, Sumitomo Shunsui, rather than on a modern business model such as that of a general contractor or an agent for asset management.

Ultimately, the Ueji organization remained intermediate in form, never developing into a modern group of skilled professionals—a consequence, perhaps, of Hakuyō's premature death. It was Ogawa Jihei's nephew Iwaki

Sentarō who would transition to form a modern group of skilled professionals during the next generation. While apprenticed to his uncle, Iwaki had been responsible for the garden at Yōwadō (the Atami villa of Iwasaki Koyata) as well as some of the many gardens that Nagao Kin'ya had created in the Tokyo area. After the war, he struck out on his own. Iwaki said that he had learned how to combine rocks in waterfalls by walking the 48 waterfalls of Akame, a famous scenic spot in the Kinki region, in his youth. After the war he established a modern landscaping business by building great gardens and golf courses using heavy machinery and by creating rooftop gardens. In learning how to arrange rocks for waterfalls by studying those in Akame, Iwaki was creating natural waterfalls rather than symbolic ones, and in this he followed the course set by Ueji.

Still, it is because Ogawa Jihei went no further than an intermediate form of organization that his work was able to continue to protect the private world of his patrons. In fact, this organizational form—intermediate between the early modern and the modern—seems often to have appeared during the budding phase of the process of modernization. It may seem the polar opposite of the world of *sukiya* carpenters, tea ceremony masters, and landscape gardeners, but Josiah Conder, the foreign advisor who brought Western architecture to Japan, is known to have directly managed his architectural design and construction projects in a similar manner, personally directing a group of tradesmen.

The father of Atsuta Yūharu, renowned master cameramen under movie director Ozu Yasujirō, was apparently a member of the group of tradesmen led by Josiah Conder, as described in the following recollection: "Back then [at the end of the Meiji period when Atsuta was born] there was this British fellow named Conder who taught Western-style architecture. He did all the big mansions for families like the Iwasakis and the Shimazus, and formed a members-only group called the Conder Society. My father became a member and worked as a plumber." [From *Ozu Yasujirō monogatari* (The Ozu Yasujirō story)]

Here we have an organization of tradesmen designed for accomplishment in the world of architecture, a genre unlike artistic pursuits that have individual creators. Conder never moved beyond this to form a modern group of skilled professionals. He was not seeking to found a general contracting business. Instead, an intermediate form of organization, one that was not a modern group of skilled professionals, better served to realize his vision—he needed a team of craftsmen to make what he imagined real.

Ōe Shintarō, an architect who worked with Ogawa Jihei, is said to have had an organization called the Kōryū-kai that was made up of tradesmen who were drawn to his skills, while architect Murano Tōgo, who brought a rich variety of architectural expression to the world of post-war Japanese architecture, also had groups of tradesmen and subcontractors with whom he worked. For Ogawa Jihei, too, it was only because he had such a group working for him that he was able to achieve the massive gardens demanded by an age that was rushing headlong into the modern. The Ogawa Jihei of this period should probably be considered a collective designed to realize an individual vision, one that could have only have emerged in a society on the cusp of modernity.

General Producer Ōgi Rodō

I would like to introduce one other person who is indicative of this kind of approach: Ōgi Rodō (given name: Ōgi Keiichirō). Born in what is now Fukuoka Prefecture in 1863, he was involved in many *sukiya* construction projects up to the time of his death in 1941 at the age of 79. I will present an overview of Rodō's work as described in *Sōkyoan ki* (A record of Sōkyo-an), the memoirs of Fujii Kisaburō, who studied under Rodō as manager of his office. Rodō seems to have established a residence in Kyōbashi-ku Minami-saya-chō in 1902 and gotten involved in *sukiya* work using *sukiya* carpenters such as Suzuki Jinzō and his father Mokichi. He established Ōgi Architectural Office in 1907 and began engaging in *sukiya* construction in earnest.

In *Sōkyoan ki*, Fujii Kisaburō writes that he assumed the post of manager at Rodō's office in 1937, the year of its thirtieth anniversary. He recalled, "What put Ōgi Rodō's name on the map as a *sukiya* architect was the completion of a villa in Kazamatsuri on the outskirts of Odawara in 1911 for Mr. Nakano, who made his fortune in oil. The establishment of Mr. Masuda's Sōundai villa in Odawara in 1906, and Mr. Yamagata's Koki-an in 1907, had started a trend among those in the business world for second homes in Odawara."

The "Mr. Nakano" referred to here is Nakano Kan'ichi, who mined for oil at Kanazu in Niigata and became known as the "Oil King." Nakano had an uncommon passion for architecture. His main residence in Niigata is now open to the public as the Nakano House Art Museum and for a time he owned a residence in Tokyo—a nationally designated important cultural property nicknamed the Copper Mansion—that he obtained from Isono Kei, who had entrusted its construction to Kitami Yonezō, a young, 21-year old master carpenter. A three-story, wood-framed building, it got its nickname because its roofs and exterior walls were completely covered with copper sheeting.

The Copper Mansion later came into the possession of Ōtani Teppei, the son of Ōtani Yonetarō, founder of Ōtani Heavy Industries, and is now owned by the Ōtani Museum. This museum, by the way, is also known for owning the residence of Furukawa Toranosuke, which was designed by Josiah Conder with gardens landscaped by Ogawa Jihei. The worlds of *sukisha* connoisseurs and the wealthy were tied together by many layers of intersecting strands.

As described in *Sōkyoan ki* (A record of Sōkyo-an), there was an imperial villa in Odawara at the time as well as massive villas owned by Masuda Takashi (art name: Donō) and Yamagata Aritomo. The area had also become home to a throng of second homes for many other powerful figures such as Ōkura Kihachirō (art name: Tsuruhiko), Uryū Sotokichi (a naval admiral and the brother-in-law of Masuda Takashi), and Nozaki Kōta. For Ōgi Rodō, Odawara, where he built a villa for Nakano Kan'ichi, was surely an incomparable stage for demonstrating what he was capable of.

Ōgi Rodō was deeply involved in fostering an interest in the tea ceremony among Mitsui-affiliated business executives such as Dan Takuma (art name: Rizan), Masuda Don'ō, and Takahashi Sōan, to whom he was introduced by Chōshū native Sugi Magoshichirō. It was Sugi's patronage that led to the later broadening of Ōgi's activities. Sugi was friendly with Inoue Kaoru, another Chōshū native who was said to be Mitsui's protector; Sugi played the role of intermediary between the two. Dan and Rodō also shared common ground in that both were originally from Fukuoka.

Ōgi Rodō is known for having built numerous tea ceremony rooms at Gokoku-ji temple in Tokyo's Otowa neighborhood. Takahashi Sōan from Mitsui, who was something of a spokesman for the *sukisha* connoisseurs of the early Showa period, served as the temple's parishioner representative and sought to revive its fortunes through the way of tea. Ōgi also had the Gekkō-den reception hall relocated to Gokoku-ji and constructed a *tahōtō* pagoda. In later years he also enjoyed friendly relations with figures such as Hara Tomitarō (art name: Sankei) of Yokohama and Matsunaga Yasuzaemon (art name: Jian). Most of the large residences that he built in central Tokyo have been lost to redevelopment, but his tea ceremony rooms can be seen at sites including Gokoku-ji in Otowa, Kōrin-in temple in Hiroo, and Gōra Park in Hakone.

Said to have been skilled in architecture, landscaping, evaluating utensils, and making arrangements for tea ceremonies, Ōgi Rodō was not so much an artisan schooled in one particular skill as a producer who created a comprehensive world of *suki* connoisseurship.

Sōkyoan ki (A record of Sōkyo-an) describes Ōgi Rodō's approach to his work as follows:

Ōgi was particularly strict about kiwari [the system of proportional relationships among different elements]. *He always said, "Kiwari isn't something that can be conveyed in words, or through notation in plans" and insisted on directing things himself. During a project's final stretch, he would have tatami mats laid out on the unfinished building site and calculate the dimensions of the details based on how things looked from eye level when sitting on the tatami. There were no set rules or theories to this method; the measurements always varied slightly case by case.*

In *Ogawa Jihei*, the head priest of Shōzō-in temple describes the work of Ogawa Jihei in similar terms:

> *He carried himself like a master, always dressed in serge* hakama *trousers and a* haori *coat of pongee with a simple family crest. When landscaping the entrance at my place, he suggested planting a single pine, then sat with my mother and father on the veranda watching his apprentices plant the tree. Suddenly he said, "That's not very appealing" and joined right in with the planting despite his* haori *and* hakama. *I can remember my parents saying, "Such a strange man. I guess that's the mark of a master."*

Ōgi Rodō and Ueji shared a concrete grasp of both the broad view and the fine details, based on which they gave specific direction. Neither was a craftsman limited to a single domain; each occupied a more holistic position. Both attracted many groups of tradesmen and tied them together with clients. Incidentally, Kitami Yonezō, master carpenter for the Copper Mansion of Nakano Kan'ichi, who gave Rodō his first work in Odawara, later transformed himself from carpenter to tea ceremony master. He, too, would go on to become a general producer in the realm of *suki* connoisseurship.

On the grounds of Gokoku-ji temple quietly stands a stone monument erected to Ōgi Rodō in 1928, one of natural Tsukuba stone inscribed with the name Rodō in calligraphy attributed to "Ryōkō the Seeker."

Adjacent to this monument, just behind it on the left, is a smaller stone inscribed with the words and names of tradesmen from many occupations who supported Rodō in his work as a general producer of *sukiya*-style buildings and who had the monument erected (Fig. 6-2).

Looking at this list makes clear that Ōgi Rodō, too, was surrounded by a group of tradesmen covering fields as diverse as construction, landscaping, and handicraft. Incidentally, the Ōgi Seisai listed among the special supporters was Rodō's younger brother, a sculptor who was appointed as an Imperial Household Artist. The list also mentions ceramicist Ōno Donna, who produced tea bowls called *Donna-yaki* under Masuda Takashi, the president of Mitsui. That the list also includes occupations such as tinsmith, tiler, Western furniture dealer, and construction hardware dealer teaches us that Rodō worked in a realm of eclectic *sukiya* construction that might best be described as a modern Japanese style.

To understand the nature of Ogawa Jihei VII, it seemed necessary to mention in this way the scope and breadth of the worlds of the *sukiya* style and the construction industry.

[Front Face]
Rodō, whose family name is Ōgi and given name is Keiichirō, was born in northern Chikuzen. He made architecture his life's work. Having profound knowledge of this country's ancient architecture and a particular mastery of the essence of landscape gardening, he is truly adept at applying these in modern ways. With a warm disposition and a love for people, his influence over the many who have worked for him during more than two decades has been ↗

	Ajioka Yūnosuke	Tokita Yasugorō
Proposers and Organizers	Shimizu Tetsutarō	Hayashi Jōtarō
	Yamamoto Teiji	Minohara Zenjirō

[West Face]
Ōgi Architectural Office
Ōgi-kai

Roof Tiler	Ajioka Yūnosuke
Paper Hanger	Shimizu Tetsutarō
Tatami Maker	Tokita Yasugorō
Plumbing Contractor	Yamamoto Teiji
Joiner	Fujii Shigeru
Electrical Contractor	Tsuchiya Kazuyoshi

[**North Face**]

Concrete Work	Hayashi Jōtarō
Plasterer	Otaka Mataichirō
Plasterer	Kawase Eijirō
Lumber Dealer	Hotta Kintarō
Lumber Dealer	Itō Yasokichi
Plant Buyer	Yanagita Tokutarō
Gardener	Iida Yasohachi
Stonemason	Satō Shigeru
Landscaper	Sekino Rinzō
Landscaper	Sekino Saiichi
Tinsmith	Monna Okuzō
Joiner	Minamitani Kumakichi
Sawyer	Kamata Manzō
Electrical Contractor	Kurokawa Giichirō
Garden Stones	Suzuki Susumu

Register of Special Supporters

Artisan	Ōgi Seisai

[**East Face**]

Painter	Ino Seishin
Ceramicist	Ōno Donna
Lacquer Painter	Watanabe Zenzaburō
Lacquer Painter	Ikushima Tōgo
Western Furniture	Terao Mon
Construction Hardware Dealer	Tanaka Kashichi
Construction Hardware Dealer	Yoshikawa Risaburō
Scaffolding Foreman	Uchida Rinzō

Fig. 6-2: Text of the inscription on the monument to Ōgi Rodō at Gokoku-ji temple

that of a loving father attending to his children. Taking the opportunity provided by the conclusion of the relocation of the Gekkō-den during the same auspicious month as the Emperor's enthronement, we came together and discussed erecting, in modest tribute, a monument made of the Tsukuba stone of which he is so fond, asking Bishop Ryōkō to provide the exquisite calligraphy for which we express our gratitude.

Erected November 1928

Register of Supporters

Ōgi Architectural Office	Minohara Zenjirō
Ōgi Architectural Office	Ōshiba Kisō
Ōgi Architectural Office	Kawanishi Mankichi
Ōgi Architectural Office Master Carpenter	Honma Umezō
Ōgi Architectural Office Master Carpenter	Furukawa Tsunekichi
Ōgi Architectural Office Master Carpenter	Sakatsume Kiyomatsu

Ōgi Architectural Office Leader	Kobayashi Genroku
Carpenter	Harada Shichisaburō
Carpenter	Honma Gonbei
Carpenter	Kobayashi Sakuhei
Carpenter	Konishi Gisaburō
Carpenter	Komiyama Tamisaburō
Carpenter	Matsuda ■ichi
Carpenter	Ogiwara Sōzō
Carpenter	Den Chikashi
Carpenter	Suehiro Seinosuke
Carpenter	Tashiro Shōsaku
Carpenter	Tashiro Gengo
Carpenter	Honda Chōzaburō
Carpenter	Igarashi Kōkichi

Scaffolding Foreman	Fukui Yasugorō

Lumber Dealer	Itō Kōichi
Bathtub Maker	Tsuruoka Denbei
Polisher	Uemura Sentarō
Artificial Tile Setter	Hosoya Kiyoshi
Mover	Tsuchiya Ichirō
Tatami Maker	Hirose Fukujirō
Garden Stones	Nakazawa Rokunosuke
Roofer	Mizuno Heijirō

Chapter Seven

The Last Patron

Nagao Kin'ya

In Ogawa Jihei's later years, a patron appeared who might, in a sense, number among his greatest. Nagao Kin'ya was the purveyor of a medicine known as Wakamoto tablets. Marketed using Chinese characters meaning "source of youth," these yeast tablets made from beer lees were both a nutritional supplement and a medication for the prevention of gastrointestinal disorders. Nagao is said to have begun producing the tablets in 1929 with thirteen hired female workers in the kitchen at Jōun-ji temple next to the Shiba Daimon gate in Tokyo. His company was energetic in promoting its product, advertised in the magazine *Fujin kurabu* (Women's club), and rapidly expanded throughout the national market. In 1931, the orthography of the product name was changed so that the word was purely phonetic. Wakamoto's popularity was also fueled by the various services offered to customers by Nagao's company, the Wakamoto Honpo Society for Nutrition and Raising Children.

The year after Wakamoto began production, Nagao Kin'ya established a 500-*tsubo* [1,650-square-meter] residence in the Sakura Shinmachi area of Tokyo's Setagaya ward. Over the course of a series of subsequent expansions, it grew into an enormous residential estate covering nearly 8,000 *tsubo* [26,400 square meters].

Nagao Kin'ya was born in 1892 in the Iba area of Yubune village in Kyoto Prefecture's Sōraku district. After profiting handily by making both a new

211

whitening cream for the treatment of acne and by manufacturing aspirin, he was nearly ruined by the panic of 1920. The enormous success of Wakamoto, however, instantly turned him into a member of the nouveau riche.

Not only was Wakamoto a strong seller before the war, it continued to sell well in the post-war period as Kyōryoku Wakamoto [Strong Wakamoto] after passing from the hands of Nagao and his wife. An advertisement combining the words Kyōryoku Wakamoto in Japanese with a woman's face is one of the enigmatic images that appeared in Ridley Scott's 1982 movie *Blade Runner* as part of his vision of a Japan-like future circa 2020. *Blade Runner* continues to have a strong following as a near-future film filled with mysterious imagery, but what does it mean for Kyōryoku Wakamoto to have appeared in the film? Japanese fans interpreted the appearance in a variety of ways. People apparently even passed out packets of Kyōryoku Wakamoto at screenings of the film. Wakamoto's iconic status can be felt in the way it shows up in such odd places. The use of Kyōryoku Wakamoto was, of course, probably no more than an arbitrary choice of images made by someone who was not Japanese.

Nagao Kin'ya's wife was named Nagao Yone. Born in 1889 in Asakusa's Umamichi-chō neighborhood, she was two years Kin'ya's senior, but much about her background remains a mystery. Tanaka Mitsuaki, a patriot of the Restoration who came to occupy a position of authority in the Meiji government, later acknowledged Yone as his daughter, but the truth of that claim is unknown. Yone was born when her mother Shika was 35 and Tanaka Mitsuaki was 47. At the age of 15, she moved to Kyoto with her uncle Yaokichi, a paperhanger, and at the age of 18 is said to have opened up a teahouse in Gion. Almost immediately, however, she eloped with Kawada Matajirō, a graduate of the Department of Civil Engineering in the Faculty of Engineering at Tokyo Imperial University, and returned to Tokyo.

Kawada Matajirō is supposed to have had a substantial income from his civil engineering work, but Yone had a poor head for money and they apparently found it difficult to make ends meet. Kawada appears to have introduced Kin'ya to Yone around 1926. At the time, Nagao was involved in various pharmaceutical businesses as noted above. Together with Kawada and Nagao, Yone rented a house in Den'en Chōfu and the three began a curious life together.

In December 1929, the year Wakamoto was launched, Yone divorced Kawada Matajirō. This did not, however, end their relationship and Kawada remained involved in managing the company. Nagao Kin'ya and Yone, meanwhile, registered their marriage in December 1933. Oddly, the relationship between Nagao, Yone, and Kawada continued even after such changes. Our primary interest, however, lies not in analyzing their psychodrama but rather in how the Nagaos ended up asking Ogawa Jihei to landscape their gardens.

Those among Ueji's patrons who we have seen so far sought to pour the wealth acquired through their success into gardens as a way to inject the richness of their public lives into their own private worlds as well. These gardens, however, were also charged to play roles in the activities of their patrons' public worlds, as political gardens, as places for the private discussion of financial matters, or as palatial guesthouses for crowning moments in their lives.

By creating a succession of Ueji gardens, the Nagaos prepared a stage for history. By inviting so many performers to walk across that stage, they hoped to see history played out before them. There is little doubt that it was Nagao Yone, said to have had a big-sisterly disposition, who urged the performance forward. In this, their personal drama seems to have advanced together with the path of history.

The primary residence in Sakura Shinmachi was developed by architect Ōe Shintarō and landscape gardener Ogawa Jihei. A graduate of Tokyo Imperial University who had been involved in repairs to the Nikkō Tōshōgū shrine, Ōe was thoroughly versed in traditional architecture. Among his work with Ogawa Jihei that we have already seen, the primary residence of Iwasaki Koyata at Toriizaka in Tokyo's Azabu neighborhood is a well-known example.

In addition to their primary residence at Sakura Shinmachi, the Nagaos would also go on to maintain second homes at Kamakurayama in Kamakura and at Karasaki on the shores of Lake Biwa in Shiga Prefecture. Ogawa Jihei was responsible for the gardens at all three sites. At Sakura Shinmachi, it was Ueji's nephew Iwaki Sentarō who actually engaged in the landscaping on the ground. Iwaki had taken part in the construction of the garden at Nomura Tokuan's Hekiun-sō in Kyoto and was involved in all of the gardens for the Nagao family. As the scope of the business expanded, the work of Ogawa Jihei came to be taken over by his son Hakuyō and his nephew Iwaki.

According to interviews I conducted with Iwaki Sentarō, Ueji's head gardener was Otani Eitarō while Takeshima Manjirō was a regular on Sumitomo projects, Kuroda Hisakichi and Suwa Shunkichi were active in Okayama, and Doi Tatsuo handled things in Fushimi. Inoue Masaharu, meanwhile, participated in work on the Nagao villa at Karasaki. In this way, many gardeners came together beneath the Ueji banner.

The primary Nagao residence at Sakura Shinmachi became known as Kōden-sō, the villa at Kamakurayama as Senko Sansō, and the villa at Karasaki in Shiga Prefecture as Rinshō-en. Some say Kōden-sō was actually called Giu-sō, but the name Kōden-sō follows the testimony of Iwaki Sentarō. According to Iwaki, the Nagao gardens were known among the workers by nicknames that played on near homonyms, as in "someone's on their deathbed (*rinjū*) so we'd best take a monetary offering (*kōden*) and light some incense (*senkō*)." This episode seems to lend credibility to the notion that the name of the residence was Kōden-sō. Where, though, did Nagao Kin'ya get the financial resources to continue to build such large residences and magnificent villas in rapid succession between 1931 and 1934?

Clearly these activities were sustained by the explosive sales of Wakamoto, but what was behind the political influence, or perhaps the conscious political patronage, that also derived from this wealth?

Author Tsutsui Yasutaka wrote a book titled *Wakamoto no chie* (The wisdom of Wakamoto) in 2001 that he says was based on *Oboete oku to isshō toku suru chōhō hiketsu ehon* (A picture book of useful tricks that will serve you well for life), published in 1938 by the Wakamoto Honpo Society for Nutrition and Raising Children. Around that time, Wakamoto published ten or so such booklets in its *Wakamoto monoshiri ehon shirīzu*

(Wakamoto picture books of knowledge series), which included militaristic titles such as *Rikugun monoshiri ehon* (Army picture book of knowledge), *Kaigun monoshiri ehon* (Navy picture book of knowledge), *Nippon yakushin ehon* (Picture book of Japan's remarkable progress), *Shōgakusei kokoroe ehon* (Picture book of rules for elementary school students) as well as *Chiri monoshiri ehon* (Geography picture book of knowledge), *Kioku uta ehon* (Picture book of mnemonic songs), and *Shukō asobi ehon* (Picture book of handicraft play), all of which Tsutsui notes are filled with content that would have been popular at the times. More than just a nutritional supplement for children, Wakamoto was also a vehicle for distributing the era's propaganda. Indeed, deliveries of Wakamoto tablets to the military increased when Japan invaded the Asian mainland. Nagao Kin'ya spared no effort in his cooperation with the military, even donating fighter planes.

After the war, Sugawara Tsūsai recorded the following recollection, which seems germane:

Later—and fortunately things misfired—Nagao Kin'ya, the manufacturer of Wakamoto, tried to take advantage of my ignorance of such matters and work through me to get permission to purchase opium. The first time, [...] he took the opportunity of a visit to my home in Kamakura by Ashida Hitoshi, who was minister of welfare in the Shidehara Cabinet, to come over from next door and try and ingratiate himself to Ashida and find a way to obtain permission to import opium.

I didn't know anything about it and was surprised to hear him recite such enormous figures, saying he would provide tens of millions or even hundreds of millions in campaign funds. I did some investigating and learned that adding opium to Wakamoto would make it addictive and make it as effective as Jintan so I turned him down, though not on any particular humanitarian grounds.

I think Nagao was looking to opium as a way to apply to the post-war period his previous experience ingratiating himself to military authorities, getting them hooked on Wakamoto, and making a fortune. [From Tsūsai jiden (The autobiography of Tsūsai)]

A supplementary note marks this as written in 1952, and the events described appear to have happened after the Second World War. On the whole, the account feels unreliable and probably is closest to a simple rumor. In his later years, Sugawara Tsūsai campaigned to "drive out the three evils"—that is, for the eradication of drugs, prostitution, and venereal disease—but spreading such tales makes them seem patently dubious. Still, Ashida lived in the Kamakurayama residential area that Sugawara had developed, and Nagao Kin'ya's Senko Sansō villa was also in Kamakurayama, so the part about Nagao being "next door" is based in fact.

Nagao Kin'ya certainly expanded his business during the early Showa period by cultivating relationships with politicians and soldiers. At the end of the Showa period, long after Senko Sansō had passed from the hands of the Nagao family, I saw for myself that it still displayed framed calligraphy by Admiral of the Fleet Nagano Osami. Nagao Kin'ya was a politically connected businessman whose business grew through deep ties to the military as Japan invaded the continent. Such is the man who appeared as Ogawa Jihei's final patron.

Although Kōden-sō, the primary residence of Nagao Kin'ya in Sakura Shinmachi, has been lost, maps and other sources indicate that it had a vast garden with a large pond. *Nihon no teien* (*A Secret of Japanese Gardens*), published by Iwanami Shashin Bunko, contains three photographs showing parts of the garden at the Nagao residence; these suggest that it incorporated numerous small bridges of varying design. The book also explains that, "the stream at the Nagao residence is only run when needed." My interviews with Iwaki Sentarō also confirm that the water in the pond was adjusted through the opening and closing of a water faucet.

Located in Tokyo's suburban Sakura Shinmachi area, Nagao Kin'ya's primary residence Kōden-sō was ill-suited for incorporating an external "borrowed landscape." The garden was an open one, with a pond and lawn, but made up a self-contained world that presumably served as a place for garden parties and other gatherings (Fig. 7-1).

Today, much of the site is occupied by the Tokyo Metropolitan Fuka-

Fig. 7-1: The garden at Kōden-sō, the primary residence of Nagao Kin'ya in Sakura Shinmachi

sawa Senior High School. The campus still contains a building called Sei-mei-tei that was part of the residence at Kōden-sō and is known to have been designed by Ōe Shintarō. Apparently, this detached annex held the bedroom and other private spaces used by Nagao Kin'ya and his wife Yone. Part of the structure is raised on a platform of steel-reinforced concrete. Ōe frequently employed this method, including at the primary residence of Iwasaki Koyata at Toriizaka and, as we will see later, at Nagao's Senko Sansō villa at Kamakurayama.

Looking at the layout of the property as reconstructed from remaining photographs and from interviews, both Seimei-tei and the main residence seem to have been located some distance from the pond, which suggests the importance placed on the lawn. A pavilion called Eiki-tei was located on the shore of the pond at the north corner of the property (Fig. 7-2).

Kōden-sō still existed for a while after the end of the Second World War, and there is a story about John D. Rockefeller III praising its garden during a visit to Japan. The dates are unclear, but Rockefeller, who support-ed the project to transform the former site of Iwasaki Koyata's primary resi-dence at Toriizaka—the work of Ōe Shintarō and Ogawa Jihei—into the International House of Japan, may have visited Kōden-sō to see another ex-ample of a site that had been developed by the same architect and land-scape gardener.

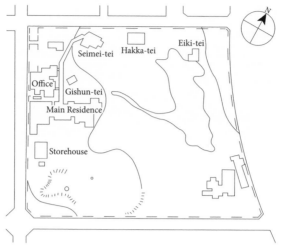

Fig. 7-2: Conceptual rendering of Kōden-sō

The suburban Sakura Shinmachi area was developed in 1913 by the Tokyo Trust Company, whose headquarters were in Nihonbashi, on roughly 230,000 square meters of woodland spanning the Fukasawa area in the village of Komazawa and the Shimonoge enclave in the village of Tamagawa. When originally divided into lots the land generally sold for 1 yen per *tsubo* [3.3 square meters], with the most expensive lots going for 5 yen per *tsubo*. A quiet, residential quarter, it was even referred to as "Tokyo's Karuizawa." The name, meaning "cherry new town," comes from the more than 1,000 cherry trees planted along the roads, which were outfitted with drainage channels. The area is said to have been divided into more than 100 lots, which must have averaged about 300 *tsubo* [990 square meters] each, a size appropriate to a high-end neighborhood.

Even amid such surroundings, the nearly 8,000-*tsubo* [26,400-square-meter] site of the Nagao Kin'ya residence surely must have stood out as something exceptional. Those in the area are said to have referred to it as "the mansion" or as "Wakamoto." A booklet summarizing the history of Sakura Shinmachi contains the following recollection from a resident named Nagasawa Yoshiaki:

The Wakao family held a garden party every year, inviting notable figures from various fields, with beauties from the Akasaka geisha district that were even more delightful to the eye than the blossoms of spring. Fireworks would be set off during the day and the children would use long bamboo rods to see who could catch the large paper dolls that came fluttering down first. Those were happy days. [From *Watakushitachi no machi Sakura Shinmachi no ayumi* (A history of our town Sakura Shinmachi)]

The "Wakao family" mentioned here is probably not the well-known Wakao family of business leaders from Kōshū but rather the Nagao family. Reading "Wakao" as a mix of "Nagao" and "Wakamoto" resulting in "Wakao" makes it easy to imagine Nagao Kin'ya and Yone, live wires fond of showiness, as enthusiastic participants in the garden party shenanigans described. It also suggests that the name of the wealthy neighbor was, as is so often the case with the nouveaux riche, not very well known.

The Garden Club of America's Visit to Japan

On 13 May 1935, 123 notables from the United States—members of the Garden Club of America—disembarked from the *Chichibu Maru* at the port of Yokohama. Some came as couples, but the majority were women. The Garden Club of America is not a single unified club but an association of regional member clubs. The 123 participants who arrived in Japan included representatives from 53 regional clubs established across the United States. The group's visit to Japan came about as the result of an invitation extended to Garden Club of America President Mrs. Jonathan Bulkley by Prince Tokugawa Iesato, then president of the America-Japan Society, when she visited Japan in 1933. Participants came from Massachusetts, Texas, California, and other locations around the country.

The arriving group was met by a reception committee that included not only Prince Tokugawa Iesato but also Prince Konoe Fumimaro and other members of the Society for International Cultural Relations, which had only just been formed the previous year. The America-Japan Society, which played a central role, was a private-sector international exchange organization founded in 1917. The Society for International Cultural Relations was similar in nature. Konoe, who had visited the United States the year before to attend the graduation of his eldest son Fumitaka from high school, was looking for ways to improve relations between Japan and the United States. For him, the visit of the Garden Club of America to Japan was an important opportunity to set the future course of Japan-American relations.

Previously, though, Konoe had a slightly different relationship with the United States. His original position can be found in *Eibei hon'i no heiwa shugi o haisu* (Reject an Anglo-American-centered pacifism), an article he wrote for the November 1918 issue of *Nihon oyobi Nihonjin* (Japan and the Japanese) shortly after graduating from Kyoto University. The title is enough to suggest that Konoe's position was not a pro-American one. The same year the article was published, Konoe accompanied Japan's delegation to the Paris Conference where Saionji Kinmochi served as ambassador plenipotentiary. For someone like Konoe, head of one of Japan's leading aristocratic families, his inclusion in the delegation may have seemed perfectly natural. He wrote "Reject an Anglo-American-centered Pacifism," therefore, as a message in anticipation of attending the conference.

After the peace conference, Konoe visited Germany, Belgium, England, and the United States before returning to Japan in November 1919. He later did an about-face, declared a pro-American position, and even discussed living in the United States as a family. This, as it turned out, was not to be, but his eldest son Fumitaka did head off to study at an American high school in 1932. Konoe then made his second journey to the United States in the year of his son's graduation. By then, he was already recognized as a young politician with a pro-American stance.

Japan's political horizons were growing more and more risky by the day due to the situation in mainland China. Tensions were rising between those who wished to form an alliance with Germany and Italy and the liberals who prioritized Japan's relationship with the United States and the United Kingdom. It was in this environment that the visit to Japan by the Garden

Club of America took place the year after Konoe's return. Making the most of such a golden opportunity, Tokugawa Iesato, Konoe Fumimaro and others put together a huge welcome as a matter of private-sector diplomacy. The Garden Club of America represented a group of unprecedented size from a social class with enormous influence. From the Japanese perspective, the visit offered the opportunity to share the culture of Japan with America through members of the visiting group and to create a foundation for cooperation between the two countries. To this end, they enlisted Japan's political and business elite in rolling out an endless series of welcome events that would showcase Japanese culture.

Having disembarked from the *Chichibu Maru*, the group was invited to a garden party at the home of Hara Tomitarō in Yokohama, after which they traveled to Tokyo, where they completed their registration as members of the visiting delegation and attended a reception at the Imperial Hotel.

The following day they visited the Meiji Jingū shrine, were welcomed at a cottage in the nearby gardens of the late Baron Dan Takuma, attended a garden party hosted by Prince Takamatsu at the Shinjuku Gyoen Imperial Garden, and were invited by the America-Japan Society to a dinner party at the Kasumigaseki Imperial Villa.

In this way, the waves of welcome continued unabated until the group's departure from Japan on 2 June. Many residences were opened up to host the large group, which was often divided into smaller parties when invited to lunch or to tea.

The group visited not only Yokohama and Tokyo but also locations such as Ōmiya, Nikkō, Hakone, Nagoya, Kyoto, Osaka, Nara, and Lake Biwa. *Beikoku teien kurabu daihyō hōnichi kinen shashin chō* (A photographic diary of the visit of the Garden Club of America to Japan) provides a glimpse of the parties that the group attended at each location, and reveals the world of the gardens that the group visited. Although perhaps a bit tedious, I provide a list of these destinations below. Locations that follow personal names and are bound by square brackets indicate what occupies the site today.

Places Visited in the Tokyo Area

Meiji Jingū shrine / Shinjuku Gyoen Imperial Garden / United States Embassy / Peer's Club / St. Luke's International Hospital / Residence of Hara Tomitarō [Sankei-en Garden] / Residence of Baron Dan Inō / Residence of Baron Shidehara Kijūrō / Residence of Nezu Kaichirō [Nezu Museum] / Residence of Asano Ryōzō / Residence of Baron Mitsui Hachirōemon Takamine [United States Embassy Staff Housing] / Residence of Dan Takuma's widow Yoshi / Residence of Miwa Zenbei / Residence of Fukui Kikusaburō / Residence of Baron Ōkura Kishichirō's wife Kumiko [Hotel Okura] / Residence of Hara Kunizō [Hara Museum of Contemporary Art] / Residence of Shiobara Matasaku / Residence of Horikoshi Kakujirō / Residence of Prince Tokugawa Iesato / Residence of Marquis Maeda Toshinari's wife Kikuko [The Museum of Modern Japanese Literature] / Residence of Tsumura Jūsha (villa) / Residence of Baron Fujita Heitarō [Hotel Chinzansō] / Residence of Fujiyama Raita [Sheraton Miyako Hotel Tokyo]

Places Visited in Ōmiya

Katakura Industries Textile Factory

Places Visited in Nikkō

Lake Chūzenji / Nikkō Tōshōgū shrine / Kanaya Hotel

Places Visited in Hakone

Iwasaki family villa / Fujita family villa / Mitsui family villa / Fujiya Hotel

Places Visited in the Nagoya Area

Nagoya Castle / Residence of Aoki Kamatarō / Residence of Morikawa Kan'ichirō / Residence of Asano Jinshichi / Residence of Okaya Sōsuke / Residence of Itō Jirōzaemon / Residence of Sekido Arihiko / Residence of Kasuya Nuiemon / Residence of Suzuki Sōichirō (Ryūmon-en villa) / Residence of Katō Katsutarō / Residence of Takahashi Masahiko / Residence of Matsuo Sōgo / Residence of Takamatsu Sadaichi

Places Visited in the Kyoto Area

Kyoto Hotel / Miyako Hotel [Westin Miyako Hotel Kyoto] / Daitoku-ji temple / Ryōan-ji temple / The Silver Pavilion / Katsura Imperial Villa / Saihō-ji temple / Tenryū-ji temple / The Golden Pavilion / Daikaku-ji temple / Kyoto Imperial Palace / Nijō Castle / Heian Jingū shrine / Shūgakuin Imperial Villa / Residence of Hirai Jinbei / Residence of Ichida Yaichirō (Tairyū Sansō) / Residence of Watanabe Toji / Residence of Yagi Seihachi / Residence of Sumitomo Shunsui (Yūhō-en) / Residence of Nomura Tokushichi II (Hekiun-sō) / Residence of Inabata Katsutarō (Waraku-an) [Kaiu-sō]

Places Visited in the Osaka and Nara Area

Osaka Kabuki Theater/ Hōryū-ji temple / Tōdai-ji temple / Kasuga Taisha shrine / Imperial Household Museum of Nara

Places Visited in the Lake Biwa Area

Biwako Hotel / Residence of Nagao Kin'ya [Rinshō-en]

It is a long list, but offers insights into how gardens were seen at the time. That the tour covered the recognized master works among the historical gardens in Kyoto (Fig. 7-3) as well as Hōryū-ji, Tōdai-ji, and Kasuga Taisha in Nara, is no doubt the result of planning to cover as many of the most important gardens as limited time would allow. That the group also went to Nikkō, Hakone, and Lake Biwa suggests how ambitious the itinerary was.

Fig. 7-3: The Garden Club of America visit to Ryōan-ji temple

Underlined items in the list include gardens landscaped by Ogawa Jihei.

Together with this tour of historical gardens, the group also visited the homes of the bourgeoisie and the aristocracy. Most of the Japanese members of the reception committee were wealthy owners of large gardens. The itinerary left the impression of gardening as the ultimate extravagance, and *sukisha* connoisseurs representing Tokyo, Nagoya, and Kyoto put on a real display of hospitality. The group's excursion to Lake Biwa was made to facilitate a visit to Nagao Kin'ya's Rinshō-en, the expansive garden that Ogawa Jihei designed in his later years (Fig. 7-4).

Nagao Kin'ya continued to build great gardens—at Kōden-sō, his primary residence in Tokyo's Sakura Shinmachi area; at his Senko Sansō villa in Kamakura, and at Rinshō-en on the shores of Lake Biwa—as if in the hope that doing so would establish for him a foothold in the world of *suki* connoisseurship. Gaining greater prominence in business circles, and friendly with Konoe Fumimaro, Nagao very much wanted to be part of receiving the Garden Club of America during their visit to Japan. He was no doubt deeply moved that the group made its way to Lake Biwa to visit Rinshō-en.

Returning again to the Garden Club's itinerary, it is striking how many residences with gardens designed by Ogawa Jihei the group visited in Kyoto: the Miyako Hotel, the Heian Jingū shrine, Ichida Yaichirō's Tairyū Sansō, Sumitomo Shunsui's Yūhō-en, Nomura Tokushichi II's Hekiun-sō, and Inabata Katsutarō's Waraku-an. In those days, to have an Ueji garden was proof that one had arrived as a wealthy *sukisha* connoisseur.

But what of the members of the Garden Club of America who were treated to this series of welcome events? They no doubt returned to the United States quite happy after a very pleasant trip. Other than enjoying their memories of Japanese gardens, however, they did little else. Their visit to Japan led to no discernable change in the diplomatic stance taken by political and business circles in the United States. Gardens were gardens, and in the United States they occupied a world that went no further than a quiet hobby.

Konoe Fumimaro and the other powerful figures in Japan had engaged

From left, Mr. and Mrs. Nagao
Kin'ya and Mrs. Jonathan Bulkley

Fig. 7-4: The Garden Club of America visit to Rinshō-en

in such an over-the-top charm offensive because they hoped the members of the Garden Club of America would exercise some influence in repairing a relationship between Japan and the United States that was already beginning to fray.

Those in the Orbit of the Nagao Gardens

Drawn by the Nagao's wealth, the area around the Nagao residence in Sakura Shinmachi became home to many others in their orbit. Suzuki Sōho, the Urasenke School tea master responsible for Nagao family tea ceremonies, lived in the area beginning in 1940. Ogawa Jihei's nephew Iwaki Sentarō, who was responsible for the Nagao family gardens, established a workplace nearby and later located the headquarters of his Iwaki Landscape Company in the area.

In his own memoirs, Suzuki Sōho recalls:

It was 1934 when I began visiting the Nagao residence to conduct training. Up until then, Grand Master Tantansai had undertaken these visits but back in the days before bullet trains and air travel it was impossible for him to continue traveling from Kyoto once a week given the other commitments attendant to his position.

When he instructed me to visit the Nagao residence in his stead, I thought to myself that I was really in for it this time. Mr. Nagao had a reputation for listening to the Grand Master, but not being so attentive to others. [From *Chanoyu zuisō* (Thoughts on the tea ceremony)]

And yet, he would go on to spend the latter half of his life with the Nagaos. Suzuki Sōho wrote that he first met Tanaka Mitsuaki, who is said to have recognized Nagao Yone as his daughter, at the Nagao residence. He also noted that, "I served tea for Count Tanaka Mitsuaki at the cottage in Kamakura, and it was after this that I began substituting for the Grand Master for training." When Tanaka visited Rinshō-en, the Nagao villa in Karasaki, Suzuki went along to arrange the tea ceremony.

There are also records of a tea gathering called the Enmei-kai whose members included Kobayashi Ichizō, Matsunaga Yasuzaemon, Hatakeyama Issei, Ishii Mitsuo, Dan Inō, Hattori Genzō, Nagao Kin'ya, and Gotō Keita. Such records suggest that Suzuki Sōho had complete responsibility for tea ceremonies among a business elite centered on the Nagao household.

Others who found favor with the Nagaos and lived near them were writer Satomi Ton; art historians Kojima Kikuo and Yazaki Yoshimori; Honma Junji, a sword expert who used the art name Kunzan; and Miyata Shōji, an expert on the history of crafts. Members of this group would gather at the primary residence in Sakura Shinmachi or at the Senko Sansō villa at Kamakurayama and enjoy discussing art and dining together. Through them, the Nagaos quickly established an impressive art collection. The collection was broad in scope, including paintings, ceramics, and swords, and high in quality, with many gorgeous pieces such as the tea jar with wisteria design by Nonomura Ninsei that is currently in the collection of the MOA Museum of Art in Atami.

Nagao Kin'ya and his wife not only took such scholars as followers but even gathered sumo wrestlers nearby. Patronizing the Nishonoseki stable, they cheered for the wrestler Kamikaze and, after the war, were supporters of the first Wakanohana. Fond of flashiness and able to spend freely, the Nagaos were all but indiscriminate in gathering members of the military, politicians, scholars, and sumo wrestlers to their side.

According to the diary of Satomi Ton, in 1941 he "became an advisor to Nagao Kin'ya's Wakamoto and earned 300 yen." Entries for 1942 include:

15 Apr.: 5 PM at Nagao's Giu-sō [Kōden-sō]. Kinoshita Mokutarō, Kojima (Kikuo), Shiga (Naoya), Musha, Yasui (Sōtarō), Satta Kotoji, Miyagawa Tadamaro, Morita (responsible for museum fabrics), and Gotō (Zauho Press).
3 Nov.: Nagao residence. Kinoshita Mokutarō, Kojima, Satta, Uson, etc.
15 Dec.: Nagao residence. Kinoshita, Uson, Kojima, and Satta.

Entries for 1945 include

5 Mar.: Visited Shiga with Nagao Kin'ya.
Before 11 Jun.: Called to Kamakurayama by Nagao and headed off
with Kawabata, Takami, and Nagai Tatsuo.
From 21 Jun.: Visited Konoe Fumimaro and Harada by automobile
with Nagao Yone and Kojima.

The biography of Konoe Fumimaro by Yabe Teiji, meanwhile, includes passages that indicate Konoe, "went from Odawara to Kamakura on 29 April 1944 and met Prince Higashikuni at the villa of Wakamoto's Nagao Kin'ya on the 30th," that "Prince Higashikuni was called to Nagao's residence in Setagaya one day and met Prince Konoe...then later met Prince Konoe again at Nagao's villa in Kamakura where the two had tea together," that "a conference of senior statesmen was held on 22 June 1944, with Konoe meeting Prince Higashikuni that night at the Nagao residence," and that "in addition to Hosokawa, Konoe was also accompanied by Yamamoto Yūzō and Nagao Kin'ya on a trip to the Kansai region that began on 22 October 1944."

Honma Junji mentions Nagao Yone in his book *Kunzan tōwa* (Kunzan's sword stories). In an episode that illustrates the depth of the Nagaos' connections, he describes the crisis he faced immediately following Japan's defeat in the Second World War when the occupation ordered the confiscation of Japanese swords. Honma sought Yone's advice, upon which Kin'ya approached Prince Higashikuni (then the prime minister) through Kojima Kikuo, and Konoe Fumimaro through Hosokawa Morisada, to have them work on the occupation forces, with the result that things turned out all right for Honma. Such political connections had probably also been leveraged now and then during the war.

Nagao Kin'ya and his wife Yone were surrounded by members of the Shirakaba-ha literary coterie such as Kojima Kikuo and Satomi Ton, people involved with art and antiques such as Honma Junji and Suzuki Sōho, and aristocratic politicians such as Tanaka Mitsuaki, Konoe Fumimaro, and

Prince Higashikuni. The stages that drew such players were Kōden-sō in Sakura Shinmachi, Senko Sansō at Kamakurayama, and Rinshō-en in Karasaki.

Nagao Kin'ya's Senko Sansō villa occupied a spot at the back of the Kamakurayama residential area. The area began being subdivided for development in 1929 and despite the name (which means "Mt. Kamakura"), geographically it was linked by a dedicated roadway running between Ōfuna and Enoshima. The area was intended as a development for second homes, and a policy of making lots no smaller than 500 *tsubo* [1,650 square meters] led to the birth of a large-scale luxury resort area. The development was a success, and soon powerful members of the political and financial elite such as Konoe Fumimaro were all building villas in the area.

The development was the work of Sugawara Tsūsai. Born in 1894, he had success as a young man running a rubber plantation in Johor on the Malay Peninsula and traveled around the world. After returning to Japan he seems to have led a turbulent life. He profited handily from reconstruction work in the wake of the 1923 Great Kanto Earthquake, however, before going on to develop the toll road and residential area between Ōfuna and Enoshima. In 1942 he established the Tokiwayama Bunko Foundation in Kamakurayama in order to maintain his own collection of calligraphy and artwork.

Senko Sansō was an enormous villa even by the standards of the Kamakurayama development. As with the primary residence in Sakura Shinmachi, the villa in Kamakurayama dwarfed its surroundings. That they built such large residences in rapid succession suggests how energetic the suddenly wealthy Nagaos were. The Sakura Shinmachi and Kamakurayama areas where they built their residences were also both examples of new resort developments that appeared in the early years of the Showa period. They chose to build homes of their own not in established neighborhoods filled with grand old mansions or in traditional resort areas but on newly developed land. Opinions may differ as to whether this was indicative of their vigorous style or simply typical behavior of the *nouveau riche*.

The Senko Sansō site is said to cover 130,000 *tsubo* [429,000 square meters]. After passing beneath the gate, the road cuts through rock and then a tunnel (Fig. 7-5). Kamakura is home to a number of estates with such road cuts, and in this, too, the Nagao residence has a distinctive Kamakura feel. Among Ueji's other work, it recalls Yōwadō, Iwasaki Koyata's villa in Atami, which was also laid out with an approach that passed through a tunnel before arriving at the residence. The main building at Senko Sansō is an old vernacular house that was relocated from Hida Takayama and rebuilt on a concrete platform (Fig. 7-6). The view from the residence to the south reveals the ocean at Shōnan through the leaves of the trees. The name of the villa ("Senko" means "folding fan lake") comes from the notion that the expansive view of the ocean suggests a fan-shaped lake.

In relocating the house from Takayama to the vast estate, architect Ōe Shintarō applied the same approach that he used at the primary residence of Iwasaki Koyata in Toriizaka and at Seimei-tei, the primary residence of Nagao Kin'ya in Sakura Shinmachi. Again, what distinguishes the site is

Fig. 7-5: The entrance to Senko Sansō, the Kamakurayama villa of Nagao Kin'ya, seen from the inside

Fig. 7-6: Senko Sansō

that the vernacular house was rebuilt on a concrete platform.

Relocating a farmhouse from a rural area and repurposing it as a villa or part of one is something seen with some frequency during this time period, as described in the work of Ishikawa Yūichi (*Kindai Nihon ni okeru minka no hyōka ni kansuru kenkyū* [Research on the evaluation of vernacular houses in modern Japan]) and Tsuchiya Kazuo (*"Inakaya" no fūkei* [The landscape of the rural cottage]). Yamanaka & Co., Ltd., an art dealer whose sales network extended overseas in the early twentieth century, is said to have acted as a go-between for the relocation of such farmhouses. Both Senko Sansō in Kamakurayama and Rinshō-en in Karasaki strongly reflect this taste of the times for rustic structures. The framework at Senko Sansō is that of a magnificent farmhouse, but Ōe Shintarō adds an atmosphere of gorgeous elegance through the use of ornamental transoms and other decorative elements in the Japanese-style rooms. This sense of refinement is what makes the villa at Kamakurayama so appealing.

Suzuki Sōho described the primary Nagao residence in Sakura Shinmachi as having "a tea ceremony room relocated from Prince Fushimi's palace in Akasaka" that "measured four-and-a-half standard mats plus a smaller *daime* mat, with a broad entrance and roof tiles decorated with the chrysanthemum crest. Out of deference the crests were hidden with a strip of cement before the war, but this was later removed" [From *Chanoyu zuisō* (Thoughts on the tea ceremony)]. Today, this tea ceremony room has been relocated to Kamakurayama.

Because Senko Sansō was located in the hills of Kamakurayama, the topography was unsuitable for creating a large pond, although there was a stream near a corner of the house that Nagao Yone used as a dressing room. Built mostly around trees and privileging the ocean view off Kamakura, the garden lacks the atmosphere of those Ueji created near Nanzeni-ji temple in Kyoto. If anything, it is perhaps more like the garden at Iwasaki Koyata's villa Yōwadō in Atami, but with a less expansive lawn.

That Nagao Yone made Senko Sansō her final place of residence after the family's later downfall suggests that it was probably where she felt most at home. The primary residence at Sakura Shinmachi has been lost, but this villa still stands quietly deep in the hills of Kamakurayama today.

On the shores of Lake Biwa, far from both their primary residence and their villa in Kamakurayama, the Rinshō-en villa that the Nagaos maintained in Karasaki was infused throughout with a playful spirit (Fig. 7-7). The name, which means "garden by the pine," refers to the villa's location adjacent to a celebrated scenic site known as the Pine of Karasaki.

Karasaki has been a topic of poetic expression since ancient times. One famous example is by seventh-century poet Kakinomoto no Hitomaro:

sasanami no	Cape Karasaki
Shiga no Karasaki	At Shiga of the rippling waves
sakiku aredo	Remains as ever before
ōmiyabito no	But waits in vain
fune machikanetsu	For the pleasure boats of courtiers to return

Another is Matsuo Bashō's haiku:

Karasaki no	The pine tree at Karasaki
matsu wa hana yori	Hazier
oboro nite	Than cherry blossoms

Fig. 7-7: Rinshō-en, the Karasaki villa of Nagao Kin'ya

In addition, the "night rain at Karasaki" is counted among the Eight Views of Ōmi.

The layout seen at Rinshō-en, with rustic cottages lined in a row, indicates that the villa was centered on the garden and on enjoying views of the lake. As the name of the villa suggests, its garden was an open one built largely around pines, its central feature a lawn extending toward groves of pine near the lake where reeds grew thickly along the shore (Fig. 7-8).

Suzuki Sōho recalls that Rinshō-en had a tea ceremony room modeled on the Urasenke school's Kan'un-tei, which was known to have been favored by Sen no Sōtan. Located on the grounds of the Urasenke estate in Kyoto, Kan'un-tei does not follow the simple, rustic style of a *wabicha* tea room but rather the more ostentatious *shoin* style, with eight tatami mats, a one-mat-sized *hondoko* formal alcove, a one-mat anteroom, and a built-in *tsukeshoin* table. Perhaps this style was best suited to the tastes of the Nagaos.

However, according to Yagasaki Zentarō, who surveyed Rinshō-en in 2004 (*Nagao Kin'ya bettei Rinshōen no chashitsu ni tsuite* [On the tea ceremony rooms at Rinshō-en, the Nagao Kin'ya villa]), the site contained a main residence, three detached tea ceremony rooms, waiting shelters, and assorted outbuildings. One of the tea ceremony rooms measured four-and-a-half mats and appears to have been a replica of the Urasenke estate's Yū-in. Another measured four mats with a half-mat alcove and had a built-in

Fig. 7-8: The garden at Rinshō-en

mizuya dōko cabinet similar in form to that at the Urasenke estate's Kon-nichi-an tea ceremony room. The overriding approach, it seems, was to build something combining a variety of models. The master carpenter was Kimura Seibei.

A concrete boathouse enabled boats to be launched directly from the garden onto Lake Biwa. The Nagaos apparently enjoyed entertaining their guests with motorboat tours of the lake that included pulling in at Hama-ōtsu (Fig. 7-9). Concrete structures were not very common during the peri-od and it was perhaps Nagao's style to build a boathouse using such new structural techniques. His fondness for new things and luxurious enter-tainment had less in common with the austere refinement of *sukisha* con-noisseurs than with the modern nouveau riche.

Many people enjoyed themselves at Rinshō-en, including Tanaka Mitsuaki and the Grand Master of the Urasenke school, but it probably shone the brightest in 1935 on the day that the Garden Club of America visited. As mentioned above, *Beikoku teien kurabu daihyō hōnichi kinen shashin chō* (A photographic diary of the visit of the Garden Club of Amer-ica to Japan) devotes five pages to the visit to the Nagao villa, including photographs of Mrs. Bulkley standing with Nagao Kin'ya and Yone, of *geiko* and *maiko* walking in the garden with open parasols, of American women playing games such as battledore and shuttlecock, of people fishing by the shore, and of guests painting ceramics (Fig. 7-4). No other destination on

Fig. 7-9: The boathouse at Rinshō-en

the tour is given as much page space.

The visit to Rinshō-en at Karasaki on the shores of Lake Biwa, however, is not included on the Garden Club of America's itinerary in Japan as listed at the front of this "photographic diary," nor is the name Nagao Kin'ya. Indeed, the name Nagao only appears in the captions to the photographs. What this means is that the visit to Rinshō-en was not part of the official itinerary but rather an unofficial stop. Within a reception committee organized by princes such as Tokugawa Iesato and Konoe Fumimaro that put national resources to the task, the Nagaos—who had rapidly risen to prominence through Wakamoto but whose prosperity was still less than a decade old—were simply too nouveau riche. Industrialists such as Hara Tomitarō (art name: Sankei) who lacked noble titles were included in the list of official members, but the position of the Nagaos was less firmly established. The only reason they were able to welcome the Garden Club of America, even in an unofficial capacity, was because they owned a large garden by Ogawa Jihei.

Here, the meaning of an Ogawa Jihei garden had been reversed. Ueji first made a name for himself in the world because Yamagata Aritomo used him for the garden at Murin-an during the mid-Meiji period. Gaining the Sumitomo, Saionji, and Iwasaki families as regular clients, he created gardens for many cultured businesspeople in the Kyoto area and beyond, becoming the first name in modern Japanese landscape gardeners in both name and fact. Through his involvement in public works such as two enthronement ceremonies, the Momoyama Imperial Mausoleum, maintenance at the Katsura and Shūgakuin Imperial Villas, and the Heian Jingū shrine, he came to occupy an unshakeable position of authority.

That the newly wealthy Nagao Kin'ya and his wife asked Ogawa Jihei to create a succession of large gardens for them was that they thought owning Ueji gardens would be the most effective, visible demonstration of their admission into established society.

Nagao and his wife were energetic about continuing to add to their art collection, which was high in quality and included many important pieces and national treasures. They also applied themselves to the tea ceremony. What enabled them to draw the broadest cross-section of society in order to make an impression were their large gardens and the garden parties held there. With the exception of a small number of prestigious nobility and sophisticated industrialists, businessmen, writers, soldiers, and sumo wrestlers were generally most impressed by great gardens. It was the presence of such a vast entourage that ultimately led even the prestigious nobility and sophisticated industrialists to come knocking.

The large gardens owned by the Nagaos, can perhaps be thought of as nouveau riche ornamentation—stage settings for those who worship money—or analogous to the mansion where the Great Gatsby held massive parties every night. This, too, suggests the essence of Ogawa Jihei's gardens.

Many of Ogawa Jihei's landscaping contemporaries were critical of his gardens, saying that they lacked ideology and were merely worldly. Such criticism is based on the view that a garden must be imbued with symbolic implications. This symbolist perspective identified the gardens of the Muromachi period as the ideal and sought to invest gardens with references to myths, sutras, worldviews, and cosmologies. The reason later landscape gardeners such as Shigemori Mirei and Nakane Kinsaku looked unfavorably upon Ogawa Jihei's work was because they were modernists who sought once again to create symbolic gardens incorporating cosmology and Buddhist stories.

The only member of the next generation who regarded Ogawa Jihei's gardens highly was Tono Takuma. Tono was the first Japanese to master landscape design in the United States and went on to teach garden design at Waseda University and the Tokyo University of Agriculture. Soon after the Second World War, he supervised the writing of *Nihon no teien* (*A Secret of Japanese Gardens*), a slim booklet filled with photographs that sought to categorize Japanese gardens by type and to introduce how they were composed. Because the selection of gardens is somewhat idiosyncratic, I would like to enumerate them here.

The book first presents two facing pages introducing the garden at "the Hirata residence in Tokyo," then moves on to the Katsura Imperial Villa, the Daisen-in sub-temple at Daitoku-ji temple, Nijō Castle, and the gardens of the Heian Jingū shrine. (Here and subsequently, underlined gardens are those with which Ogawa Jihei was involved.) The book then goes on to present categories of gardens with representative examples of each, as follows:

Boating Pond Garden	Nomura residence
Strolling Pond Garden	Katsura Imperial Villa
Viewing Pond Garden	Tenryū-ji temple
Flat Garden	Ryōan-ji temple
Tea Ceremony Garden	Part of the Nomura residence
Zen Garden	Nanzen-ji temple
Auspicious Garden	Shōden-ji temple, Konchi-in temple
Dry Landscape Garden	Saihō-ji temple
Condensed Landscape Garden	Suizen-ji temple (Kumamoto)
Borrowed Landscape Garden	Shūgakuin Imperial Villa
Literati/Cottage Garden	Middle garden at Murin-an
Contemporary Garden	Kiyosumi Gardens, Bridge pilings at Heian Jingū shrine

The book then lists garden elements including water, streams, rocks, vegetation, garden paths, stepping stones, *nobedan* stone paving, garden gates, bridges, fences, gazebos and pagodas, washbasins, wells, and lanterns. The Nomura residence is provided as an example for both streams and bridges.

Given the number of underlined gardens in the list above, one can see the high regard in which *A Secret of Japanese Gardens* held Ogawa Jihei. Because its editorial supervisor Tono Takuma had learned landscape design in the United States, instead of designing and describing gardens as visual aids for illustrating myths or narratives, he analyzed them as formal compositions. As a result, he evaluated them purely on the basis of their composition and forms, and what rose to the surface was Ogawa Jihei. It is fortunate that a book introducing gardens from this perspective was written so soon after the end of the war. At the time, the Nagao residence in Sakura Shinmachi was not yet lost and the post-war modernist view of gardens had yet to take over, to the book can be seen as an important testimony about the aesthetic to which Japan's modernization gave rise.

The gardens of Ogawa Jihei were compositions using real topography, vegetation, and stones as they were found—naturalist gardens free of symbolic implications. Water was not held in place to symbolize the sea but ran as streams that were nothing more than streams. The stones were just stones, and there was no gathering of rare examples or positioning to give them meaning. Stones were laid flat amid broad garden expanses. Lawns were vast and used for garden parties. Conspicuous plantings of rare trees were infrequent. Even when pines were used, they were used in groves, while trees such as firs and bayberries were also brought in. In this we find Ueji's modernity. The nouveaux riche and the Great Gatsby represented a spirit born of the modern. In creating gardens that were not invested with symbolism and did not rely on rare trees and rare stones, Ogawa Jihei exhibited a spirit born of a Japanese modernity. This is why his gardens have appealed to ordinary people, distinguished gentlemen, prestigious nobility, and sophisticated industrialists alike.

The Landscape at the End

Ogawa Jihei got his start around the time that the Sino-Japanese War was drawing to an end, when Yamagata Aritomo built his Murin-an villa near Nanzen-ji temple in Kyoto. Gardens were the only hobby that this stubborn, lonely man of authority allowed himself, and he was able to lose himself when faced with them. Even in his later years, Yamagata described to *sukisha* connoisseur Takahashi Sōan how captivated he was by the flow of a cascading waterfall: "One expects the shape of the waterfall to always remain the same, yet it seems different every time I look and I never grow tired of watching. I sometimes stand here [at Koki-an in Odawara] gazing at it for a long while." [From *Sankō iretsu* (Distinguished deeds of the late Prince Yamagata)]

When this lonely, powerful figure was forced to confront himself, the atmosphere of the garden was a little universe that sustained him. Ogawa Jihei, landscaper of the garden at Murin-an, created environments where the people who built modern Japan could show themselves, meet people, make decisions, and be lost in solitude.

Yamagata Aritomo met with Katsura Tarō and others at Murin-an and committed to the Russo-Japanese War. Sumitomo Shunsui maintained gardens by Ueji in Kyoto, Osaka, Kobe, and even Tokyo. Saionji Kinmochi employed Ueji gardens as an inseparable part of his own political style. Many gentlemen of business, too, sought to express their own status and style through Ueji gardens. No gardens were as loved by the people who propelled Japan's modernization forward as those of Ogawa Jihei. Born of the Lake Biwa Canal, a product of modernization, Ueji's gardens spread throughout the Kyoto, Osaka, and Kobe region and then eventually on to Kurashiki, Nagahama, Okitsu and Atami, Kamakura, and Tokyo.

In the same way that Japan launched itself out into the world with the Meiji Restoration, so Ueji's gardens were the broadest expression of the lifestyles of those who sustained Japan in the Restoration's wake.

One other figure would shine a final light on the gardens of Ogawa Jihei: Konoe Fumimaro. This light, however, was neither rosy, festive, nor open to the future.

We have already seen how the last of Ueji's great garden patrons, Nagao Kin'ya, gradually drew closer to Konoe Fumimaro. On the occasion of the Garden Club of America's visit to Japan in 1935, Nagao invited the group to his Rinshō-en villa at Karasaki in Shiga Prefecture and held a grand garden party. Although not included as part of the official itinerary, it was an opportunity for the merely nouveau riche Nagaos to make their presence felt among the prestigious nobility.

Eventually, by the mid-1940s, Nagao Kin'ya had come so far as to bring Konoe Fumimaro and Prince Higashikuni together at his Senko Sansō villa in Kamakura and to accompany Konoe on his visit to the Kansai region with Yamamoto Yūzō and Hosokawa Morisada. Nagao's financial resources were probably lavishly applied in such matters, and his primary residence and villas with their expansive Ueji gardens probably made comfortable venues for Konoe and the others.

Konoe Fumimaro had studied at Kyoto Imperial University, so he was already familiar with the world of Ogawa Jihei's gardens. While Konoe was a student in Kyoto, his classmates from the Peers' School such as Harada Kumao and Kido Kōichi were also studying there. Konoe eventually became a politician while Harada played a role as what might be described as Saionji Kinmochi's personal secretary and Kido became lord keeper of the privy seal. Konoe, Harada, and Kido would form a tightly knit group within the imperial court of the early Showa period, a group whose close association had its roots in their time together in Kyoto. As children of the aristocracy, of course, the three knew each other during their secondary education at the Peers' School, but it was in Kyoto where they first became close. Because they would get together at Harada's lodgings in Kitashirakawa, they called themselves the Shirakawa Party. Considering that the Shirakawa River would have been used as a lower canal had the Lake Biwa Canal been used to power water turbines, and that water from the gardens of Ogawa Jihei actually flowed into the Shirakawa River, it seems that Konoe began his life as a student in an area that overlapped with Ueji's cultural realm. The time when Konoe and his friends formed the Shirakawa Party was roughly the period when the Philosopher's Walk emerged from the Lake Biwa Canal constructed by Tanabe Sakurō—part of the process by which the modernization achieved by means of canal technology was transforming culture.

Kyoto was also home to Saionji Kinmochi's Seifū-sō villa. The first time Konoe visited Saionji there was in 1913 while he was still a student at Kyoto Imperial University. At the time, Saionji had resigned as prime minister of the second Saionji Cabinet over the issue of increasing the army by two divisions, had retired as president of the Seiyūkai political party, and was living a quiet life at Seifū-sō.

One day, thinking that he would like to meet Saionji, his much older predecessor in aristocratic society, Konoe knocked on the door of Seifū-sō dressed in his school uniform and without a letter of introduction. Inviting Konoe in, Saionji, a man who had formed two cabinets, treated the young Konoe in his gold-buttoned uniform respectfully and addressed him as *kakka* ("Your Excellency"). Even though the Saionji family ranked among the *seigake*, the second tier of the nobility, the Konoe family was the highest-ranked among the five regent families at its pinnacle. Because Fumimaro had assumed the position of head of his family, it was only natural that he should be called *kakka*, but Konoe seems to have felt that to be addressed in such a manner upon first meeting a man older than his father meant instead that he was being made light of. After this, Konoe never visited Saionji again while he was a student in Kyoto. Such a form of resistance was characteristic of Konoe, who although head of one of the five regent families was also a progressive intellectual.

He also had other memories related to the term *kakka* as a form of address. While he was studying at Kyoto Imperial University, he rented a villa at the hot springs in Arima in order to escape the summer heat. His brother Hidemaro and other younger brothers also stayed there. Apparently, hearing that Prince Konoe was in residence the local chief of police paid a visit and asked, "Is Konoe *kakka* in the neighborhood?" to which Fumimaro's younger brothers replied, "Never heard of any such *kakka*" and sent him on

Fig. 7-10: The garden at Seifū-sō, the Kyoto villa of Saionji Kinmochi

his way. After that, Fumimaro's younger brothers would tease him by calling him *kakka*, which became Fumimaro's nickname among the family.

Be that as it may, while the encounter at Seifū-sō ended badly, it must have given Konoe Fumimaro a glimpse of the Saionji Kinmochi lifestyle, that is, of Saionji enjoying a garden landscaped by Ogawa Jihei (Fig. 7-10).

After immersing himself in the world of politics, Konoe Fumimaro would come to enjoy friendly relations with Saionji Kinmochi. In truth, Konoe walked through this world under the protection of the much older Saionji. When Saionji served as ambassador plenipotentiary to the 1919 Paris Peace Conference after the end of the First World War, Konoe also went to Paris as an unusually young member of his entourage. His selection would have been unthinkable were it not for the Konoe family's high status, and suggests how great Saionji's hopes were for the head of the aristocracy.

On 23 and 26 May 1924, Konoe visited Saionji at Seifū-sō together with Mizuno Naoshi of the Kenkyūkai party in the House of Peers, and Koizumi Sakutarō of the Seiyūkai political party. The following April, Konoe also visited Zagyo-sō in Okitsu with his family. After that, Konoe would report the political situation to Saionji at every opportunity, ask for his insights, and follow or resist his instructions. In other words, as politicians from aristocratic backgrounds, the two maintained a relationship that was neither too close nor too distant. Saionji favored Konoe, and Konoe relied on Saionji. In fact, with the exception of Sanjō Sanetomi during the turbulent period of the Restoration, Saionji and Konoe were the only ones of aristocratic background to hold the position of prime minister in pre-war Japan.

In the course of what came to be called the *keien jidai* (Katsura-Saionji era)—when Saionji, who sought to engage in party politics, and Katsura Tarō, who sought to engage in the politics of Yamagata Aritomo's army faction, alternated administrations—Saionji came to entrust the future to Konoe. On Konoe's part, he served as chairman of the funeral ceremony when Saionji died. Through three cabinets, Konoe brought about a politics of accommodation, and his indecision led to the Pacific War.

Still, we can imagine that Konoe probably used Saionji as a reference not only with respect to politics but also with respect to lifestyle. Although lacking anything like Saionji's experiences in France, Konoe was, in seeking to become a pro-America internationalist politician, no doubt conscious of Saionji's cosmopolitanism. It is certain, too, that the Saionji lifestyle as Konoe understood it would have encompassed both the way he lived his life and the residences at which he did so. Konoe, too, would demonstrate a style of his own in the way he arranged his residences.

The Konoe family maintained the Yōmei Bunko Foundation in Kyoto as well as a proper residence in Tokyo. The Tekigai-sō villa in Tokyo's western suburbs is well known as a Konoe residence, but the family's primary residence in Tokyo since the Meiji period was actually located in Ochiai. This house continued to be maintained, but Konoe Fumimaro preferred the more suburban Tekigai-sō and effectively made it his primary residence.

Strictly speaking, Tekigai-sō was not a home that Konoe built for himself but one that he acquired. It was originally the home of Irisawa Tatsukichi. A physician who taught internal medicine at Tokyo Imperial University, Irisawa was known as a skilled doctor and served as court physician to Emperor Taisho. The residence that Konoe turned into Tekigai-sō was the one that Irisawa had built on the outskirts of Ogikubo, a western suburb of Tokyo, and had been designed by architect Itō Chūta. Known for buildings such as the Heian Jingū shrine in Kyoto and Tsukiji Hongan-ji temple in Tokyo, Itō also designed large estates such as that of Asano Sōichirō. The Irisawa home, a masterpiece of Itō Chūta's residential architecture, and one for which he had Kaneko Seikichi serve as site manager, was completed in 1927.

Taking a liking to the house, Konoe Fumimaro acquired it from the Irisawa family and made it his own, but it is unclear what it was about the house that appealed to him. Irisawa had examined Konoe, who was sickly, on occasion in the past, and appears to have recommended that he live somewhere with clean, dry air. This then seems to have led him to offer Konoe the house in Ogikubo where he lived. Irisawa was a proponent of a lifestyle built around sitting on chairs rather than on the floor, and his own residence was made up of rooms with the high ceilings he preferred. He also owned a villa in Suginami that had been designed by William M. Vories, so he may not have minded turning his primary residence over to Konoe. Wanting to live in the suburbs away from the tumult of Tokyo, Konoe was probably pleased by the well-built Japanese-style residence designed by Itō Chūta that stood on a south-facing slope, and felt it suitable in status to serve as his primary residence. He acquired the site in 1937. It was Saionji Kinmochi who gave it the name Tekigai-sō. Irisawa lived until 1939, and Konoe must have been grateful to him for enabling his acquisition of the house. In *Itō Chūta kenchiku sakuhin* (The architectural works of Itō Chūta), the building is listed as "Tekigai-sō (Formerly the Irisawa residence)." At the time of this book's publication, the residence had already passed from Irisawa's hands, but there was probably an effort to avoid identifying the building as Konoe's residence. The book contains six photos of the exterior, entrance, guest room, Chinese-style parlor, study, and dining room, but no floor plans. The photos are testament to the building's elegant, high-ceilinged design that mixed Japanese style with a touch of the Chinese. On the building's south side was an inelegant pond whose shoreline was reinforced with boards (Fig. 7-11).

Although Konoe made Irisawa Tatsukichi's home his own, his attitude was not that of someone indifferent about where he lived. He probably

Fig. 7-11: Tekigai-sō, the residence of Konoe Fumimaro

chose his residence based on a single aesthetic and his image of an ideal lifestyle. The Irisawa residence was not done in the *sukiya* style but rather a fairly rigid version of the more formal *shoin* style. The addition of Chinese-style elements further strengthened the impression of severity. It seems likely that Konoe's desire to obtain the property was underpinned by a conscious desire to give expression to a lifestyle of his own. It is easy to imagine that the Saionji lifestyle probably took on great significance in this regard. Although Tekigai-sō exhibits a rigid style with Chinese influence, taking it as his residence first and foremost enabled Konoe to acquire his own style. He used the Chinese-style entrance and guest rooms just as they had been when the building was owned by Irisawa, but remodeled the living room, bedrooms, and other private spaces extensively, lowering the ceilings and changing the position of the central hallway. To do this work, he called Hasebe Eikichi, an architect from the Sumitomo Eizen Design Office. While retaining what was good about the Irisawa residence, Konoe also created a home to suit his own tastes.

Konoe Fumimaro established the Yōmei Bunko Foundation in Kyoto in 1938, the year after he acquired the Irisawa Tatsukichi residence. On behalf of the foundation, he had the *sukiya*-style Kozan-sō villa built in 1944. He entrusted the building's design to Sumitomo architect Hasebe Eikichi and the garden to Ogawa Jihei's grandson Ogawa Jirō (Ueji IX). The project was entirely in keeping with the Saionji style. Saionji had, after all, with the support of the Sumitomo, always had Ueji landscape his gardens and Sumitomo architects and master carpenters build his buildings.

At the time Konoe built Kozan-sō, Saionji Kinmochi and Ogawa Jihei VII had both already left this world. Nevertheless, just as Saionji had done, Konoe entrusted the garden to Ueji and the building to a Sumitomo architect, suggesting how deeply Saionji's living environment had resonated with him. Had Ogawa Jihei VII been alive, Konoe might also have had him take on a major renovation of the garden at Tekigai-sō.

In the latter half of his life, Konoe Fumimaro became friendly with Nagao Kin'ya. If the term "friendly" invites misunderstanding, then we could also say that Konoe did not keep Nagao at a distance. After all, Nagao's wealth and the Ueji gardens that he maintained here and there presumably offered Konoe opportunities to relax and unwind, and places to meet people discreetly.

Going a step further, in addition to the pride and ill temper of an aristocrat, we can also see in Konoe a worldliness that played well with the common man. Take sumo wrestling, for example. Konoe was famous for his love of sumo and often went to see wrestlers train and compete. Visiting sumo competitions provided an excellent opportunity for him to gain popularity among the masses. Such preferences of Konoe's were a good match with the worldliness of Nagao Kin'ya. Patronizing wrestlers such as Kamikaze before the war and spending lavishly on the first Wakanohana after its end, Nagao probably never lacked for things of common interest to talk about with Konoe.

The relationship between Konoe Fumimaro and Nagao Kin'ya reached its climax just before Konoe's death.

Konoe heard the radio broadcast of the imperial rescript announcing Japan's surrender while at his villa at Iriuda in Odawara. Two days later, on 17 August 1945, he joined the cabinet of Prince Higashikuni as a minister of state without portfolio and attended his swearing-in ceremony at the

Akasaka Palace. In this way, he indicated that he would participate in the construction of the post-war regime. Konoe and Prince Higashikuni were familiar with one another and, prior to Japan's defeat, had often used the residences of Nagao Kin'ya as places to meet and talk.

The next month, on 2 September, a ceremony was held on the deck of the battleship *Missouri* for the signing of the instrument of surrender.

On 11 September, orders were issued to arrest thirty-nine people for war crimes. Konoe Fumimaro was not among them. On 13 September, Konoe visited and met with Supreme Commander of the Allied Powers Douglas MacArthur in Yokohama. Konoe took this action in advance of the emperor's visit to MacArthur. Konoe appears to have been confident that he would be well received by the Americans as a politician who had staked out a liberal position. His meeting in Yokohama, however, seems not to have gone well, due in part to poor interpretation.

On 4 October, Konoe met again with MacArthur, this time at the occupation's general headquarters (GHQ) that had been set up at the Dai-ichi Life Insurance Building in Tokyo. At this meeting, MacArthur is said to have suggested that Konoe gather Japan's liberal camp and seek to undertake the revision of Japan's constitution. Konoe immediately began to set about the work of constitutional reform, but the following day brought the resignation of the entire Higashikuni Cabinet and the establishment of a new cabinet under Shidehara Kijūrō. No longer serving as a minister of state and removed from national government, Konoe was able to devote himself to constitutional reform. On 11 October, Konoe was made a special appointee to the office of the lord keeper of the privy seal and commissioned to draw up a draft constitution.

Reform of the constitution, however, was the cabinet's job, and the voices of those who argued that it was improper to have someone who had served as prime minister multiple times during the war draw up the post-war constitution gradually grew louder. On 29 October, Japanese newspapers reported on an article in the New York Times insisting that those like Konoe who had served as prime minister during the war must not re-emerge in post-war Japan. On 9 November, Konoe was summoned to the amphibious command ship *Ancon* and questioned by the Strategic Bombing Survey. At this session, said to have been more an interrogation, rather than being addressed as "Prince Konoe" as in the past, he was repeatedly addressed as "Mr. Konoe." Apparently, he was thoroughly worn down by the time the questioning came to an end.

In fact, prior to this "interrogation," a memorandum on Konoe written by Herbert Norman, a Canadian diplomat knowledgeable about Japan, had been submitted to GHQ on 5 November. Norman also submitted a second memorandum to GHQ on 8 November, this time about Lord Keeper of the Privy Seal Kido Kōichi. Norman is said to have denigrated Konoe and defended Kido in explicit terms. As a fellow communist, Norman was friendly with Tsuru Shigeto, who he met while a student at Harvard, and one theory has it that Norman defended Kido because Kido was related to Tsuru by marriage. Although this interpretation seems fairly compelling, the particulars largely go no further than the realm of speculation. Some say a vision of Kido's face might have flashed through Konoe's mind as he was undergoing "interrogation" on the *Ancon*, but I have my doubts about whether we can go that far. I suspect Konoe would have had no way of knowing about the Norman-Tsuru relationship. Still, Konoe could tell that his own position was becoming objectively less favorable with each passing day. On 22 November he submitted his draft revised constitution to the emperor and resigned the peerage. Had he been convinced that Kido was behind his "interrogation" on the *Ancon*, he would surely have decided to take his own life at that point. Nevertheless, he continued to twist and turn with regard to his own position until the very end. And in this, an Ueji garden would play a major role.

On 27 November, Konoe left Tokyo for his villa in Karuizawa. Having submitted his draft revised constitution and resigned the peerage, he probably felt a profound sense of having finished everything. The end, however, was yet to come. On 2 December, orders were issued for the arrest of 59 people including Prince Nashimoto. Konoe is said to have been shocked to see this member of the imperial family respond by turning himself in to the authorities. Then, on 6 December orders were issued to arrest a further nine people including Kido Kōichi. This time, Konoe's name was also on the list. The deadline to turn himself in was 16 December.

On 11 December, Konoe left Karuizawa and headed back to Tokyo. Instead of arriving home at Tekigai-sō, however, he went to Kōden-sō, the primary residence of Nagao Kin'ya in Sakura Shinmachi, where he spent three days. Much about his reasons for staying there, the deep psychology behind this decision, is beyond the limits of interpretation. Perhaps he thought that if he returned to Tekigai-sō he would have no choice but to decide immediately whether to turn himself in or resist. If so, his time at Kōden-sō may have offered a final postponement, a final opportunity to decide what to do.

nyūgoku no	As prison
majika ni semaru	Draws near
yosamu kana	How cold the night!

Konoe Fumimaro is said to have written this verse at Kōden-sō and sent it to Kiya Ikusaburō. It suggests that Konoe had resigned himself to turning himself in. One theory has it, however, that it was during his time at Kōden-sō that Konoe received from the mistress of the house, Nagao Yone, the potassium cyanide that he would soon use to take his own life. As an owner of the pharmaceutical company that manufactured Wakamoto, so it goes, Yone would have had the means to obtain such chemicals.

Before returning to Tekigai-sō, while at Kōden-sō Konoe Fumimaro contemplated his choices—whether to turn himself in or resist, to live or die—while gazing upon a garden landscaped by Ogawa Jihei. Keeping his decision to himself, he left Kōden-sō for Tekigai-sō on 14 December. There, on the night of 15 December, just before the 16 December deadline for turning himself in, he committed suicide by potassium cyanide.

The garden at Kōden-sō may well have recalled the gardens at Saionji Kinmochi's various estates. Indeed, it offered a view that stretched as far as the garden at Murin-an that Yamagata Aritomo had built exactly fifty years before. Although it is difficult to imagine that Konoe was fully aware of this, perhaps at the end he looked upon this garden by Ogawa Jihei and sensed, beneath the level of consciousness, the indelible spirit that flowed in the background across the history of Japan's pursuit of modernization.

Born together with the Lake Biwa Canal that sought to modernize Japan, the gardens of Ogawa Jihei emerged at Murin-an, where Yamagata Aritomo first gave expression to Japan's modernization, and went on to create an expansive world. Fifty years later when the Empire of Japan that Yamagata had built came crumbling down, it was the gardens of Ogawa Jihei upon which Iwasaki Koyata gazed while secluded at his residence in Toriizaka before dismantling his zaibatsu, and that Konoe Fumimaro regarded at the end.

Ogawa Jihei created gardens that completely circumscribed the great Yamagata-Saionji-Konoe triangle that framed the process of Japan's modernization, a process that started with victory in the Sino-Japanese War and ended with defeat in the Pacific War, a process that started with Yamagata Aritomo, passed through Saionji Kinmochi, and ended with Konoe Fumimaro.

Afterword

I cannot remember now when or where I first saw a garden by Ogawa Jihei. It might have been Murin-an in Kyoto, or perhaps it was through the weeping cherry in Tanizaki Jun'ichirō's *Sasameyuki* (*The Makioka Sisters*).

In any case, there was a period when I became deeply absorbed with Ueji's gardens. I mentioned this to Nishizawa Fumitaka, an architect who surveyed gardens, and can remember him saying, "Ueji's really fascinating." When I spoke to Nakane Kinsaku, a landscape gardener who was serving as President of the Osaka University of Arts, he bluntly said, "Those gardens have no philosophy." Still, I interviewed people like Ōe Hiroshi and Iwaki Sentarō and went to visit Ogawa Jihei's gardens one by one whenever I could find the opportunity. The result of such efforts was an article titled "Meiji kara shōwa ni itaru sukiya: Ueji no sekai" (Sukiya architecture from the Meiji through Showa periods: The world of Ueji) in the Architectural Institute of Japan's *Kenchiku zasshi* (Journal of architecture and building science). This was at a time before any researchers from Kyoto or the Kansai region had written academic papers on Ueji.

After that I continued to visit gardens, research the clients who commissioned them, and try to imagine the worlds behind them. I never made much progress, however, on the work of putting it all together. Up to that point I had researched the formation of modern architecture in England and Japan, and everyone looked puzzled whenever I spoke of Japanese gardens. When the paperback version of my book *Tōkyō no geniusu roki* (Genius loci in Tokyo) came out, Fujimori Terunobu, who wrote the introduction, even teased, "Suzuki, a scholar of modernism, slips and speaks of Yamagata Aritomo."

I myself had the feeling that it would be difficult to continue on in writing about Ogawa Jihei and his world, and that I might never get things put together. Most of his gardens are private, which makes visiting them a challenge. Over time I took the opportunities that happened to come my way and little by little added to the gardens I had seen. I am very grateful for the assistance provided by Ōtani Toshikatsu and his wife, and by their daughter Miyoko while visiting the Furukawa residence at Nishigahara in Tokyo, where I benefitted from an explanation of the garden provided by the current Ueji, Ogawa Jihei XI.

Still, decades passed without ever compiling things into book form, and I even came to take pleasure in imagining the task to be something forever unattainable as in Kafka's *The Castle*.

Eventually *UP*, the magazine of the University of Tokyo Press, permitted a serialization and I was given space on alternate months from August 2010 through February 2012. This greatly opened up the potential for putting together a book on Ueji. Still, the opportunity for serialization wasn't without limits, so as soon as it was done I set about compiling the book. At first I thought I could just touch things up a little bit and be done, but things did not work out that way. During the summer of 2012 I had the chance to see the garden at the Ōhara villa in Kyoto, for which I am much indebted to Ōhara Ken'ichirō and Shōda Yasuko. Ueji XI also kindly rushed over to help. Then, in 2013, ownership of Konoe Fumimaro's Tekigai-sō villa passed to the City of Suginami and I was able to visit the property thanks to the goodwill of the folks at Kenbun, Inc. who had been contracted to conduct a survey of the site. With each such new opportunity, completion of the book kept being pushed further off into the future. Having decided that further postponements are best avoided, I now find myself writing this afterword.

This book would never have taken shape without the assistance of literally countless people, for whose help I am deeply grateful. I owe a particular debt of gratitude to Komuro Madoka, who has been on the project since the serialization for *UP*. Finally, I wish to thank my wife Tokiko, who has been a constant source of support throughout.

Suzuki Hiroyuki
May 2013

Bibliography

Ogawa Jihei

Amasaki, Hiromasa. *Nanadaime Ogawa Jihei: Sanshi suimei no miyako ni kaesaneba* [Ogawa Jihei: We must return the capital to a place of scenic beauty]. Kyoto: Minerva Shobo, 2012.

———. "Nanadaime Ogawa Jihei (Ueji): Kindai teien no senkakusha" [Ogawa Jihei VII (Ueji): Pioneer of the modern garden]. *Journal of the Japanese Institute of Landscape Architecture* 58, no. 2 (1994): 107–110.

———, ed. *Ueji no niwa: Ogawa Jihei no sekai* [Ueji's gardens: The world of Ogawa Jihei]. Kyoto: Tankōsha, 1990.

"Iwaki Sentarō sakutei kyūjūnen" [Ninety years of Iwaki Sentarō's landscaping]. *Niwa*, April 1990.

Kuroda, Yuzuru (Tengai). *Meika rekihō roku* [A record of visits to distinguished homes]. Tokyo: Kuroda Yuzuru, 1901.

———. *Zoku kōko kaishin roku* [A record of pleasant scenes in and around the capital, vol. 2]. Kyoto: Yamada Geisōdo, 1907.

———. *Zoku zoku kōko kaishin roku* [A record of pleasant scenes in and around the capital, vol. 3]. Kyoto: Kuroda Yuzuru, 1913.

Nihon no teien [The gardens of Japan]. Supervised by Takuma Tono. Tokyo: Iwanami Shoten, 1955. (English version: *A Secret of Japanese Gardens*. Tokyo: M. Onizuka, 1958.)

"'Ueji' kenshūkai hōkoku" [Report of the Ueji study group]. *Ōtani bijutsukanhō* [Bulletin of the Ōtani Museum], no. 8 (2001).

Yamane, Tokutarō, ed. *Ogawa Jihei*. Kyoto: Ogawa Kinzō, 1965.

Lake Biwa Canal

Cunningham, John T. *Newark*. Newark: New Jersey Historical Society, 1988.

Hashimoto, Itsuo, ed. *Onkiken shujin shōden* [A short biography of Kawashima Jinbei]. Kyoto: Kawashima Orimono, 1964. First published 1913.

An Industrial Landscape Observed: The Lachine Canal. Montreal: Canadian Center for Architecture, 1992.

Jarvis, Adrian. *Hydraulic Machines*. Aylesbury: Shire Publications, 1985.

Jinkai Kenkyūkai, ed. *Kitagaki Kunimichi nikki "Jinkai"* [Jinkai: The diary of Kitagaki Kunimichi]. Kyoto: Shibunkaku Shuppan, 2010.

Kyōto-shi Denkikyoku Shomuka, ed. *Biwako sosui oyobi suiryoku shiyō jigyō* [The Lake Biwa Canal and hydropower project]. Kyoto: Kyōto-shi Denkikyoku, 1940.

Kyōto Shimbunsha, ed. *Biwako sosui no hyakunen* [A century of the Lake Biwa Canal]. Kyōto-shi Suidōkyoku, 1990.

Lee, James. *The Morris Canal: A Photographic History*. Easton, PA: Delaware Press, 1988.

Nishikawa, Shōjirō, ed. *Tanabe Sakurō hakase rokujūnenshi* [A sixty-year history of Dr. Tanabe Sakurō]. Kyoto: Yamada Chūzō, 1924.

O'Connell, James C. *Inside Guide to Springfield and the Pioneer Valley*. Springfield, MA: Western Massachusetts Publishers, 1973.

Shank, William H. *Towpaths to Tugboats: A History of American Canal Engineering*. York, PA: American Canal and Transportation Center, 1982.

Shimizu, Yasukichi, ed. *Biwako sosui enkakushi* [A history of the Lake Biwa Canal]. Ōtsu: Biwako Chisuikai, 1925.

Yoshikawa, Tamiji. *Otokunigunshi* [A history of Otokuni district]. Kyoto: Otokunigunshi Hensankai, 1940.

Yamagata Aritomo

Inoue, Toshikazu. *Yamagata Aritomo to Meiji kokka* [Yamagata Aritomo and the Meiji state]. Tokyo: Nippon Hōsō Shuppan Kyōkai, 2010.

Itō, Takashi, ed. *Yamagata Aritomo to kindai Nihon* [Yamagata Aritomo and modern Japan]. Tokyo: Yoshikawa Kōbunkan, 2008.

Koki-an Kiroku Hozon Chōsadan, ed. *Yamagata Aritomo kyūtei Odawara Kokian chōsa hōkokusho* [Report on the survey of Koki-an, the former Yamagata residence in Odawara]. Tokyo: Chiyoda Kasai Kaijō Hoken, 1982.

Kumazawa, Kazue. *Seizan yoei: Tanaka Mitsuaki haku shōden* [Traces of Seizan: A short biography of Count Tanaka Mitsuaki]. Tokyo: Aoyama Shoin, 1924.

Oka, Yoshitake. *Yamagata Aritomo: Meiji Nihon no shōchō* [Yamagata Aritomo: A symbol of Meiji Japan]. Tokyo: Iwanami Shoten, 1958.

Suzuki, Makoto, Takashi Awano, and Wakana Inokawa. "Yamagata Aritomo no teienkan to Chinzansō [Chinzan-sō and Yamagata Aritomo's view of gardens]. *Journal of the Japanese Institute of Landscape Architecture* 68, no.4 (2005): 339–350.

Takahashi, Sōan, ed. *Tōto chakaiki* [A record of tea gatherings in Tokyo]. Tokyo: Keibundō Shoten, 1920.

Takahashi, Yoshio. *Sankō iretsu* [Distinguished deeds of the late Prince Yamagata]. Tokyo: Keibundō Shoten, 1925.

Yoshida, Sadako. *Shinshinshū*. Tokyo: Yoshida Sadako, 1941.

Sumitomo Tomoito

Kawada, Jun. *Sumitomo kaisōki* [Remembering Sumitomo]. Tokyo: Chūōkōronsha, 1951.

Ōsaka-shi Bunkazai Kyōkai, ed. *Sumitomo dōfukishoato hakkutsu chōsa hōkoku* [Report on the archaeological survey of the Sumitomo copper refinery site]. Osaka: Ōsaka-shi Bunkazai Kyōkai, 1998.

Ōsaka-shi Kyōiku Iinkai Jimukyoku Shakai Kyōikubu Bunkazai Hogoka, ed. *Ōsaka shinai shozai no kenchiku bunkazai: Kyū Sumitomo hontei tamatsukiba no chōsa to zenshin tatemono no kōsatsu* [Architectural heritage in Osaka City: Survey of the billiards hall at the former Sumitomo primary residence and its predecessor building]. Osaka: Ōsaka-shi Kyōiku Iinkai Jimukyoku Shakai Kyōikubu Bunkazai Hogoka, 2000.

Sakamoto, Katsuhiko. "Kyū Tanabetei no kenchiku to Noguchi Magoichi" [Noguchi Magoichi and the architecture of the former Tanabe residence]. In *Kyū Tanabetei ichiku saisei hozon chōsa hōkokusho* [Survey report on the relocation, restoration, and preservation of the former Tanabe residence]. Kyoto: Kyū Tanabe-tei Ichiku Saisei Iinkai, 1997.

Sumitomo Shiryōkan, ed. *"Sumitomo Nagahori dōfukisho to Sumitomoke jūtaku" no sekkei to enshutsu: Sumitomo Yūhōen rekishi tenjikan tenji mokei* [The design and direction of the Sumitomo Nagahori copper refinery and Sumitomo residence: Exhibition models at the Sumitomo Yūhō-en history museum]. Kyoto: Sumitomo Shiryōkan, 1998.

Sumitomo Shunsui Hensan Iinkai, ed. *Sumitomo Shunsui*. Kyoto: Sumitomo Shunsui Hensan Iinkai, 1955.

Saionji Kinmochi

Andō, Tokuki. *Enkō hiwa* [The secrets of Saionji Kinmochi]. Tokyo: Ikuseisha, 1938.

Kyōto Daigaku Meishō Seifū-sō Teien Seibi Katsuyō Iinkai, ed. *Shiryō kara mita Seifūsō no kenchiku: Kenzōbutsu chōsa hōkokusho* [The architecture of Seifū-sō as seen in historical records: Report on a survey of the buildings]. Kyoto: Kyōto Daigaku Meishō Seifū-sō Teien Seibi Katsuyō Iinkai, 2011.

Saionji, Kinmochi. *Tōan zuihitsu* [Tōan essays]. Edited by Doppo Kunikida. Tokyo: Chūōkōronsha, 1990.

Uchiyama, Keinoshin, ed. *Saionji kō tsuioku* [Remembering Prince Saionji]. Tokyo: Chūō Daigaku, 1942.

Iwasaki Koyata

Iwasaki Koyata Den Hensan Iinkai. *Iwasaki Koyata den* [A biography of Iwasaki Koyata]. Tokyo: Iwasaki Koyata Den Hensan Iinkai, 1957.

Iwasaki Koyata shokanshū [The collected letters of Iwasaki Koyata]. Tokyo: Seikadō, 2004.

Mitsubishi Keizai Kenkyūjo Fuzoku Mitsubishi Shiryōkan, ed. *"Iwasakike denki" sakuinshū* [Index to biographies of the Iwasaki family]. Tokyo: Mitsubishi Keizai Kenkyūjo, 2008.

Mitsubishi Kōhō Iinkai. *Iwasakike yondai yukarino teitaku, teien* [The residences and gardens of four generations of the Iwasaki family]. Tokyo: Mitsubishi Kōhō Iinkai, 1994.

Suzuki, Hiroyuki. "Iwasaki Koyata no niwa" [The gardens of Iwasaki Koyata]. *Karamu*, no. 100 (1986): 75–78.

Murai Kichibei

Nagata, Tatsuo. *Hina no nagori*. Tokyo: Nagata Tatsuo, 1917.

Ōtani, Motochiyo. *Tabakoō Murai Kichibei: Tabako min'ei no jittai* [Tobacco king Murai Kichibei: The actual state of private-sector tobacco]. Tokyo: Sekai Bunko, 1964.

Takanashi, Yoshitarō, ed. *Sannōsō zushū* [Images of Sannō-sō]. Tokyo: Kōyōsha, 1927.

Furukawa Toranosuke

Furukawa Toranosuke-kun Denki Hensan Iinkai, ed. *Furukawa Toranosukekun den* [A biography of Furukawa Toranosuke]. Tokyo: Furukawa Toranosuke-kun Denki Hensan Iinkai, 1953.

Kitamura, Nobumasa. *Kyū Furukawa teien* [The Kyū-Furukawa Gardens]. Tokyo: Kyōgakusha, 1981.

Nara, Akihiko. "Kyū Furukawa tei ni tsuite: Kondoru no jūtaku isaku no kenkyū" [On the former Furukawa residence: Research on the last house designed by Conder]. *Shiseki to bijutsu* 40, no. 3 (1970): 92–103.

Ōtani Bijutsukan. *Tōkyōto shitei meishō kyū Furukawa teien honkan shūri kōji hōkoku-sho* [Report on repairs to the main building at the Kyū-Furukawa Gardens (A Tokyo Metropolitan Government Designated Place of Scenic Beauty)]. Tokyo: Ōtani Bijutsukan, 2001.

Suzuki, Makoto. "Kyū Furukawa teien no wayō to kindai" [The Japanese-Western style and modernity of the Kyū-Furukawa Gardens]. *Bunkazai no hogo*, no.36 (2004).

Nagao Kin'ya

Honma, Junji. *Kunzan tōwa* [Kunzan's sword stories]. Tokyo: Tōkyō Shuppan, 1974.

Setagaya Machinami Hozon Saisei no Kai, ed. *Tōkyō toritsu Fukasawa kōtōgakkō Sei-meitei chōsa hōkokusho* [Report of the survey of Seimei-tei at Tokyo Metropolitan Fukasawa High School] Tokyo: Setagaya Machinami Hozon Saisei no Kai, 2001.

Shirasaki, Hideo. *Tōsei kijin den* [Biographies of contemporary eccentrics]. Tokyo: Shinchōsha, 1987.

Suganuma Motoji, ed. *Watakushitachi no machi Sakura Shinmachi no ayumi* [A history of our town, Sakura Shinmachi]. Tokyo: Tōyōdō Kikaku Shuppansha, 1980.

Sugawara, Tsūsai. *Tsūsai hōdan: Bakemono hikkomu* [Tsūsai speaks his mind: Where monsters fear to tread]. Tokyo: Nihon Shuppan Kyōdō, 1951.

———. *Tsūsai jiden: Rekidai saishō kenpō hiwa* [The autobiography of Tsūsai: secrets of successive prime ministers and the constitution]. Tokyo: Tokiwayama Bunko Shuppanbu, 1977.

Suzuki, Hiroyuki, ed. *Nagao Kin'ya kyū bettei Senko Sansō* [Senko Sansō, the former villa of Nagao Kin'ya]. Tokyo: Tōkyō Daigaku Suzuki Hiroyuki Kenkyūshitsu, 2002.

Suzuki, Sōho. *Chanoyu zuisō* [Thoughts on the tea ceremony]. Kyoto: Tankōsha, 1975.

Tsutsui, Yasutaka. *Wakamoto no chie* [The wisdom of Wakamoto]. Illustrations by Yōko Kitayama. Tokyo: Kinnohoshisha, 2001.

Yagasaki, Zentarō. "Nagao Kin'ya bettei Rinshōen no chashitsu ni tsuite: Sukiyashi Kimura Seibei no kenkyū (2)" [On the tea ceremony rooms at Rinshō-en, the Nagao Kin'ya villa: A study of *sukiya* carpenter Kimura Seibei (2)]. *Nihon kenchiku gakkai Kinki shibu kenkyū hōkokushū keikakukei* 46 (2006): 777–780.

Konoe Fumimaro

Konoe, Hidemaro. *Fūsetsu yawa*. Tokyo: Kōdansha, 1967.

Kudō, Miyoko. *Ware Sugamo ni shuttō sezu: Konoe Fumimaro to tennō* [I won't turn myself in to Sugamo: Konoe Fumimaro and the emperor]. Tokyo: Nihon Keizai Shimbunsha, 2006.

Nagao, Kazuo. *Konoe Fumimaro*. Tokyo: Kōyō Shuppan, 1979.

Torii, Tami. *Konoe Fumimaro moku shite shisu: Surikaerareta sensō sekinin* [Konoe Fumimaro died in silence: A shift of responsibility for the war]. Tokyo: Sōshisha, 2007.

Tsutsui, Kiyotada. *Konoe Fumimaro: Kyōyōshugiteki popyurisuto no higeki* [Konoe Fumimaro: The tragedy of a cultured populist]. Tokyo: Iwanami Shoten, 2009.

Yabe, Teiji. *Konoe Fumimaro*. Tokyo: Yomiuri Shimbunsha, 1976.

Other

Atsuta, Yūharu, and Shigehiko Hasumi. *Ozu Yasujirō monogatari* [The Ozu Yasujirō story]. Tokyo: Chikumashobō, 1989.

Beikoku Teien Kurabu Shōtai Iinkai. *Beikoku teien kurabu daihyō hōnichi kinen shashin chō* [A photographic diary of the visit of the Garden Club of America to Japan at the invitation of Prince Iyesato Tokugawa, May 13th to June 2nd, 1935]. Tokyo: Beikoku Teien Kurabu Shōtai Iinkai, 1935.

Fortune, Robert. *Edo to Pekin: Eikoku engei gakusha no kyokutō kikō.* Translated by Kaoru Miyake. Tokyo: Hirokawa Shoten, 1969.

(English version: *Yedo and Peking; A Narrative of a Journey to the Capitals of Japan and China, with Notices of the Natural Productions, Agriculture, Horticulture and Trade of those Countries and Other Things Met with By the Way.* London: John Murray, 1863.)

Fujii, Hatsuo. *Doboku jinbutsu jiten* [The encyclopedia of civil engineers]. Tokyo: Atene Shobō, 2004.

Fujii, Kisaburō. *Sōkyoan ki* [A record of Sōkyo-an]. Self-published, 1955.

Fukuda, Yoshie. "Shōwa shoki no Japanese Garden: 'Beikoku teien kurabu daihyō hōnichi kinen shashin chō' o tōshite" [Japanese gardens in the early Showa period: Seen through *A photographic diary of the visit of the Garden Club of America to Japan*]. PhD diss., University of Tokyo, 2001.

Harigaya, Kanekichi. *Teien zakki* [Miscellaneous notes on gardens]. Tokyo: Nishigahara Kankōkai, 1938.

Hashimoto, Kizō. *Kyōto to kindai bijutsu* [Kyoto and modern art]. Kyoto: Kyōto Shoin, 1982.

Heian Jingū Hyakunenshi Hensan Iinkai, ed. *Heian jingū hyakunenshi* [A century of the Heian Jingū shrine]. Kyoto: Heian Jingū Shrine, 1997.

Hirakawa, Sukehiro. *Wakon yōsai no keifu: Uchi to soto kara no Meiji Nihon* [A genealogy of "Japanese spirit and Western learning": Meiji Japan from inside and out]. Tokyo: Kawade Shobō Shinsha, 1987.

Inabata Katsutarō-ō Kiju Kinen Denki Hensankai, ed. *Inabata Katsutarō kun den* [A biography of Inabata Katsutarō]. Osaka: Inabata Katsutarō-ō Kiju Kinen Denki Hensankai, 1938.

Inabata Sangyō Kabushiki Kaisha, ed. *Inabata hachijūhachinenshi: 1890–1978* [The Eighty-eight-year history of Inabata: 1890–1978]. Osaka: Inabata Sangyō, 1978.

Inoue, Ritsuko. *Saigo no iromachi Tobita* [Tobita: The last pleasure quarters]. Tokyo: Chikumashobō, 2011.

Ishikawa, Yūichi. "Kindai Nihon ni okeru minka no hyōka ni kansuru kenkyū" [Research on the evaluation of vernacular houses in modern Japan]. PhD diss., Kyoto Institute of Technology, 2008.

Itō Hakase Sakuhinshū Kankōkai, ed. *Itō Chūta kenchiku sakuhin* [The architectural works of Itō Chūta]. Tokyo: Jōnan Shoin, 1941.

Itō, Yukio, ed. *Kindai Kyōto no kaizō: Toshi keiei no kigen 1850–1918* [The remaking of modern Kyoto: The origins of urban management 1850-1918]. Kyoto: Minerva Shobō, 2006.

Kanesaka, Yukihiko. *Tairyū Sansō no jiwari to ishigumi no kumikata* [Land allotment and rock arrangement at Tairyū Sansō]. Self-published, 2002.

Katō, Tetsuhiro, Osamu Nakagawa, and Seishi Namiki, eds. *Higashiyama Kyōto fūkei ron* [On the landscape of Higashiyama, Kyoto]. Kyoto: Shōwadō, 2006.

Kawahigashi, Yoshiyuki, ed. *Josaia Kondoru kenchiku zumenshū* [A collection of architectural drawings by Josiah Conder]. 3 vols. Tokyo: Chūōkōron Bijutsu Shuppan, 1980–1981.

Kido, Kōichi. *Kido nikki: Kido hikokunin sensei kyōjutsusho zenbun kyokutō kokusai gunji saiban kenkyū* [Kido diary: Affidavit by defendant Kido to the International Military Tribunal for the Far East]. Edited by Kyokutō Kokusai Gunji Saiban Kenkyūkai. Tokyo: Heiwa Shuppan, 1947.

Kobayashi, Takehiro. *Meiji ishin to Kyōto: Kuge shakai no kaitai* [Kyoto and the Meiji restoration: The dissolution of aristocratic society]. Supervised by Hiroyuki Suzuki. Kyoto: Rinsen Shoten, 1998.

Kōshitsu kenchiku: Takumiryō no hito to sakuhin [Imperial architecture: The people and works of the Takumi-ryō]. Tokyo: Kenchiku Gahōsha, 2005.

Ko Yamanaka Sadajirō-ō Den Hensan Iinkai, ed. *Yamanaka Sadajirō den* [A biography of Yamanaka Sadajirō]. Osaka: Ko Yamanaka Sadajirō-ō Den Hensan Iinkai, 1939.

Kuchiki, Yuriko. *Hausu obu Yamanaka: Tōyō no shihō o ōbei ni utta bijutsushō* [The house of Yamanaka: The art dealer who sold the greatest treasures of the East to Europe and the United States]. Tokyo: Shinchōsha, 2011.

Kumakura, Isao. *Kindai sukisha no chanoyu* [The tea ceremony of modern *sukisha* connoisseurs]. Kyoto: Kawara Shoten, 1997.

Machihara, Ryō. *Asami Matazō den* [A biography of Asami Matazō]. Tokyo: Nakasako Iwajirō, 1902.

Maejima, Yasuhiko. *Kōkyo gaien* [The outer gardens of the Imperial Palace]. Tokyo: Kyōgakusha, 1981.

Mainichi Shimbunsha, ed. *Kyōto jinbutsu sanmyaku* [The mountain range of Kyoto personalities]. Tokyo: Mainichi Shimbunsha, 1956.

Maruyama, Hiroshi, Tsutomu Iyori, and, Hiroshi Takagi, eds. *Kindai Kyōto kenkyū* [Studies of modern Kyoto]. Kyoto: Shibunkaku Shuppan, 2008.

Murakami, Junji, ed. *Nomura Tokuan shumihen* [Nomura Tokuan: Hobbies]. Kobe: Nomura Tokuan-ō Denki Hensankai, 1951.

Nakahara, Tessen. *Kyō shippō mon'yōshū* [A collection of Kyoto cloisonné designs]. Kyoto: Tankōsha, 1981.

Nara Bunkazai Kenkyūjo Keikan Kenkyūshitsu, ed. *Kyōto Okazaki no bunkateki keikan chōsa hōkokusho* [Report on a survey of the cultural landscape in Okazaki, Kyoto]. Kyoto: Kyōto-shi Bunka Shiminkyoku Bunka Geijutsu Toshi Suishinshitsu Bunkazai Hogoka, 2013.

Nihon Engei Kenkyūkai, ed. *Meiji engei shi* [A history of Meiji gardening]. Tokyo: Nihon Engei Kenkyūkai, 1915.

Niwa, Teizō. *Nihon no shiba to shibafu* [Grasses and lawns in Japan]. Tokyo: Meibundō, 1958.

Okayama, Rika. "Ōgi Rodō no sukiya ni tsuite (1): Sukiya kenkyū" [On the *sukiya* style of Ōgi Rodō (1): Studies of *sukiya*]. *Nihon kenchiku gakkai kenkyū hōkokushū* 71 (2000): 573–576.

Ono, Kenkichi. *Kyōto o chūshin ni shita Nihon teien no kenkyū* [A Study of modern Japanese gardens in and around Kyoto]. Nara: Nara Kokuritsu Bunkazai Kenkyūjo, 2000.

Oshitani, Moritoshi. *Ōmi shōnin to Nagahama shōnin* [Ōmi merchants and Nagahama merchants]. In *Shimogō kyōsai sōritsu hyakushūnen kinen oyobi Shōshūkan saikō ki-*

nen. Nagahama: Shimogō Kyōsaikai, 2002.

Sakai, Takashi. *Tsūtenkaku: Shin Nihon shihon shugi hattatsu shi* [Tsūtenkaku: A new history of the development of Japanese capitalism]. Tokyo: Seidosha, 2011.

Sugita, Hiroaki. *Kindai Kyōto o ikita hitobito: Meiji jinbutsushi* [The people who lived in modern Kyoto: A record of Meiji personalities]. Kyoto: Kyōto Shoin, 1987.

Suzuki, Hiroyuki. *Nihon no kindai 10: Toshi e* [The modern period in Japan 10: To cities]. Tokyo: Chūōkōron Shinsha, 1999.

———. *Vikutorian goshikku no hōkai* [The collapse of Victorian Gothic]. Tokyo: Chūō kōron Bijutsu Shuppan, 1996.

Suzuki, Makoto. "Tono Takuma: Nihon no "randosukēpu ākitekuto" daiichigō" [Tono Takuma: Japan's first "landscape architect"]. *Journal of the Japanese Institute of Landscape Architecture* 60, no. 4 (1997): 291-294.

Takagi, Hiroshi, and Kunikazu Yamada, eds. *Rekishi no naka no tennōryō* [Imperial mausoleums in history]. Kyoto: Shibunkaku Shuppan, 2010.

Takahashi, Yoshio. *Garakuta kago* [Basket of odds and ends]. Tokyo: Sōbusha, 1914.

———. *Hōki no ato* [After the broom]. 2 vols. Tokyo: Shūhōen Shuppanbu, 1933.

———. *Shumi bukuro* [Bag of hobbies]. Tokyo: Shūhōen Shuppanbu, 1935.

Takeda Hakase Kanreki Kinen Jigyōkai, ed. *Takeda hakase sakuhinshū* [The collected works of Dr. Takeda]. Tokyo: Takeda Hakase Kanreki Kinen Jigyōkai, 1933.

Tanaka, Hidetaka. *Kindai sadō no rekishi shakaigaku* [A historical sociology of the modern tea ceremony]. Kyoto: Shibunkaku Shuppan, 2007.

Tsuchiya, Kazuo. "'Inakaya' no fūkei: Tabunkateki jōkyō o tōshite hakken sareta minka no kachi" [The landscape of the rural cottage: The value of folk dwellings as discovered in a multicultural context]. *Tokoha Gakuen University Research Review* 30 (2010): 67–89.

———. "Kindai sukisha no bessō kenchiku ni okeru bashosei to sugata: Inakaya o meguru tabunkateki jōkyō to biishiki" [The form and sense of place of villas owned by modern *sukisha* connoisseurs: The aesthetics and multicultural context of rural cottages]. *Tokoha Gakuen University Research Review* 28 (2008): 59–86.

Ueda, Keiji, ed. *Shōken kōtaigō shi* [A biography of Empress Shōken]. Tokyo: Teikoku Kyōiku Kenkyūkai, 1914.

Ueda, Yasutsugu. *Ārudeko no kenchikuka Yakushiji Kazue* [Art Déco architect Yakushiji Kazue]. Okayama: San'yō Shimbunsha, 2003.

Yagasaki, Zentarō. "Kindai Kyōto no Higashiyama chiiki ni okeru bettei teitakugun no keisei to suki kūkan ni kansuru kenkyū" [A study of spaces for *suki* connoisseurship and the formation of villas and residences in the Higashiyama district of Kyoto during the modern era]. PhD diss., Kyoto Institute of Technology, 1998.

———. "Daiku Shimada Tōkichi no shigoto to sakufū" [A study of the work and style of carpenter Shimada Tōkichi]. *Nihon kenchiku gakkai Kinki shibu kenkyū hōkokushū keikakukei* 49 (2009): 709-712.

Yamazaki, Mikihiro. "Itō Chūta no kyōdō sekkeisha Kaneko Seikichi no ryakureki ni tsuite" [A brief profile of Kaneko Seikichi, design assistant to Itō Chūta]. *Summaries of Technical Papers of Annual Meeting, Architectural Institute of Japan* (2005): 205–206.

Yokoyama, Keiko, and Makoto Suzuki. "Yūrinsō no hen'yō ni miru gendai teien dezain no mebae" [The beginnings of modern Japanese garden design as seen in the transformation of the garden at Yūrin-sō]. *Journal of the Japanese Institute of Landscape Architecture* 67, no. 5 (2004): 393–396.

APPENDIX 1: Ogawa Jihei VII's Main Works

Yamagata Aritomo	Kyoto villa Murin-an (1894–1896)
Sumitomo Tomoito	Chausuyama primary residence Keitaku-en (1908–1915) Sumiyoshi residence [Former residence of Tanabe Sadakichi] (1908) Shishigatani villa Yūhō-en (1913–1920) Kinugasa villa (1919) Unagidani former primary residence (1933)
Saionji Kinmochi	Kyoto villa Seifū-sō (1913) Surugadai residence (1918–1919) Okitsu villa Zagyo-sō (1920)
Ōhara Magosaburō	Amase villa (1922–1923) Kurashiki villa Yūrin-sō (1928–1931) Sumiyoshi villa (1932)
Iwasaki Koyata	Kyoto villa (1925–1928, 1933) Toriizaka residence (1928) Atami villa Yōwadō (1935)
Nagao Kin'ya	Sakura Shinmachi residence Kōden-sō (1931) Kamakurayama villa Senko Sansō (1931–1934) Karasaki villa Rinshō-en (1932–1934)
Nanzen-ji Area	The Hishida residence (1897) Ichida Yaichirō's villa Tairyū Sansō (1902–1905) Inabata Katsutarō's villa Waraku-an (1905) Someya Kanji's villa [Matsushita Kōnosuke's villa Shinshin-an] (1908) Fujita Kotarō's residence (1909) Nomura Tokushichi II's villa Hekiun-sō (1917–1928) The Hamazaki residence (1919) The Okumura villa (1919) Shimogō Denpei's villa Seiryū-tei (1920) The Yoshida villa (1921) Ogawa Chikanosuke's residence (1922) The Satsuma villa (1925) Hosokawa Moritatsu's villa I-en (1927–1930) The Matsumoto villa (1929–1930) Miyako Hotel (1933–1934)

Kyoto	Heian Jingū shrine (1894–1926) Imperial Museum of Kyoto (1896) Kyoto Commercial Museum (1909) Maruyama Park (1910) Kyoto Kaikō-sha (1910) Imperial Palace in Kyoto and the Katsura, Shūgakuin, and Nijō Imperial Villas (1912, beginning an ongoing position working on Imperial Household Ministry gardens) Fushimi Momoyama Mausoleum (1913) The brushwood fence around the Yukiden and Sukiden buildings (1914) Fushimi Momoyama East Mausoleum (1915) Prince Kuni's villa (1920) The south garden at Kiyomizu-dera temple (1923) Ōkura Tsunekichi's villa in Fushimi (1924–1927) Yasaka Shrine (1926–1927) Matsugasaki reservoir (1927) Kōun-ji temple (1927) Denhō-in at Daigo-ji temple (1929) Higashiyama Ryōzen shrine (1930–1931) Ninna-ji temple (1931) Tō-ji temple (1931) Konpuku-ji temple (1932) Goō Shrine (1932) Daitoku-ji temple (1933) Monument to the Kyoto 16th Division (1933) The graveyard at Bukkō-ji temple [Gravesite of the Ogawa family]
Other	Prince Kaya's villa in Suma (1897) Asami Matazō's villa Keiun-kan (1912) The official residence of the governor of Yamaguchi Prefecture (1919) Yamashita Tarō's villa in Kobe (1919) Murai Kichibei's residence Sannō-sō in Tokyo (1919–1920) Furukawa Toranosuke's residence in Tokyo (1919–1920) Ataka Yakichi's villa in Sumiyoshi (1925) Ogura Masatsune's residence in Tokyo (1933–1934)

This list was made based on *Ogawa Jihei* (Ogawa Jihei), *Ueji no niwa: Ogawa Jihei no sekai* (Ueji's gardens: The world of Ogawa Jihei), and the author's interview with Iwaki Sentarō.

APPENDIX 2: The World of Modern Japanese-style Architecture

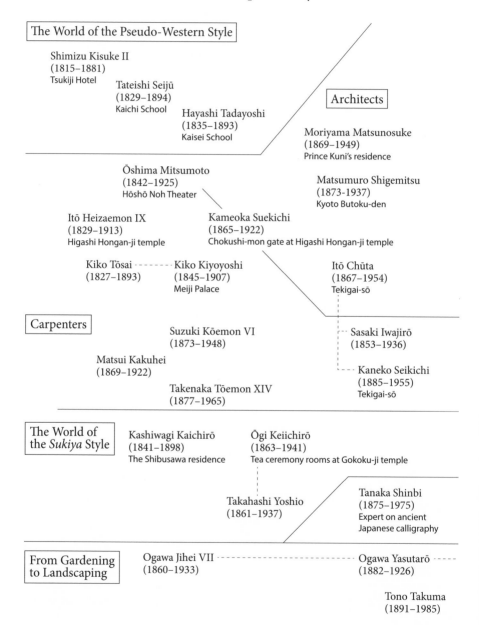

The World of the Pseudo-Western Style

Shimizu Kisuke II
(1815–1881)
Tsukiji Hotel

Tateishi Seijū
(1829–1894)
Kaichi School

Hayashi Tadayoshi
(1835–1893)
Kaisei School

Architects

Moriyama Matsunosuke
(1869–1949)
Prince Kuni's residence

Ōshima Mitsumoto
(1842–1925)
Hōshō Noh Theater

Matsumuro Shigemitsu
(1873-1937)
Kyoto Butoku-den

Itō Heizaemon IX
(1829–1913)
Higashi Hongan-ji temple

Kameoka Suekichi
(1865–1922)
Chokushi-mon gate at Higashi Hongan-ji temple

Kiko Tōsai
(1827–1893)

Kiko Kiyoyoshi
(1845–1907)
Meiji Palace

Itō Chūta
(1867–1954)
Tekigai-sō

Carpenters

Suzuki Kōemon VI
(1873–1948)

Sasaki Iwajirō
(1853–1936)

Matsui Kakuhei
(1869–1922)

Kaneko Seikichi
(1885–1955)
Tekigai-sō

Takenaka Tōemon XIV
(1877–1965)

The World of the *Sukiya* Style

Kashiwagi Kaichirō
(1841–1898)
The Shibusawa residence

Ōgi Keiichirō
(1863–1941)
Tea ceremony rooms at Gokoku-ji temple

Takahashi Yoshio
(1861–1937)

Tanaka Shinbi
(1875–1975)
Expert on ancient
Japanese calligraphy

From Gardening to Landscaping

Ogawa Jihei VII
(1860–1933)

Ogawa Yasutarō
(1882–1926)

Tono Takuma
(1891–1985)

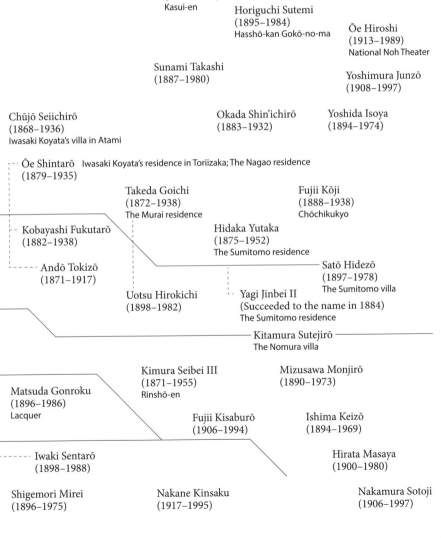

Taniguchi Yoshirō
(1904–1979)

Murano Tōgo
(1891–1984)
Kasui-en

Horiguchi Sutemi
(1895–1984)
Hasshō-kan Gokō-no-ma

Ōe Hiroshi
(1913–1989)
National Noh Theater

Sunami Takashi
(1887–1980)

Yoshimura Junzō
(1908–1997)

Chūjō Seiichirō
(1868–1936)
Iwasaki Koyata's villa in Atami

Okada Shin'ichirō
(1883–1932)

Yoshida Isoya
(1894–1974)

Ōe Shintarō   Iwasaki Koyata's residence in Toriizaka; The Nagao residence
(1879–1935)

Takeda Goichi
(1872–1938)
The Murai residence

Fujii Kōji
(1888–1938)
Chōchikukyo

Kobayashi Fukutarō
(1882–1938)

Hidaka Yutaka
(1875–1952)
The Sumitomo residence

Andō Tokizō
(1871–1917)

Satō Hidezō
(1897–1978)
The Sumitomo villa

Uotsu Hirokichi
(1898–1982)

Yagi Jinbei II
(Succeeded to the name in 1884)
The Sumitomo residence

Kitamura Sutejirō
The Nomura villa

Kimura Seibei III
(1871–1955)
Rinshō-en

Mizusawa Monjirō
(1890–1973)

Matsuda Gonroku
(1896–1986)
Lacquer

Fujii Kisaburō
(1906–1994)

Ishima Keizō
(1894–1969)

Iwaki Sentarō
(1898–1988)

Hirata Masaya
(1900–1980)

Shigemori Mirei
(1896–1975)

Nakane Kinsaku
(1917–1995)

Nakamura Sotoji
(1906–1997)

Index

About the Author and the Translator

Suzuki Hiroyuki

Born in Tokyo in 1945, Suzuki completed the doctoral course at the University of Tokyo Graduate School of Engineering in 1974 and was later awarded the Doctor of Engineering degree. After studying overseas at the University of London Courtauld Institute of Art and working as a full-time lecturer at the University of Tokyo Faculty of Engineering, in 1990 he began working as a professor at the University of Tokyo Graduate School of Engineering. After retiring from this position, he was named professor emeritus at the University of Tokyo. In April 2009 he began working as a professor at the Aoyama Gakuin University School of Cultural and Creative Studies. In April 2010 he was appointed director of the Museum Meiji-mura, a position he held until his death in Tokyo in 2014.

Publications include: *Tōkyō no geniusu roki* [Genius loci in Tokyo] (Bungei Shunjū, 1990, Suntory Prize for Social Sciences and Humanities); *Vikutorian goshikku no hōkai* [The collapse of Victorian Gothic] (Chūōkōron Bijutsu Shuppan, 1996, Architectural Institute of Japan Prize); *Toshi e* [To cities] (Chūōkōron Bijutsu Shuppan, 1999, Society of Architectural Historians of Japan Prize); *Toshi no kanashimi* [The sadness of cities] (Chūōkōron-Shinsha, 2003); *Kenchiku no idenshi* [The genes of architecture] (Ōkokusha, 2007); and *Kenchiku: Mirai e no isan* [Architecture: A legacy for the future] (A posthumous collection of manuscripts edited by Itō Takeshi, University of Tokyo Press, 2017).

Hart Larrabee

An American translator who lives with his family in the little town of Obuse in northern Nagano, Japan, Larrabee fondly remembers exploring the Philosopher's Walk and the gardens of Kyoto while a student in that city long ago. He translates non-fiction widely in the fields of art, design, and architecture, most recently *Japan's Wooden Heritage: A Journey Through a Thousand Years of Architecture* by Fujimori Terunobu and Fujitsuka Mitsumasa for the Japan Library series. His translations of short stories by Takano Fumio and Kakuta Mitsuyo have appeared, respectively, in the anthologies *Tomo: Friendship Through Fiction* and *The Book of Tokyo: A City in Short Fiction*. His most recent literary translation is *Haiku: Classic Short Japanese Poems*, a selection of verse by the "big four" haiku masters Matsuo Bashō, Yosa Buson, Kobayashi Issa, and Masaoka Shiki.

（英文版）庭師　小川治兵衛とその時代

Landscape Gardener Ogawa Jihei and His Times: A Profile of Modern Japan

2018年3月27日　　第1刷発行

著　者　鈴木　博之
訳　者　ハート・ララビー
発行所　一般財団法人 出版文化産業振興財団
〒101-0051 東京都千代田区神田神保町3-12-3
電話　03-5211-7282（代）
ホームページ　http://www.jpic.or.jp/

印刷・製本所　大日本印刷株式会社